Invisible Suburbs

Invisible Suburbs

Recovering Protest Fiction in the 1950s United States

Edited by Josh Lukin

University Press of Mississippi

Jackson

www.upress.state.ms.us

The University Press of Mississippi is a member of the Association of American University Presses.

Manufactured in the United States of America

First printing 2008
∞
Library of Congress Cataloging-in-Publication Data

Invisible suburbs : recovering protest fiction in the 1950s United States / edited by Josh Lukin.
p. cm.
Includes bibliographical references (p.) and index.
ISBN 978-1-934110-87-4 (alk. paper)
1. American fiction—20th century—History and criticism. 2. Protest literature, American—History and criticism 3. Politics and literature—United States—History—20th century. 4. Protest in literature. 5. Dissenters in literature. 6. Identity (Psychology) in literature. I. Lukin, Josh.
PS228.P73I58 2008
813'.540935873—dc22

2007045824

British Library Cataloging-in-Publication Data available

In memory of my brother

Contents

INTRODUCTION

Thirty-Three Years of the Fifties

Josh Lukin

In 1997, Joel Foreman began his anthology *The Other Fifties: Interrogating Midcentury American Icons* by lamenting how little change the previous ten years of fifties studies had made in the public consciousness, which still regarded that decade either as a "simple, innocent, happy" time or as "radically separated from the 1960s by a culture of complacence" (1). Foreman and his contributors, by contrast, sought to frame the era as characterized by "the emergence of oppositional forces that, in subsequent decades, achieve[d] either dominance or general acceptance" (5). The Foreman anthology's essays on such topics as television, Elvis, Ayn Rand, and the Salinger craze work brilliantly toward that goal. But that schema of "emergence" runs a great risk of reduplicating the misconceptions Foreman sought to combat: his conclusion that "Well before Bob Dylan had anything to sing about, the times they were a-changin'" (21) threatens to push back the origin story of America's liberatory movements by ten years without altering the basic trope of an *origin*.[1] The approach works admirably to disavow and challenge conservative nostalgia for an imaginary fifties—that simple, innocent, and happy age when the American people were filled with faith in their leaders, fear of the Communist menace, and gratitude for the comforts of the nuclear family, when no one worried terribly much about racism, poverty, homosexuality, or the rights of women. But it risks confirming, to use Jacques Derrida's critique of origin stories, "an ethic of archaic and natural innocence, of a purity . . . [the celebrant of which] has dreamed of full presence, the reassuring foundation, the origin and the end of the game" (264–65). Foreman, to explain how the fifties generated the movements we associate with the sixties and seventies, invokes changes that "deflected [Americans] from the trajectories of habit, custom, received belief, and tradition" (6) and even uses birth metaphors—calling for "histories of nascent liberation and rebellion" and praising those who "see the fifties as an incubator for the activities of the women's movement" (3–4). Thus his introduction's rhetoric implies a stable, foundational, maternal presence from which the turbulent decade emerged.

But history, of course, tells us otherwise, exposing the blind spots in Foreman's introduction. In particular, the idea of sixties rebellion as having been born in the fifties stops far too soon in its backward historical trajectory. Far from being in their infancy, a number of "sixties" movements and ideas entered the fifties fully grown, or at least past the toddler stage. Longtime civil rights activist Chandler Davis made that point in a 2003 interview:

> CD: Phil Klass was once talking to somebody about the Civil Rights Movement in the Sixties, and he said, "When I was a Freedom Rider in the early Fifties—" And they said, "You mean Sixties," and he said "Fifties." The Negro Congress had demonstrations, and everyone got the shit beaten out of them—I don't know if Phil ever got the shit beaten out of him—but they started ten years before the famous ones started, and some people were present at both.
>
> My sister had exactly the same conversation in a class she was taking as an older graduate student at the University of California in Berkeley. She said, "When I was arrested in a demonstration against discrimination in hiring in 1949—" They said, "You mean 1969"; she said, "I mean 1949."
>
> JL: *Racial discrimination.*
>
> CD: Yeah. She was arrested outside a store in Boston, where she then lived, which wouldn't hire black people. So she and Phil Klass both had this experience of being in the Movement before it was known to exist. Of course, it was for the same reason: it was because the Movement prior to the New Left, which means prior to 1960, was redbaited not out of existence—
>
> JL: *But out of history.*
>
> CD: Yeah. To the point where people felt that they could dismiss it, because "Oh well, it's just those Communists." And of course, some of us *were* Communists. . . . [But] even the ones that were organized entirely by Trotskyists were written out of history . . . (79)

1949 was also the year in which Davis attacked ethnic and gender stereotyping in genre fiction ("Critique & Proposals"). The following year, New York City's United Parents Associations issued a complaint that public school textbooks "showed no Negroes except in the role of servants. The books' illustrations showed no Chinese-Americans, Mexican-Americans or any other group except white . . ." and suggested that such omissions were inimical to "creat[ing] in a child . . . a feeling of the worth and dignity of human beings, of the worth and dignity of himself and his family" ("Parents Urge Inter-Group Textbooks").

Such initiatives, the likes of which are stigmatized today as "political correctness," naturally incurred the hostility of redbaiters in the fifties. More strikingly, they also elicited impatience on the part of the Left, nostalgic for its own imagined purity. In 1950 Mary McCarthy expressed dismay that Greenwich Village society had become focused upon the self-assertion of the Negroes and homosexuals when it had thirteen years earlier been exclusively concerned with discussion of class conflict.[2] Country singer "Haywire Mac" McClintock, a longtime IWW organizer and Marxist proselytizer,[3] recorded a track entitled "Darky Uncle Ned," presenting an old traditional song and a newly euphemized version:

"Wellll, it used to be fun to be in radio—we used to be able to sing songs the way we wanted to sing 'em or the way they were originally written and the first thing ya know, well they got to organizing these pressure groups all over the country and I don't care what kind of a song you sing . . . you know you're going to step on somebody's toes . . . ," he lamented, proceeding to sing the original version of a song about "an old darky [whose] name was Uncle Ned . . . [who] hadn't any wool on the top of his head" and whom we mourn since "He's gone where the good darkies go. Now, you couldn't sing that song like that today. You'd have to" perform it as a song concerning "Uncle Edward," a worthy "of Afro-American extraction" lacking "capillary substance on the apex of his cranium. . . . Yeah, there's been great changes. Good times comin'" ("Haywire Mac").

Hence, two related controversies that seem very current—the issue of "Inter-Group Representation" (now "Diversity"), which in fact can be traced back to the 1930s,[4] and the concern that the "politics of recognition" are a trivial distraction from more substantial inequities, if not a destructive tool of "these pressure groups" (See Gitlin, and, for a rebuttal of the argument, Duggan)—appeared in recognizable form at the very beginning of the 1950s. How, then, long after the Red Scare ended, did such facts remain obscure, such that Reagan conservatives and Left fundamentalists could mobilize the myth of simpler times? I propose that the answer involves persistent shortcomings in the ways scholars have sought to model the fifties, particularly from the seventies onward.

In 1977, Doubleday & Co. published Douglas T. Miller and Marian Nowak's *The Fifties: The Way We Really Were*, a book with the stated purpose of debunking nostalgic depictions of the "Fabulous Fifties" and presenting and characterizing the decade as "materialistic, militaristic, frightened, conformist, conservative, stuffy, [and] trivial" (12). Billed as "the first in-depth study of America's social and cultural history during that decade" (411), the volume used an immense range of literary, journalistic, governmental, cinematic, and musical sources to support its conclusion that "fear and prosperity [had] combined to make us a mediocre people" (385). In his 1974 book, *Cold War America: From Hiroshima to Watergate*, historian Lawrence Wittner wrote that at the height of the Cold War, "literary rebellion was virtually nonexistent. Popular fiction stressed the themes of individual acquisition, business success, conformity, and anti-Communism. . . . Even 'serious' fiction skirted America's social problems. . . . Of all the novels published between 1945 and 1960, perhaps only Ralph Ellison's *The Invisible Man* [*sic*] could be called a significant work of social criticism. Here, the protagonist confronts and finally understands the real world; then, rejecting it in horror, he retreats underground" (129–30).

Such broad generalizations contrast sharply with the meticulousness with which Wittner documents economic and political history, but they are not unusual. Marty Jezer's *The Dark Ages: Life in the United States 1945–1960* suggests that "At a time of political silence, the Beats were, in actuality, the only rebellion around" (274). Even Miller and Nowak, immersed in the era's culture, claim that Kerouac and Ralph Ellison were the only exceptions to the decade's abandonment of the social novel, although they give a nod to Norman Mailer: "*Barbary Shore* . . . bore a message of socialist hope and struggle. Unfortunately, it was an elephantine, clumsy work" (372).[5] Morris Dickstein in *Gates of Eden* locates the rise of social protest not in the Beats but in the Black Humorists who emerged at the end of the decade to contest "[t]he literary intellectuals [who had] simply abandoned politics to pursue private myths and fantasies, to devote their work to the closet intensities of the isolated self" (40).

These views of fifties culture, like most attempts to impose a unitary view upon the culture of a large group of people, bear only occasional connections to historical reality. A significant weakness of the "culture of complacence" view of the fifties, beyond the condescending tone of its adherents, is the extent to which it takes fifties social critics at their word. For the critiques of "conformity" and "political silence" are very much products of that decade: Robert Lindner's *Prescription for Rebellion*, William H. Whyte's *Organization Man*, Mary McCarthy's "The new coercion finds us without the habit of protest. . . . We are dissident but inactive" (15), and Lionel Trilling's "the world is a complex and unexpected and terrible place" (*Liberal Imagination* xii) were neither after-the-fact criticisms nor challenges to the prevailing fifties *zeitgeist*: they were exemplary of the decade's self-criticism. This was the decade that began by labeling its youth "The Silent Generation" and ended by making a bestseller of Vance Packard's *Status Seekers*. The accusation that their era was characterized by conformity and fear would have come as no surprise to the fifties commentariat; they would have been delighted to see how history vindicated their self-image.

The Conformity Model seems to have dominated discussions of the fifties into the mid-eighties; even mild demurrals such as Paul A. Carter's 1983 *Another Part of the Fifties* covered many of the same themes and addressed the same arguments as more aggressive attempts to contest *Happy Days* nostalgia for the era.[6] Useful as such volumes were for the broad outlines of political and economic history, they left much to be desired in their description of the decade's culture and their analyses of its conflicts. But in 1989, the pattern of historians telling themselves the same story repeatedly was decisively broken, thanks largely to the efforts of a single Minneapolis household. Lary May's anthology, *Recasting America: Culture and Politics in the Cold War*, and the 1987–88 University of Minnesota conference it documented, effectively ended attempts to reduce the fifties to a monolithic age of oppression. In 1988, Elaine Tyler May began her study *Homeward Bound: American Families in the Cold War Era* with the words, "In 1959, a young couple married and spent their honeymoon in a bomb shelter" (3). Connecting the nuclear family to the nuclear arms race[7]—framing consumerism, the cult of domesticity, anticommunism, and sexual repression as aspects of a general Cold War Containment Culture—Elaine Tyler May popularized a schema that could unify the diverse accounts in her husband's anthology of how the fifties saw dominant paradigms change in the social sciences, history, legal theory, and the arts.

Once the Mays and their collaborators had promulgated the Containment Model, few books about the fifties continued to claim that we had been a timid, prosperous, mediocre people in that age; instead, we were a diverse and creative people who were reined in by specific institutional forces and ideologies. Authors could no longer credibly present the fifties as the decade in which everyone was either a victim of the Red Scare or an enthusiastic accomplice of McCarthy, no one questioned the myth of universal prosperity, Herman Wouk's novels were seen as the peak of literary achievement, and suburban women—all of them housewives—were only dimly aware that there could be other sources of ecstasy than a new Frigidaire. The Containment Model was, and remains, an effective tool for analyzing such aspects of the fifties as domestic political repression, ideological censorship, and especially gender relations in an era of which Ann Douglas has aptly stated, "Never before or since in American cultural life has so little support or credence been given to the independent female intellect. Researching this period sometimes feels like coming upon a terrain that has been sprayed for women, as woods and backyards are sprayed for insects" (86). Such volumes as Stephen Whitfield's 1991 *The Culture of the Cold War* and Stephanie Coontz's 1992 *The Way We Never Were: American Families and the Nostalgia Trap* contain rich historical accounts of containment on the national and interpersonal level. Andrew Hoberek's recent *The Twilight of the Middle Class: Post-World War II American Fiction and White Collar Work* is in part an astute extension of the Containment Model, as Hoberek discusses what the fifties did to mitigate class-consciousness, analyzing and exposing the fantasies of autonomy created by mental laborers (artists among them) loath to admit that they inhabited the same economic sphere as, and often were, employees. Both Hoberek and Coontz seek in their researches to explain how damaging legacies of fifties containment have hurt American political discourse in more recent decades, enabling our leaders to exploit false consciousness and false nostalgia.

When applied by less discriminating intellects than those of Coontz and Hoberek, however, the Containment Model runs a significant risk and possesses a serious limitation. The risk is exemplified by what Hoberek has styled "studies [that] tend to see all texts as a vehicle for anticommunist politics" ("Cold War" 83)—in short, it is easy for a containment study to slip back into the dogmas of the conformity school, finding tools of oppression everywhere and denying the possibility of oppositional ideas turning up in successful media. Containment's limitation is related to this risk: its emphasis on the intensity of fifties oppression can lead one to wonder how any change could have occurred at all. T. J. Jackson Lears wrestled with this problem in *Recasting America* and drew the surprising conclusion that it would be wrong to overestimate the role of the counterhegemonic private sphere in the fifties: "It made no difference how eloquently convictions were expressed around kitchen tables or in church basements if those private points of view were never admitted into the charmed circle of 'responsible opinion.' Some groups had more power than others, including the power to set the boundaries of permissible debate, to legitimate some ideas and values while declaring others 'tasteless' or 'irresponsible'" (49). Lears went on to explain that good things happened in the early sixties because the fragile alliance of hegemonic forces began to crumble and "many intellectuals and academics" were prompted to become counterculture leaders.

While Lears identified some important forces for societal change,[8] his account, emphasizing the containment effected by those who could "set the boundaries," left unanswered the question of where those intellectuals and academics got the idea to go down to Mississippi, to oppose the war, to write about sexual politics, and generally to raise a ruckus. They were often inspired by a small number of journalists and activists who told them what was going on at those kitchen tables and church basements and thus moved them to participate. If intellectuals and academics played a vital role, it was in bearing witness to the actions of the consciousness-raisers and bus-boycotters, such that the word of their protest was spread to those who would otherwise have been unaware or dismissive of those activities. The transformation of a popular movement to a public movement can be helped greatly by endorsements and advocacy on the part of powerful individuals, but it begins and endures because the disempowered unite to advocate their own interests at those very kitchen tables.

What is necessary to prevent the Containment Model from slipping into overestimations of the breadth and intensity of containment's power is a complementary school of thought emphasizing resistance. Such a perspective is well represented by *The Other Fifties*, but it predates the Foreman anthology, going back at least to the early eighties: when Foreman wrote that critical accounts of the fifties were unduly dominated by "studies that depict the early years of the cold war in terms of massively invasive systems of repression operating most powerfully at the level of ideology" (3), he did not include books that, without specifically or solely addressing the fifties, offered histories of specific subcultures and movements that spanned the mid-century decades and persisted in the face of the containment years. Barbara Ehrenreich on male rebellion, John D'Emilio on gay movements, and Leila Rupp and Verta Taylor on the women's movement are exemplary of eighties scholarship. By the nineties' end, Alan Wald had written on and revived work by fifties Leftists of various stripes; Michael Denning had touched upon the fifties legacy of Popular Front culture; and Robert Caserio had uncovered eight books in the postwar decade that portrayed gay characters sympathetically. Writing in the mid-nineties, Foreman used as exemplary of his ideals Joanne Meyerowitz's *Not June Cleaver: Women and Gender in Post-War America, 1945–1960,* which had demonstrated how immense the gap was between the dominant fifties discourse of white middle-class domestic fulfillment and the actual range of activities performed by women in that era. The years since *The Other Fifties* have seen astute work on the decade's children's literature, Asian-American culture, *noir* fiction, and African American radicalism.[9]

The Emergence Model, then, has proven immensely useful and inspiring to cultural historians. To the extent that it too runs certain risks, they are the risks inherent in any historical generalizations: the farther its claims stray from analysis of specific experiences and movements, the more likely they are to make errors of rhetoric, emphasis, or characterization, as in the case of Foreman's tending to understate in his introduction the continuity between fifties liberatory movements and their antecedents. Emergence risks a parallel excess to that of Containment: it can fall into the everything-is-subversive school of cultural studies and ignore oppressive ideological forces, or at least overestimate the freedom fifties Americans had to move outside them. Morris Dickstein's 2002 *Leopards in the Temple: The Transformation of American Fiction 1945–1970* reverses his previous characterization of fifties fiction to celebrate twenty canonical male authors such as Bellow and Kerouac, arguing that what was gained in the turn away from prewar literary values has too long been ignored, and that although the era's sociopolitical atmosphere was "like a damp, gray fog," its major novelists provided a few lampposts.

A telling argument between the Emergence and Containment views recently occurred in the pages of the journal *Extrapolation,* where novelist L. Timmel Duchamp addressed the gap between how younger feminist scholars perceive the feminist content of 1950s science fiction and how her own generation, which observed the era firsthand, frames the genre. Younger feminist critics[10] have in recent years confronted the stereotyping of fifties SF by women as "sweet little domestic stories" that supported the era's gender roles and have concluded that the characterization is neither accurate nor fair. These revisionist scholars argue that mid-century women's SF covered a range of themes and topics, and that the stories that *did* present galactic housewives often did so in the service of serious social critique, working to define the possibilities for audiences that had not previously existed as fully self-acknowledged communities. The younger scholars' ability to reclaim the texts of "housewife SF" without discomfort, Duchamp argues, demonstrates a blind spot when it comes to understanding the hostility Joanna Russ and other second-wave feminists displayed toward work that acquiesced to the feminine mystique, and in grasping the experience that informed that hostility. Duchamp's essay, "Old Pictures: The Discursive Instability of Feminist Science Fiction," explains for the benefit of the younger generation what Russ and her ilk were so riled up about; more broadly, she seeks "to consider how continual shifts in the social meaning of certain concepts and discursive constructions can radically alter the . . . possible ways in which a story is read" (32). Using autobiography, women's history, and a late-fifties feminist SF story by Chandler Davis, "It Walks in Beauty," Duchamp's piece presents a strong critique of scholarship that presumes women had the resources freely to adopt or decline the housewife "role" when in fact every voice in the era's dominant discourse persistently reminded women that to give priority to non-housewifely pursuits was to relinquish their very femaleness. Duchamp analyzes Davis's dramatization of this fact and concludes with a reflection on how, especially when the constraints and possibilities of gender are at issue, science fiction must be read with an attention to how its meaning and verisimilitude reflect the "ideological baggage" its readers and authors bring.[11]

Hence for the Emergence Model to avoid anachronism and eschew the assumption that one can, as Lionel Trilling and Alfred Kazin claimed to do, stand outside ideology, it may need the Containment Model to quell its excesses, just as the Containment Model needs the Emergence Model to curtail its pessimism. And indeed, much discussion of the fifties in the present decade has attempted to find a model synthesizing the two views. Perhaps the most important work on the U.S. fifties as a whole since *Recasting America* is "Fifties Culture," a nine-part "Special Section" of the *minnesota review*'s 2002 issue, edited by Andrew Hoberek and containing contributions by Hoberek, Christina Klein, Leerom Medovoi, Paul Young, Maria Farland, and others. Hoberek, Klein, and Medovoi each propose new ways to schematize fifties culture that could resolve the question of where sixties rebellion came from without ignoring the forces of containment or overestimating the independent power of grassroots rebellion in the U.S.

Hoberek, following Ann Douglas's landmark essay "Periodizing the American Century: Modernism, Postmodernism, and Postcolonialism in the Cold War Context," notes a number of limitations in earlier fifties studies, one being the tendency to equate the fifties with the Cold War. Not only does that equation ignore the role of that war in three subsequent decades, it ignores the agency of most of the world's population, framing the developing world as little more than the place where the U.S. and USSR found hapless peoples to victimize.[12] Klein and Medovoi, by contrast, each propose a Three World Model, in which both the Third World and American perceptions of our country's relationship with it play an important role in the organization of fifties culture. Klein's "The Sentimental Culture of Global Integration," later incorporated into her *Cold War Orientalism: Asia in the Middlebrow Imagination, 1945–1961*, uses "integration" in a domestic as well as an international sense, asserting that the agenda of "integrating the economies of the non-communist world into a U.S.-dominated world capitalist economy" changed the internal discourse on race, as "Americans justified their new global dominance by pointing to their unique status as a multiracial, multi-ethnic nation of immigrants committed to the principle of tolerance and inclusion" (154, 156). Presenting itself as a warm, friendly place capable of vast sympathy and eager to give developing nations a helping hand, the U.S. fostered a discourse of sentimental affiliation at least as powerful as its aggressive and fearful anticommunism. Cold War ideology was buttressed not only by fear but by the alluring promise of transcending difference to connect emotionally with free peoples at home and abroad. Even the macho Cold War liberal Arthur Schlesinger Jr. "recast the Cold War as an attractive project of forging bonds with people vulnerable to communism, rather than a fearful project of opposing communists" (160).

Medovoi articulates his version of the Three World Model in more ambitious terms: whereas Klein emphasizes the utility of the integration discourse in selling the Cold War to the American people, Medovoi openly asserts that he is adapting a hitherto incoherent Emergence Model (my term) so that it will for the first time make sense. He makes a persuasive case. Elaine Tyler May and Jackson Lears asserted that the age of containment collapsed under its own contradictions; subsequent scholars have demonstrated the presence of many emergent challenges to the containment state. But Medovoi and Hoberek argue that rebellion is extremely undertheorized by contrast with containment, and indeed it had no Elaine Tyler May to write its foundational analysis, no George Kennan to cite as its inventor, no wedding in a bomb shelter to serve as its synecdoche. Medovoi invokes a familiar argument to demonstrate the weakness of our understanding: we still talk about rebellion like the fifties itself did. "By and large, critics have celebrated the figures in question . . . by taking their self-professed status as rebels at face value. . . . [They] have been touted as lonely voices in the night who lashed out against the Cold War order, but whose capacity to do so was not in any way itself a product of that order. . . . Such explanations for the appearance of postwar 'rebels,' in retaining the repressive hypothesis of the Cold War order, cannot help but reactivate the very discourse of subversion that was always already a corollary of the discourse of containment" ("Cold War America" 171).

Medovoi points out that the U.S. had, in presenting its public face, to accommodate the fact that between 1945 and 1960, "forty countries with a total of eight hundred million people—more than a quarter of the world's population at the time—revolted against colonialism and won their independence" (Von Eschen 125). Much more than in decades past, the country's rhetoric was anti-imperialist, and the use of force either rationalized in the name of helping peoples achieve their freedom or effected covertly. U.S. leaders repeatedly reminded the world that our country had been the first to overthrow European colonial government and that we were uniquely placed to sympathize with newly liberated countries. Moreover, we were distinct from Old Europe by virtue of our youth as a nation and from the Soviets by virtue of our freedom. Medovoi traces tropes of rebellion, youth, and freedom as they pervade fifties official discourse and popular culture, showing how the Beats, the rock 'n' rollers, and the

Method actors were celebrated as representative of America. Further, he links the successes of the civil rights movement with the powerful impetus America had to support its claim to be freer than its Cold War rival in the eyes of the Third World: "If youth figured America in its newness, as a young nation akin to the Third World, then blacks signified America as a space for the achievement of racial emancipation, aligning it once again with the new African and Asian nations" ("Cold War America" 179).

Deftly avoiding the everything-is-liberatory school, Medovoi acknowledges both sides of the Three Worlds coin: he explains that "the triangular structure of the Cold War globe produced simultaneously repressive and emancipatory results across the breadth of American culture in the 1950s" ("Cold War America" 182). If anything, he underestimates the number of worlds involved—America, more than ever before, was also concerned that its newly liberated allies in the *First* World think well of us, lest they end up electing Communists; and concern over the country's image in Europe paralleled worry over Africa's and Asia's views.[13] The Three World Models of the fifties promise to be productive in many areas, schematizing a Cold War culture that accounts for both containment and emergence. Still, like Foreman's introduction to *The Other Fifties*, and unlike some of the scholars whom I have associated with the Emergence Model, they run the risk of bogging down in origins at the expense of continuities. I wish to propose a supplementary perspective, inspired by the accounts given by people with first-hand experience of anticommunist and sexist containment, but acknowledging rebellious and liberating experiences as well.

A striking passage in Medovoi's article states that "Though without question the Cold War closed down numerous prewar and wartime political possibilities (perhaps most overtly a cross-racial working-class radicalism), it must be acknowledged that it opened up a new kind of symbolic and political impetus to Civil Rights struggles" ("Cold War American" 179). What did it feel like to have one's possibilities closed down, or foreclosed, at that time? Or to have new possibilities "opened up"? With respect to the former, screenwriter Howard Koch wrote as early as 1947, "When I hear the current attacks on free education, when I read articles from all over the country pouncing on any remaining vestige of progressive thought . . . I realize I'm living in a strange, strange time. What only two years ago was virtue is now vice; what was a friend is now foe; what was then patriotic is now often subversive. That's not a very easy adjustment. We find ourselves trying to maintain our sanity—trying to stand mentally upright in a world that's turned upside down" (May, *The Big Tomorrow* 215). The syndrome is what Helene Cixous, writing as a Jew in Algeria during the same era, called "anachronia," using similar terms: ". . . the sufferer isn't sick, she suffers from the mental anachronia of her entourage, she is surrounded by blatant puppets, she is the only one to see that everything is reversed upside down, reversed and claiming to be the other way up. There is a general mental and semantic slippage. The demented believe themselves normal. Untruth has uncontested authority. Everyone believes what is not. Everyone unsees what is. The program is uninterrupted" (Yee 196–97).

The effects of having new possibilities open are rarely described at such length, and may indeed be harder to articulate. Martin Luther King Jr. recounts the desegregation of the Montgomery buses: "At this hour my heart began to throb with an inexpressible joy. The darkest hour of our struggle had indeed proved to be the first hour of victory" (160). John Allen Ryan reports of the first public reading of *Howl*, "the people gasped and laughed and swayed, they were psychologically had, it was an orgiastic occasion" (Watson 187). Early Mattachine society member Geraldine Jackson states that, among fellow gay radicals, "people were able to bloom and be themselves . . . [you could] say what you wanted to say and feel accepted. . . . You felt like you had a mission in the world. . . . You felt that you were doing something terribly worthwhile for our people" (D'Emilio 67, 69). And there are scores of accounts wherein individual encounters with artifacts—Beat poetry, science fiction stories, rock 'n' roll—leave them ecstatic with a sense of possibility.[14]

This was, then, the experience of the individual aware of oppression: on the one hand "trying to stand mentally upright"; on the other, successful attempts to make the world around you stand upright or to find a milieu in which your own co-ordinates were accepted, where the authority of untruth is contested. The question, on a larger scale, is this: in an era where older modes of resistance were discredited, stigmatized, or destroyed, how did marginalized groups try to salvage or to reconceptualize their struggles for rights and recognition? For the purposes of this anthology, in particular, how did literature work as a critique, a reflection, or an anticipation of those struggles?

Medovoi's example of the black civil rights struggle finding new tools in the U.S.'s need to present the image of a free society, presumably after that struggle had to sever its ties with socialism, has analogies in other movements and indeed in individuals' reinvention of themselves and their work.[15] But "reinvention" is not the most apt word. Readers may recall in their geometry class having had to tinker with the equation for a curve so as to rotate or move the curve to a different position on the Cartesian plane: feminism, the civil rights movement, protest fiction, and other artifacts and agendas had to undergo similarly arduous tinkering to occupy the Cold War quadrant of the historical grid, as it were: sometimes the tinkering was successful, and sometimes it was beyond the mathematical skill of the tinkerers. The evocative mathematical term for the process is "deformation": hence I style my approach the Deformation Model.[16]

By "deformation" I mean to refer to the adoption of new strategies, positions, or media which militate in favor of already-extant goals, rather than the use of extant tools for new purposes. To the extent that Raymond Chandler used a form created by the radical Hammett to tell conservative stories, or Jack Kerouac adopted elements of the Popular Front migrant narrative to glorify individualism, they were not engaged in deformation but in refunctioning. Shirley Jackson, as Ann Douglas has noted, was engaged in deforming the feminist novel; but she was also refunctioning the Gothic genre. Neither deformation nor refunctioning is completely dependent on intentionality: in the case of deformation, the values preserved by a work can be determined in part by its audience, as in the case of the many mothers of mentally retarded children who wrote to Elizabeth Spencer that her *Light in the Piazza* relieved their feelings of isolation.

The first essay in this volume, Harry Thomas's "Good Old Boy Masculinity and Same-Sex Desire in *Cat on a Hot Tin Roof* and *The Bitterweed Path*" considers the persistence of a class-based perspective the existence of which was insufficiently acknowledged in the fifties, as he traces the refunctioning of an old Southern populist trope to accommodate a homophilic position. Although the canonical work Thomas discusses ends unhappily (Big Daddy, the voice of tolerance and authenticity, dies, while Brick remains miserable) and the noncanonical work ends happily, both address how a residual cultural formation can be drafted into an agenda with what, by today's standards, are progressive elements: *The Bitterweed Path* uses "Good Old Boy Masculinity" for a story that approaches the condition of gay pastoral, while the Williams play incorporates that trope in a story of the fall from that innocent condition into an age of sexual anxiety.

Ian Peddie's "The Wrong Side of Town: *A Walk on the Wild Side* in an Age of Reaction" recounts an artistically successful deformation that was reviled in the public sphere, Nelson Algren's attempt to update Popular Front and Naturalist values for a critique of fifties capitalism. Algren's frontal attack on bourgeois complacency was destined to fail in the eyes of cultural mandarins who were among its targets, but its critiques foreshadowed New Left and sixties battles for social justice. Similarly, Kathlene McDonald lauds an artist who could not succeed in the fifties mainstream because of her Left baggage. Martha Dodd, as McDonald presents her in "Postwar Left Feminism and Antifascist Resistance in the Cultural Work of Martha Dodd," effects a deformation of her anti-Nazi writing into the anti-McCarthyist realm, all the while refining her feminist goals. Unlike Betty Friedan, who successfully deformed Left feminist insights into a middle-class discourse, Dodd found her feminist labors exorcised from history; like Algren's, her work expresses sentiments and depicts conflicts that would find new life in subsequent decades.

The second half of *Invisible Suburbs* focuses less upon preservation of class struggle and more upon the strategies used by oppressed minorities to gain rights and recognition in the fact of threats posed by containment. Like Harry Thomas, Stephanie Brown juxtaposes a canonical and a marginal work; in her case, they are by the same author. "Anybody's Protest Novel: Chester Himes and the Prison of Authenticity" contrasts Himes's canonical first novel, *If He Hol-*

lers Let Him Go, with his rarely discussed *End of a Primitive*. The latter was the last literary novel Himes wrote before turning to *noir* fiction; in it, he brought a black-humorist perspective to bear on the conventions of the mid-century "protest novel" and shattered them all, burlesquing the role of the protest novelist and exposing the culpability of the genre in supporting what Brown styles "the fictions of power." Caricaturing major figures of the black literary establishment (not excluding Himes himself) and disavowing literary realism, liberal pieties, and the prescribed role of an African American novelist, *The End of a Primitive* lampoons the oppressive conventions of protest novels and uses relentless gallows humor to present a unique strategy for writing under desperate and annihilating conditions in the 1950s U.S.

Himes was also no Betty Friedan: the deformations his work underwent, like those of Algren, sought not to accommodate fifties pressures but to attack them head-on, with predictable results for the mainstream reception of his novel.[17] In a famous essay on how alternative culture can operate in the shadow of hegemony, Raymond Williams observed, "There will be areas of practice and meaning which, almost by definition from its own limited character, or in its profound deformation, the dominant culture is unable in any real terms to recognize" (43). Indeed, there are always critical works of art that manage to gain currency by containing elements that publishers and reviewers can misrecognize as affirming or comforting to their expectations. Such works run the risk, unfortunately, of disguising their critique well enough that an ideological critic sympathetic to their agenda may also misrecognize them as tools of the dominant order.[18] *The Light in the Piazza*, a novella written by Elizabeth Spencer at the end of the fifties that owes its popularity to the ways it appealed to the sentimental culture of global integration, has suffered thanks to such misrecognition. The novella has elicited disdain from critics who, unable to grasp Spencer's irony or out of touch with 1960 U.S. values, see it as a celebration of the similarities between femininity and mental retardation (Delany 2006).

Meticulously historicizing the novella and paying close attention to Spencer's tone, Ladislava Khailova takes a different tack, as her title—"Rewriting Patriarchal Paradigms of Retardation in Elizabeth Spencer's *The Light in the Piazza*"—implies. Although it does not model activism on behalf of the mentally impaired or American women,[19] Spencer's story turns a critical eye on the societal assumptions about both oppressed groups as depicted in earlier literature. *The Light in the Piazza* is particularly effective in contesting the eugenic view of mentally retarded women as degenerates, sexual threats, and in need of containment; but, in the context of a fifties discourse the misogyny of which can hardly be overstated,[20] its feminist gestures are also noteworthy. The novella's narrator, seeing her mentally retarded daughter accepted among the Italians, is gripped by an ironic sense of wonder: "Isn't it amazing: America so stigmatizes my daughter that these primitive patriarchal types constitute her best hope for being treated as a human being?" But Khailova goes further, showing that the novella has substantial satiric insight into femininity and what meager exercise of female agency was available to a woman on her own in that era.

A fascinating practice of deformation for writers who, unlike Spencer, could not finesse their fiction into work for William Shawn's *New Yorker*, was to go into genre fiction, creating social protest literature under the radar of mainstream cultural critics. Alan Wald, in his contribution to Bill Mullen and Sherry Linkon's 1996 anthology *Radical Revisions: Reading 1930s Culture*, lists three postwar hard-boiled writers with Popular Front backgrounds and explains, "These examples suggest that the majority of writers produced by the 1930s radical upheaval did *not* follow the trajectory of Steinbeck or Dos Passos in their literary *or* political careers. They entered the arena of what we choose to call 'mass culture.' Here, they produced literature along the full spectrum of possibility—from landmarks to formula work—in science fiction, children's literature, romance, horror, detective, pulp, popular science, adventure, and so on. [Some, like Jim Thompson, turned to genre fiction to avoid poverty and political stigma, after having written more straightforward works of political protest]. Chester Himes's evolution was similar. So was Frank Yerby's" (18).

Wald's comments concern writers driven "underground" by the Red Scare; but the "lavender scare," i.e. the newly institutionalized homophobia of the postwar years, worked in a similar fashion. David Bergman has recorded how Greenberg Publishers, the major source of gay-themed literary fiction in the early thirties and the immediate postwar years, was forced by the federal government to stop publishing gay fiction in the early fifties; the censorship had a chilling effect on other publishers and authors alike (49–51). Only the paperback revolution enabled literature depicting gay communities to survive, by facilitating the creation of a new genre with unprecedentedly wide distribution: the gay "pulp" novel. Jennifer Worley's "The Mid-century Pulp Novel and the Imagining of Lesbian Community" explains how productive this deformation turned out to be, spewing forth books that introduced readers to the existence of homosexuality, evoked the concept of gay community, and even prefigured the anti-heteronormative positions that would inform later liberation movements. Lesbian pulps were a "trash" genre[21] that sustained a community's identity when broader societal forces would just as soon have seen it obliterated.

A model of fifties culture focused on artistic deformation and refunctioning can coexist happily with the Three World Models, acknowledging the possibilities opened up by Klein's "integration" and Medovoi's "emancipation" alongside those crushed by containment. *The Light in the Piazza* shows the power of Medovoi's beloved rebellious youth and *The End of a Primitive* depicts a man who understands all too well what the sentimental culture of integration is trying to sell people. In Algren and Dodd, containment dominates. But the novels studied by Thomas and Worley, involving as they do rootless youths finding themselves integrated into an empowering culture by older mentors who identify with them and wish to nurture and perpetuate their kind, find a surprisingly effective account in Medovoi's trope of idealized First-Third World relations.[22] To see these works in terms of deformation of old agendas and refunctioning of old forms is not to dispute the basic structural claims of Three Worlds; but such a perspective can add a better understanding of authorial agency and of continuity with earlier eras, presenting fifties authors and readers as individuals who sought, in the words of Chandler Davis, "to guard a peculiar flame through [years] of persecution" (". . . From an Exile").[23] The scholars herein honor those guardians.

Notes

1. The reference to Bob Dylan is also confusing. Of course young Robert Zimmerman was singing in the fifties, and of course he was aware, thanks to the recordings of Pete Seeger, Josh White, Big Bill Broonzy, and Odetta, that there were social issues to sing about in that decade.

2. I describe from memory a theme from a talk by Richard Kaye, "Mary McCarthy and the Politics of Impersonality."

3. Haywire Mac introduced the young Jim Thompson to Marx, and inspired him to become a novelist (Polito 128–29).

4. Lawrence Levine recounts the breadth of 1930s literary anthologies and traces the contraction of the canon from the postwar years through the early sixties (*Opening* 94–95).

5. They are wrong on both counts: *Invisible Man* was not widely classed a protest novel (see Brown, following) and *Barbary Shore* is a slim, stylistically graceful elegy for a time when socialist hope and struggle seemed viable.

6. Carter, a minor science fiction writer as well as a historian, takes pride in tracing the decade's debates over political protest in science fiction. Although a useful corrective to the Conformity school, this is another example of a point that cultural critics in the fifties were aware of: when David Riesman in 1953 ridiculed "Intellectuals [who] try to cope with their anxiety by telling each other atrocity stories about America," he made an exception for SF dystopian Cyril Kornbluth, whose pessimistic stories "can be witty and even revealing" (*IR* 124).

7. Again, a point that the era's science fiction had gestured toward, memorably in the work of Judith Merril, Philip K. Dick, and Theodore Sturgeon; but May brings a wealth of research and theoretical tools to the problem as well as evidence that things could and did change.

8. The question arises, however, of whether such theoretical innovators as Bourdieu (in his late polemical books) and such historical novelties as bloggers influencing the decisions of mainstream journalists might leave Lears's Reagan-era theorizing outdated.

9. The eighties innovators are those cited by Elaine Tyler May: Ehrenreich for *The Hearts of Men*, D'Emilio for *Sexual Politics, Sexual Communities*, and Rupp/Taylor for *Survival in the Doldrums: The American Women's Rights Movement, 1945 to the 1960s*. The major works by Wald and Denning on the subjects mentioned include Wald's *Writing from the Left* and Denning's *The Cultural Front*. Authors and editors working since Foreman's anthology include Julia L. Mickenberg, Floyd Cheung, David Cochran, Sean McCann, and Bill Mullen.

10. Duchamp specifically describes essays by Justine Larbalestier and Lisa Yaszek.

11. A major influence on Duchamp's articulation of history is her fellow Foucauldian

SF novelist, Samuel Delany, whose essay "Velocities of Change" shows how many concepts taken for granted in earlier and later years, such as the critique of "blaming the victim," were unintelligible to the fifties' dominant discourse.

12. Many "Cold War" volumes didn't even go that far. One looks in vain in the index of Miller and Nowak or J. Ronald Oakley for mentions of Iran, Guatemala, or the Congo.

13. To Europe, however, we had to prove that we were cultured and sophisticated rather than youthful and rebellious. The CIA was most active in the project of making sure we showed our best side to Europe and concealed our dirty linen: see Frances Stonor Saunders.

14. The Velvet Underground's "Rock 'N' Roll" is exemplary.

15. Ex-Marxists who attempted new modes of protest, in addition to those mentioned below, include The Futurians, an early science fiction organization among whose members were Judith Merril, Cyril Kornbluth, Isaac Asimov, and Frederik Pohl.

16. The connotations of the term are apt. Ann Douglas argues of the era's gynophobia that its "long-term consequence was the women's movement, but the immediate result, as Shirley Jackson, Carson McCullers, and Flannery O'Connor were quick to dramatize on another plane, was mutation. Fashion witnessed a return via Christian Dior and other designers to a grotesquely misshapen feminine form, pinched and pronged by stiletto heels, severely cinched at the waist and handicapped with hobbled or sheath skirts and all-points uplift bras . . ." (86). Indeed, grotesquerie, dismemberment, and dysmorphism abound in fifties protest fiction, from Nelson Algren to John Okada to Chester Himes to Ray Bradbury.

17. Algren's and Himes's innovations survive in part because their work found enthusiasts and epigones in the next generation, such as Russell Banks and Ishmael Reed. Belated rediscovery was a common fate for such uncompromising artists.

18. See Michael Rothberg for a refutation of one such ideological critic.

19. Samuel Delany has soundly observed that to depict a state of affairs in which members of the oppressed group are isolated from others of their kind, or people who might share their goals, can be seen as an act of resignation in the face of an unsatisfactory status quo. Such a criticism might be complicated, however, by the fan letters Spencer received from grateful mothers of mentally retarded children: the story *effected* some mitigation of the sense of isolation it *depicted*.

20. See Coontz and Duchamp as well as my "Cold War Masculinity in the Early Work of Kate Wilhelm."

21. Elizabeth Long points out that "'Trash' is not a fixed category, but rather a contested boundary-marker for dividing the upper levels of literary value from those books not worth discussing" (206). Often, of course, being "not worth discussing" protected "trash" authors, such as anticommunist science fiction writers, from mainstream condemnation. Even more conservative authors were not safe: Peter Rabinowitz cites a 1954 article in *Fortnightly Review* in which the author breathes a sigh of relief upon concluding that Raymond Chandler's novels are mere entertainments and not social critiques, for otherwise they would be "a serious boon to the propagandists of the Kremlin" (Rabinowitz 168).

22. Tennessee Williams's Brick, in the terms of this analogy, has gone over to the Russians. Note how Big Daddy denounces him in the same feminizing terms Arthur Schlesinger reserved for Leftists (Compare Gilbert and Cuordileone).

23. The altered word is "generations" in the original. Davis, writing in 1960 after both he and his father had spent most of the decade persecuted by the Redhunters, could not foresee that some of the worst aspects of containment culture would be defeated in the near future.

Invisible Suburbs

Good Old Boy Masculinity and Same-Sex Desire in *Cat on a Hot Tin Roof* and *The Bitterweed Path*

Harry Thomas

Aiming to Break the Double Bind

Condensing a great deal of conventional wisdom about both sexuality and American regionalism into one sentence, queer historian John Howard reminds us that "Mississippi has long been considered America's most repressive locale," and that "the 1950s have long been assumed the [country's] most repressive period" (*Men Like That* xiv). Given that in much scholarship, as Howard explains, "the history of gay and lesbian people has often mirrored the history of the city" because "gay identity and culture formation" have been "linked to capitalist industrialization," rural Mississippi seems the place least likely in which to look for fiction interested in imagining systems of sexuality and gender that lie outside of strict heteronormativity (*Men Like That* 12). Historians of sexuality have also characterized the American 1950s—the decade of John Wayne masculinity and a "lavender scare" obsessed with rooting out homosexuals within the U.S. government—as a decade marked by an intense "effort to label homosexual behavior as deviant" and a sharp intensification of "the penalties that gay men and lesbians faced" for the open expression of their desires (D'Emilio and Freedman, 288). Given these two aspects of its image, rural Mississippi in the 1950s would seem to be a particularly unlikely time and place in which to find thinking (or behavior) lying outside or beyond the heteronormative frame.

This conventional wisdom is, of course, a vast oversimplification. Howard's *Men Like That* complicates the notion that post-World War II Mississippi was a place devoid of visible same-sex desire (and behavior). One particularly compelling piece of evidence that Howard uses to make the case that "men-desiring-men were neither wholly isolated nor invisible" in Mississippi during the decades following World War II is Mississippian Thomas Hal Phillips's first novel, *The Bitterweed Path* (*Men Like That* xiii). Set on a plantation in Mississippi in the 1890s, *The Bitterweed Path* tells the story of a nearly life-long intergenerational, cross-class and same-sex love affair between Darrell Barclay, a poor white teenager and Malcolm Pitt, the owner of the plantation where Darrell's father works as a sharecropper. In addition to its subject matter, two other things about the novel seem particularly striking: its publication date and its resolution. Originally published in 1950 by respected New York literary house Rinehart (and virtually lost until Howard returned it to print in 1996), *The Bitterweed Path* resists doling out tragic endings for its male characters who love men. Unlike other mid-century literary work by more famous and commercially successful southern authors, the men who love men in Phillips's novel do not commit suicide. Nor are they punished for their desires; no wrathful lightning bolts—literal or metaphorical—ever descend from the sky.[1]

Neither perversion nor exploitation, Darrell and Malcolm's attraction to each other is portrayed as being both mutual and naturally occurring. As the years pass, Darrell labors for Malcolm and eventually becomes his business partner, his surrogate son, and his lover. Malcolm Pitt does die (when parts of the cotton gin he and Darrell run together explode) and Darrell mourns him greatly, but the book closes with Darrell inheriting Malcolm's plantation, building a big house of his own in the style of Malcolm's, and realizing that he himself has become a man. "Some day I will have another son," Darrell declares on the last page of the novel, hinting that the cycle of upper class men mentoring, and loving, working class boys can and will—and indeed, should—continue (314).

Phillips's novel complicates any conception of the 1950s (as an era) or the American South (as a region) as the site of universal and unrelenting compulsory heterosexuality. This essay attempts to map some of the strange new territory that Phillips's novel deposits its readers in. In order to do that, I will read *The Bitterweed Path* alongside another, much better known, work from the 1950s that deals with same-sex desire in the American South: Tennessee Williams's Pulitzer Prize–winning play *Cat on a Hot Tin Roof* (1955). *Cat* made its Broadway debut only five years after publication of *The Bitterweed Path* and the two works have more in common than their settings on Mississippi plantations. Williams's play and Phillips's novel both attempt to imaginatively short circuit, rewrite or repair what, drawing on the work of Eve Kosofsky Sedgwick, I will call the double bind of masculine identity.

Much of Sedgwick's theoretical work is concerned with what she calls "the continuum of male homosocial desire" (*Between Men* 1). Her now well-known claim is that, at the present time, she sees same-sex relations between women running a smooth, relatively uninterrupted gamut from friendship (the homosocial) to love and sexual desire (the homosexual), while the male version of the "continuum between homosocial and homosexual" is "radically disrupted" (*Between Men* 1–2). This disruption, according to Sedgwick, demonstrates how Western masculinity has become a kind of double bind, a paradoxical state of being constantly caught up in the exhausting process of "the stimulation and glamorization of the energies of male-male desire . . . an incessant project that must . . . coexist with an equally incessant project of denying, deferring, or silencing that satisfaction" (*Epistemology* 56).

This double bind of Western masculinity is driven by both patriarchy (in which relationships between men assume crucial social, political, and economic importance) and homophobia. I argue that this homophobia is a response to gender deviance at least as much as it is sexual deviance; it is a misogynist reaction against a conception of same-sex desire that figures gay men as internally or psychologically feminine. This way of thinking about same-sex desire and the men who experience and/or act on it arises from the medical/psychological model of homosexuality that Michel Foucault maps the birth of in his *History of Sexuality, Volume One*. According to Foucault, this late nineteenth-century medical/psychological model characterized homosexuality as "less . . . a type of sexual relations than . . . a certain way of inverting the masculine and the feminine in oneself . . . a kind of interior androgyny, a hermaphrodism of the soul" (43). Therefore, under this model of homosexuality, to be a man who desires men is to—paradoxically—cease to be a man.

In his groundbreaking *Gay New York*, historian George Chauncey complicates Foucault's categorization, expressing skepticism about exactly how widely the medical/psychological model Foucault describes might have circulated in America. Nevertheless, Chauncey's research does demonstrate that the middle decades of the twentieth century saw a shift in the ways in which Americans understood the relationship between same-sex desire and gender identity. Chauncey's claim is that, beginning in the late 1930s, American culture experienced a "reorganization of sexual categories and the transition from an early twentieth-century culture divided into "queers" and "men" on the basis of gender status to a late twentieth-century culture divided into "homosexuals" and "heterosexuals" on the basis of sexual object choice" (22). That is to say, in the pre–World War II gay world that Chauncey maps, men (particularly working class men) could have sex with other men and still be understood as men so long as they undertook the supposedly "active" role in same-sex relations and maintained a "masculine" gender performance in their day to day lives. As the shift from a queer/"normal" man binary to a homosexual/heterosexual binary became ever more increasingly widespread, it became "more difficult for men to consider themselves 'straight' if they had any sexual contact with other men, no matter how carefully they restricted their behavior to the 'masculine' role" (22). Thus the shift in binaries limited men's sexual possibilities; as a growing consensus declared that *any* same-sex contact served as proof that a man's identity was "homosexual" (and therefore, according to the medical/psychological model that Foucault maps, feminine), the double bind that Sedgwick discusses grew increasingly tight. Chauncey claims that the shift in thinking about sexual behavior and gender identity that he describes begins in the late 1930s and intensifies during and after World War II until homosexual/heterosexual eventually becomes "the hegemonic sexual regime in American culture" (23).

That said, Chauncey is clear that this shift in "sexual regimes" was not an instantaneous, day-to-night transformation that happened at the same time in every part of America; instead it was often the case that different models for understanding the relationship between sexual behavior and identity coexisted and competed. He also acknowledges that the "gay world" described in *Gay New York* should not necessarily be taken as typical. But his analysis effectively supplements *Men Like That*, wherein Howard too makes the case for a changeover in thinking about the relationship between sexual behavior and gender identity which was hardly smooth and uniform in its occurrence when he claims that "throughout the twentieth century queer sexuality [in Mississippi] continued to be understood as both acts *and* identities, behaviors *and* beings" (xviii, emphasis Howard's).

Thus by the 1950s, when both *The Bitterweed Path* and *Cat on a Hot Tin Roof* appear, they do so at a time when the homosexual/heterosexual binary (and the double bind it creates for men who desire men but wish to retain a masculine identity) is becoming increasingly hegemonic in America. Both Williams's play and Phillips's novel attempt—with differing degrees of success for their respective characters—to modify, resist or sidestep this increasingly hegemonic system of classifying male desires and identities. Each work tries, in its own way, to imaginatively untangle the masculine double bind and to remove same-sex desire from its associations with effeminacy. And while each author attempts to create and/or validate a quite different form of same-sex desire, both *Cat* and *The Bitterweed Path* feature a central male character who has the power to literally re-imagine the world, to realign sex and gender roles as he pleases. These characters—Malcolm Pitt in *The Bitterweed Path* and Big Daddy Pollitt in *Cat*—are both white men who, despite being wealthy plantation owners, practice and perform a kind of working class southern agrarian masculinity.

Like all gender/social types, the masculinity I refer to here is a slippery thing. While describing *The Mind of the South* (1941) W. J. Cash called its model practitioner "a hell of a fellow," while more recently southern sociologist John Shelton Reed has called this "authentic, indigenous working-class hero" the good old boy (50, 35). What both Williams and Phillips understand about southern culture is that within it, good old boy masculinity is a kind of cure-all: performing socially as a good old boy excuses or even naturalize all kinds of behaviors. As Reed explains: "Larry King has pointed out, 'when people designate somebody as a good ol' boy the sentence has to start something like, "Well, now, Bubba, he may beat his wife some and burn a few barns when he's drankin', and there's the time he shot his little boy's eye out with a BB gun and all that—but he sure is a *good* ol' boy"'" (Reed 38, emphasis King's). Thus it is good old boy masculinity on which the two Mississippi-born authors (born only eleven years apart) hang their separate attempts to rewrite the possibilities of white southern manhood. This essay aims to map the different ways in which both Phillips and Williams deploy this peculiarly southern form of masculinity as they attempt to secure a place for (to borrow Howard's title) "men like that" in the South.

The "Tolerance" Plantation: *Cat on a Hot Tin Roof*

Among the greatest American literary depictions of the white masculine homosocial/homosexual double bind that Sedgwick articulates, Tennessee Williams's *Cat on a Hot Tin Roof* is a cautionary tale outlining the treacherous terrain that lies ahead of American (and particularly southern) men who desire men.[2] The character most painfully caught in the paradoxical space between loving a man and still wanting to be perceived as one is Brick Pollitt, the former pro football star and son of plantation patriarch Big Daddy. Having taken up drink after the suicide of his friend and teammate Skipper, Brick insists that Skipper was the most important person in his life just as vehemently as he denies the suggestion that they might have been anything more than friends.

Indeed, it is only during the second of the play's three acts, when Big Daddy suggests that Brick might have had romantic and/or sexual feelings for his friend Skipper, that Brick's carefully cultivated alcoholic detachment is shattered. When Big Daddy tells Brick that his brother Gooper and sister-in-law Mae have "suggested that there was something not right exactly" in Brick's relationship with Skipper, something "Not, well, exactly *normal* in [their] friendship," Brick explodes with outrage (114, emphasis Williams's). "Oh, *you* think so, too, you call me your son and a queer," Brick says to Big Daddy, "Oh! Maybe that's why you put Maggie and me in this room that was Jack Straw and Peter Ochello's, in which that pair of old sisters slept in a double bed where both of 'em died!" (115, emphasis Williams's).

Jack Straw and Peter Ochello were the owners of the plantation that Big Daddy expanded and inherited. Despite their having given his father a home, a job, and a sizeable inheritance, Brick's characterization of Straw and Ochello as "that pair of old sisters" makes it clear how he feels about them. In this line and the many others that make up Brick's furious refutation of his father's suggestion—"*sodomy!*," "you think we did dirty things between us," "a pair of dirty old men?," "A couple of— . . . ducking sissies? Queers?," "a, unnatural thing"—it becomes clear that Brick sees a neat one-to-one correspondence between same-sex desire, male effeminacy, and general moral deviance (117, 118, 118, 118, 119, emphasis Williams's). Shocked by his father's casual discussion of the subject, Brick asks him: "Don't you know how people *feel* about things like that? How, how *disgusted* they are by things like that?" (119, emphasis Williams's).

If the point were not already clear, Williams's concludes Brick's homophobic tirade with both a revealing father-son exchange and an equally revealing stage direction:

> BRICK: Why can't exceptional friendship, *real, real, deep, deep friendship!* between two men be respected as something clean and decent without being thought of as—
> BIG DADDY: It can, it is, for God's sake.
> BRICK: —*Fairies. . . .*
> *[In his utterance of this word, we gauge the wide and profound reach of the conventional mores he got from the world that crowned him with early laurel.]* (120, emphasis Williams's)

What we see here—and what Williams tells us in his stage direction—is just how deeply Brick is caught up in the double bind of masculine identity. The southern culture that Brick lives in tells him that men who desire men sexually are effeminate, unnatural, and quite possibly evil.[3] That same culture also tells him that he himself—as the golden boy, a devastatingly handsome star college quarterback, former pro football player, and probable heir to an enormous Delta cotton plantation—could not possibly be effeminate, unnatural, or evil. Believing that both of these things (same-sex desire's gender-transitive and morally deviant nature, his own solid masculinity and culturally-affirmed goodness) are simultaneously true, Brick cannot agree that he might have wanted with Skipper what Skipper wanted with him, nor can he leave Skipper's memory behind.[4]

What is of course ironic in this scene—and what many Williams scholars have written about—is the fact that Brick, so busy ranting and raving in denial, misses the fact that his father is not the least bit horrified or repulsed by the idea of Brick and Skipper having shared a bond that went beyond platonic friendship. Big Daddy, who grew up poor, admits to having "knocked around in [his] time," and having "slept in hobo jungles and railroad Y's and flophouses in all cities before" he "hopped off a yellow dog freight car" and got hired by Straw and Ochello, and then goes on to say that he has "seen all things and understood a lot of them" (115, 115, 116, 116). When faced with the possibility that his youngest and favorite son might prefer men to women sexually, Big Daddy takes the news in stride, telling Brick that he himself always "lived with too much space around me to be infected by ideas of other people. One thing you can grow on a big place more important that cotton!—is *tolerance!*—I grown it!" (120, emphasis Williams's).[5] So while Big Daddy sees space ("a big place") as the source of his tolerance, the text suggests that his past of hard manual labor and his occupation as an agrarian (even if he himself no longer dirties his hands with farming) has more to do with his ability to so easily bridge the gulf between homosocial and homosexual that paralyzes and consumes his son.

Although he appears onstage in *Cat* as a fantastically wealthy plantation patriarch, Big Daddy is new money: he came from nothing and everything he has, he has earned for himself. As a man in America in the 1950s, the fact that Big Daddy earned his money through grueling physical labor gives him a great deal of both respect and power. His distinctiveness gains power in the context of an ongoing "postwar crisis of masculinity" that Robert J. Corber sees as being "precipitated by the emergence and consolidation of a Fordist organization of production and consumption . . . in the 1950s a model of masculinity that stressed domesticity and cooperation gradually became hegemonic. Men were no longer encouraged to show initiative or to exert their independence from the domestic sphere. Rather, they were expected to define themselves through their identities as consumers—an expectation hitherto confined to women . . . many men experienced the postwar shift from production to consumption as a threat to their masculinity" (5–6, 14).

Corber suggests that men in the fifties were being asked to cooperate and to consume at a time when they still remembered older models of masculinity, models based on rugged individualism and production rather than corporate cooperation and consumption. Williams, in Act I, uses a speech by Maggie "The Cat" to ensure that his audience is aware of both the nature of Big Daddy's masculinity (its roots in producing, in being an individual) and the respect afforded him because of it: "I've sort of always admired [Big Daddy] in spite of his coarseness, his four-letter words and so forth. Because Big Daddy *is* what he *is*, and he makes no bones about it. He hasn't turned gentleman farmer, he's still a Mississippi redneck, as much of a redneck as he must have been when he was just overseer here on the old Jack Straw and Peter Ochello place. But he got hold of it and built it into th' biggest an' finest plantation in the Delta.—I've always *liked* Big Daddy" (53, emphasis Williams's).

And when Big Daddy himself finally does appear on stage at the beginning of Act II, audience members see that Maggie's description of him was perfect. From the moment of his entrance forward, Big Daddy commands the stage and acts as a kind of brutish champion for truth (as opposed to the southern upper-class pretenses that Big Mama, Gooper, Mae, and sometimes Maggie perform). He calls attention to Reverend Tooker's materialistic ambitions, shouts commands (which are instantly obeyed) to turn the radio on and off, and is openly cruel to his own wife (63–67). When Big Mama objects to this treatment, Big Daddy makes a long speech to her in which he both reasserts his own mastery (of the plantation and of his family) and cites his personal history (as a manual laborer, a producer, and an autonomous individual) as a source for that mastery. Accusing Big Mama of trying to seize control from him, he says: "Bossing. Talking. Sashaying your fat old body around the place I made! I made this place! I was overseer on it! I was the overseer on the old Straw and Ochello plantation. I quit school at ten! I quit school at ten years old and went to work like a nigger in the fields. And I rose to be overseer of the Straw and Ochello plantation. . . . I did all that myself with no goddamn help from you . . ." (77).

Big Mama may have traveled to Europe and bought a basement-full of Old World antiques to decorate her plantation big house with, but Big Daddy is no southern gentleman. He is a far cry from that social type, which John Shelton Reed (himself quoting Alabamian Daniel R. Hundley's 1860 guide to southern social types) sees as having "a 'natural dignity of manner' and 'the utmost self-possession'" and whose manners are "'remarkably easy and natural, never . . . loud of voice—even when angry rarely using his voice above the ordinary tone of gentlemanly conversation'" (25).

Regardless of his bank balance or the size of his house, Big Daddy is much closer—in terms of the kind of masculinity he performs—to being one of the poor white yeoman farmers that W. J. Cash saw as the essential southern type. This type of man, according to Cash, had decidedly ungentlemanly goals: "To stand on his head in a bar, to toss down a pint of raw whiskey at a gulp, to fiddle and dance all night, to bite off the nose or gouge out the eye of a favorite enemy, to fight harder and love harder than the next man, to be known eventually far and wide as a hell of a fellow" (50). Big Daddy's brand of unpretentious masculinity thus squares neatly with the ethos of southern populism, which dates to at least the 1890s. "In brief," write historians Wayne Parent and Peter A. Petrakis: "Populists believed that certain forms of economic activity were virtuous while others were not. Moneylenders, leaders of big corporations, commodity speculators, those engaged in the stock market, and middlemen in general all shared the characteristic of not being involved in the tangible production of goods. Economic activities that did not increase concrete goods were considered to be parasitic. . . . The Populists believed that as farmers they were involved in virtuous economic activity, while business and financial elites got rich through, in their view, scams and swindles. It was the farmer and the worker who were the backbone of America" (164).

With the populist-approved, agrarian "hell of a fellow" becoming an increasingly endangered species in an increasingly urbanized and corporatized postwar America, nostalgia for Big Daddy's brand of (laboring, productive, individualistic, agrarian—and therefore, in the eyes of southern populism—natural and good) manhood set in. Cash, whose *Mind of the South* was published in 1941, observed as much. He saw such nostalgia as "an intense revulsion against the ugliness of the new industrialism . . . and a yearning back toward the colorfulness and the more or less imaginary glory of the . . . purely agricultural past" (63).

I contend that it is this nostalgia for a vanishing type of masculinity—and the power it confers to the remaining practitioners of that masculinity—that allows Big Daddy to excuse or even approve the possibility of Brick's same-sex desire. Creator and lord of all he surveys, whatever Big Daddy says is exactly what goes on his plantation. Of the characters in the play, it is he and only he that has the power to untangle same-sex desire from the associations of effeminacy and moral degeneracy to which it had been so widely linked. In an industrializing, corporatizing postwar America where men were becoming increasingly domesticized, the power to do so—to create a space for his son where the double bind of masculine identity might be resolved, where Brick might be a man *and* love one—comes to Big Daddy by virtue of his agrarian, laboring past. And if it is Big Daddy's good old boy masculinity that empowers him to make this change (at least within the world of his plantation), then it is his age that allows him to imagine that such a change could be possible. Because he is a generation older than Brick, Big Daddy grew up at a time when the homosexual/heterosexual binary that Chauncey describes as emergent in mid-century discourse lacked the hegemonic force that it has during the present action of the play, the mid-1950s. If any such binary was common in Big Daddy's youth it was the queer/normal man distinction, which would have allowed for some men to have sex with other men while retaining a masculine social identity for themselves.

The tragedy of *Cat*, of course, is that Brick does not (and perhaps cannot) see or accept the space that his father is trying to make for him. While Brick, the star quarterback beloved by women, is unquestioningly butch, even he—only one generation removed from little money and hard labor—does not possess the power to bridge the double bind in the way his father suggests. Brick cannot untangle same-sex desire from its associations with effeminacy and moral deviance. Despite being a former football hero, Brick is also a university graduate and white-collar professional laborer (once his football career ended, he worked as a sports announcer until his drinking cost him the job); he has never worked with his hands, never grown anything or held a job where he produced tangible, concrete goods.[6] In a 1950s South caught between both increasing industrialization and an older ethic of southern populism (and in a middle twentieth-century America increasingly convinced that any same-sex desire or behavior makes a man fully homosexual, and therefore feminine), Brick's decidedly postwar service-economy masculinity is already too suspect to bear the further burden of same-sex desire that his father's hard laboring past and good old boy masculinity can withstand, accommodate, and even approve.

Populism, Patrimony, and the Love of Boys: *The Bitterweed Path*

While Williams, writing in the 1950s about the 1950s, looks to Big Daddy's brand of southern working class agrarian masculinity as the position in culture that might affirm and transform same-sex desire, Thomas Hal Phillips sets the action of *The Bitterweed Path* in the 1890s and uses good old boy masculinity as a kind of armor that shields his protagonists. By consistently enacting the role of Cash's "hell of a fellow" type, Darrell Barclay and Malcolm Pitt ameliorate not one, but two behaviors that their neighbors in the 1890s (and their readers in the 1950s) would have likely found either suspicious or abhorrent: first, their introduction of industry and a market economy into the previously agrarian South by their building and joint operation of a cotton gin, and second, their ongoing intergenerational and interclass romantic/sexual relationship with one another.

The Bitterweed Path begins in Vicksburg, Mississippi, in or around the year 1895, and the novel wastes little time making clear that both same-sex desire and southern working class agrarian masculinity will be two of its major thematic concerns.[7] Eighth-grader Darrell Barclay, the son of a poor white sharecropper and Ku Klux Klansman, has come to Vicksburg to compete in a foot race with other schoolboys. When Darrell goes into a boathouse to change into his racing uniform, he encounters a naked boy his own age. The sight of "the pale fullness of [the boy's] loins" takes Darrell's breath away, and the boy later turns out to be Roger Pitt, son of plantation owner Malcolm Pitt (4). Darrell's own father, away finding land to sharecrop on, cannot be at the races to support him, but Darrell wins the race and Malcolm Pitt—"tall and strong and broad-shouldered" with a "solid brown chin"—congratulates him heartily and escorts him to the judge's stand to receive his first-place ribbons (5). When the man handing out the prizes tells Darrell not to trust Malcolm, Malcolm responds like a true southern populist, saying "He's a banker and a politician, Darrell. He's the one not to be trusted" (8).

Darrell—thoroughly entranced by both Roger and Malcolm—returns home and is greeted by his own father's cruelty and indifference, which lead him to declare that "I wish Malcolm Pitt was my father and I wish Roger was my brother . . ." (18). In many ways, the rest of the novel plays itself out in fulfilling that wish. Malcolm Pitt signs Darrell's father to a sharecropping contract and Darrell soon moves to the Pitts's plantation. Roger and Darrell begin a deep friendship (that includes skinny-dipping and naked wrestling, which causes both boys to become aroused); and when Darrell's father is shot and killed while riding with the Klan, Malcolm Pitt hires the boy on as a "hand" so that he may stay on the plantation (53, 62). Shortly after this, Roger's mother (a woman who Darrell never sees outside the house without gloves, and who insists that her son play the piano and memorize Shakespeare) arranges to continue Roger's education by sending him off to boarding school. Thus begins one of the novel's most fascinating moves: with Roger away at boarding school, Darrell works "harder in the fields . . . than he had ever worked for anyone" and, over time, becomes both Malcolm's right hand man and surrogate son (68). As this process continues, what had seemed like a novel about two boys in love gradually morphs into a novel about a man and a boy in love.

This emerging (homo)erotic triangulation—whom does Darrell love, Roger or Malcolm? whom will he choose?—becomes clear in Part 2, Chapter 3, when Malcolm tells Darrell of his plans to build and run a cotton gin on the plantation, a gin whose profits they will, according to Malcolm, "split half and half" (78). Then, just before Christmas, Malcolm takes Darrell along with him on a trip to Memphis. The goal of this trip is to buy the parts for the gin itself, but Malcolm also does some Christmas shopping, both for his family and for Darrell.

He buys Darrell an expensive tailor-made suit, and this kindness makes Darrell deeply uncomfortable. When he tells Malcolm that he cannot accept the present, Malcolm says "You can't do that. You want to be my boy, don't you?" (80). "Yessir," Darrell replies. "I want to. But I'm not your son" (80). "Are you going to be that way with me?" Malcolm counters, "I thought you loved me a little" (80). Darrell says that he does, and he ends up taking the coat.

Then, later that night, while they are sharing a room on a steamboat headed back down to Vicksburg, Darrell complains of being cold and Malcolm lifts the sheets on his own bed, inviting Darrell into it: "Darrell crossed the room and climbed into bed beside Malcolm and the warmth seemed to swallow him. He turned once and his face was against Malcolm's shoulder and Malcolm pulled him close so that Darrell could feel the great maleness of him, soft and warm and weighty. . . . His heart began to pain him with its wild beating, for now he touched the great clean strength of Malcolm Pitt. . . . Their hands rested lightly together. Then, as if to complete the ritual, Malcolm put his arm around Darrell. Darrell . . . knew that, somehow, there was nothing fleeting about the moment, that he was bound forever to the great strength against him" (83–84). While Phillips pulls a literary fade-to-black after this, denying readers explicit textual evidence that Darrell and Malcolm have sex, his writing up to the fade out manages to be both charged enough and vague enough to enable both sides of a "Did they or didn't they?" debate. What exactly, for example, is "the great maleness" of Malcolm Pitt that Darrell feels so "soft and warm and weighty"? As written, it could be Malcolm's penis just as easily as it could be the size and power of Malcolm's whole male body.

I read this scene between fifty-something man and teenage boy to be fully sexual and I contend that the situation surrounding it—the fact that Malcolm and Darrell wind up in bed together while on what amounts to a shopping trip, to purchase both Christmas presents and the parts needed to build a cotton gin—is worth paying attention to. As Michael Trask points out, early twentieth-century American culture saw a direct correspondence between deviant desire and mass culture (where a market economy provides instant gratification of presumably limitless consumer desire), so that: "If we are accustomed to thinking that we all belong to mass society but that only some of us are queer, early-twentieth-century society by contrast declares that to belong to mass society is always to enter the sphere of the illicit, the perverse, the dirty. In short, according to the major thinkers in the Progressive era and beyond, in mass culture everyone is queer" (194). Those Progressive-era thinkers would seem to be vindicated by the scene between Malcolm and Darrell on the riverboat. Despite Phillips's ceaseless attempts to remind readers that Malcolm Pitt is a good old boy through and through—he distrusts bankers and politicians! he drinks! he chews tobacco! he works the land he owns! he uses folksy aphorisms such as "If you let the rough side drag long enough it'll get smooth"! and Darrell sees him as "stronger than all the other men put together"!—the moment that he and Darrell leave the agrarian plantation and enter the world of mass consumer culture is the very same moment that they sleep together, literally and almost certainly metaphorically (77, 75).

This night on the riverboat is hardly the last place in *The Bitterweed Path* where the tensions between "hell of a fellow" southern populist masculinity and industrialization (and the place of same-sex desire) make themselves apparent. At the Pitt family Christmas party that follows Malcolm and Darrell's trip, Malcolm has too much to drink and makes a scene, a scene which reveals that Darrell's status as a good old boy in training is precisely what makes him attractive to Malcolm. Roger has returned home from boarding school for this Christmas party, and while the family is assembled around the dinner table, Malcolm asks his son, "Have you learned a whole hell of a lot, Roger? In your books, I mean" (89). Roger replies that he can factor and Malcolm, decidedly unimpressed, says "That must be fine" (89).

Later, after several more drinks, Malcolm takes both Roger and Darrell into the kitchen and makes a speech that reveals both the nature of his love for Darrell and his scorn for higher education: "Roger, you ought to see our plantation now. It's really beautiful. It's not green, being December, you see, but it's beautiful. You're going to be a doctor, but me and Darrell—Darrell and I—know how to make things grow. We work alike" (92). At this point Mrs. Pitt tries to silence Malcolm, but he only "looked at [his wife] and then crossed the room to Darrell and put his arm around Darrell's neck. 'This is my real son. We're just farmers and we can't factor, but by God we can raise the best cotton in the country. Roger is a schoolboy, soft; well let him be a doctor.' He pulled Darrell close. 'We're going to build a gin—half and half. You couldn't work like we do, Roger—us men. You're pale—like winter butter. But look at Darrell. . . .' He began to feel Darrell's arms" (93). What is of interest in these Christmas party rantings, apart from Malcolm's breathtaking cruelty towards his own son, is the way in which Malcolm uses the language and values of southern populism—"Darrell and I—know how to make things grow," "we work alike," "we're just farmers," "you couldn't work like we do,"—to defend the building of a cotton gin, an industrializing project that arguably might not square with the ethos of southern populism.

Malcolm repeats this curious pattern yet again later in the book, when Darrell is threatened by G. Roper, a peer of Malcolm's. While Malcolm and a group of other men are drinking to celebrate the completion of the gin, Darrell stays apart from them and takes a tour of the industrial marvel, looking at its "weighing platform," "ginner's stool," "copper weights," "scale-desk," "belts," "ginheads," "glass windows," "bins," and "compress" before deciding to crawl out along a pipe and wipe down the scales (105). While Darrell is suspended precariously doing this task, Roper appears and accosts him. Roper had had ambitions of building a cotton gin himself, and he is embittered that Malcolm and Darrell have beaten him to it. In his anger, Roper charges Malcolm Pitt with the cardinal sins of southern populism: cheating and swindling.

Roper tells Darrell that Malcolm is manipulating him, that Malcolm is going to give Darrell half of the gin only because Malcolm will then expect Darrell to marry his daughter Miriam, thus keeping profits from the gin wholly within the Pitt family (108). Bemoaning Malcolm's economic dominance in the area, Roper alleges that Malcolm has been inhospitable, that he has cheated him by refusing to sell him land that he (Roper) wants to build a general store on: "He'll beat me to the sawmill too, then the store. He's going to build the store for you, ain't he? That's the reason he won't sell me that acre? Ain't it?" (108).

Darrell defends himself against these charges by utilizing the labor-centric language of southern populism: "I get half of what we clear, that's all. I work for it" (108). At that moment, Malcolm Pitt appears and, in classic "hell of a fellow" style, threatens violence if Roper does not back away from Darrell. "Go ahead," Roper laughs. "Throw me off. Break my neck and go to jail—go to Parchman. No. They wouldn't put you in the pen. They would never put you in the pen . . ." (109). The implication here is that Malcolm has used—and would use—his economic power in order to cheat justice, that he is precisely one of the moneyed non-agrarian businessmen that southern populism views with such suspicion and scorn.

But while Roper's charges in this scene seem to call Malcolm and Darrell out for being what they are—powerful, upwardly mobile men who are industrializing the previously agrarian south—Malcolm answers the charges and smooths the situation over with rhetoric and action pulled straight from the southern agrarian/populist playbook. He soothes Darrell's concerns about ownership by explaining that he is selling, not giving, the half-interest to Darrell: "I want you to be proud of this gin. The worst thing in the world is for a man to work at something he's not proud of. You're going to run it and pay for your half" (110). And then the chapter ends with Malcolm making a neighborly, communitarian gesture, by "going to Vicksburg" and "deed[ing] one acre of land to G. Roper" (110).

What is hopefully clear at this point is the way in which Phillips deploys good old boy masculinity to reassure his readers that whatever else Malcolm and Darrell might be, they are good old boys first and foremost: "I never hit a drunk man before in my life," Malcolm says to Darrell after the altercation with Roper, "Certainly not somebody who drank my own whisky" (109–10). Even when they are operating counter to the ethos of southern populism (by building the gin, which processes materials rather than generating them and provides a service to consumers rather than producing tangible goods itself), Malcolm and Darrell are still able to deploy populist and agrarian language skillfully enough to forestall the suspicion (and quell the outrage) of their neighbors.

Phillips is thus asking southern populism and its approved brand of masculinity to do more work than Williams did. In the 1950s of *Cat*, good old boy masculinity has the power to sanction and transform how same-sex desire is thought of because widespread industrialization and mass culture have made it rare, and therefore alluring. In the 1890s of *The Bitterweed Path*, this same type of masculinity is more common, and it becomes both the chief reason that Malcolm is attracted to Darrell and the way in which he is able to justify/excuse his own role as industrializer.

But as some of the language quoted above has probably already made clear, good old boy masculinity is only part of how Phillips aims to rework same-sex desire in his novel. While Malcolm Pitt is almost always described in terms of his strength and cleanliness (attributes that stem directly from his status as a land-working "hell of a fellow"), of equal importance is the way in which Phillips frames same-sex desire in terms of familial bonds, so that Darrell fantasizes about Roger and Malcolm being his brother and his father, not his lovers or partners or boyfriends.

In *Men Like That*, John Howard writes that Phillips, when interviewed, said that the Biblical story of Jonathan and David had been his inspiration for *The Bitterweed Path*. Howard himself goes on to point out that "historically the notion of brotherhood often stood in for, or alongside, queer desire among Mississippians of Phillips's generation" (190–91). That said, Howard's writings about *The Bitterweed Path* overstate the centrality of the Roger-Darrell relationship to the novel and fail to recognize that even after Malcolm Pitt has died, it is to him—not Roger—that Darrell remains the most passionately attached. Darrell himself says so, after all, mere moments before going to bed with Roger.

This scene, which illustrates the hierarchy of Darrell's affections, appears toward the very end of the novel. Malcolm has been killed accidentally by an explosion in the cotton gin and Roger and Darrell, mourning him, have gone to Vicksburg for a night. They share a hotel room and as they sit together, watching the river, Roger asks Darrell: "Did you love Father? I mean really love him?" (310). Darrell answers with a question of his own: "Would you make something ugly out of that, Roger?" (310). "No," Roger says. "I think I'd be the last person in the world to do that" (310). Darrell's answer, finally, is "'Yes. I never saw him in my life but that something moved inside me. I would have done anything for him. Anything. I wish I'd been killed instead of him . . .' Suddenly he put his arm around Roger, and he said, 'I love you Roger. I always have. But not that much. Sometimes I wish I did. Sometimes I wish with all my heart I did . . .'" (310–11).

Darrell and Roger do end up sleeping with each other after this scene, and in what is probably the novel's most definitive exchange, they answer the "Did they or didn't they?" question that has lingered over both their own relationship, and Darrell's relationship with Malcolm. As they lie in bed just about to have sex, Roger asks Darrell:

> "Do you think it's right?"
> "I don't know . . . we're grown now . . ."
> "What did Father ever say?"
> "Nothing . . . he never said anything . . ." (311)

Roger and Darrell do end up having sex, traveling together into what Phillips calls "the wild tenderness," but their connection ultimately proves to be fleeting (311). In the morning they return home and part ways forever. Roger goes back to New Orleans to practice medicine, and Darrell remains, taking up his role as owner and operator of Malcolm Pitt's plantation.

Throughout the book Darrell's attraction wavers from Roger to Malcolm and back again, but in this near-final scene, Phillips finally resolves the question. It is the father/lover bond to Malcolm that endures in Darrell's heart, not the brother/lover bond that might have been possible with Roger. Indeed, it is the father/lover bond that proves to be sustainable and repeatable in the novel. It is what Darrell looks to repeat, at the end of the novel, when he vows that "Someday I will have another son" (314).[8]

Contrary to what the mainstream thought of postwar America would make of it, Darrell certainly does not experience his relationship with Malcolm as either molestation or exploitation. Darrell is drawn to Malcolm from the very first moment he sees Malcolm and Malcolm becomes both Darrell's lover and the loving, caring father he wished he'd had, "a wide muscled hand that never lashed out" (55).[9] Darrell's love for Malcolm is so strong (and so deeply tied to Malcolm-as-father-figure and the strength that his good old boy masculinity confers) that at the novel's close he must reject even Roger, who is Malcolm's son but who—as an educated, non-agrarian who does not perform manual labor—can never be the man, the father, or the lover that Malcolm was. It is only Darrell, who stays on the plantation and works the land alongside of Malcolm and inherits it from him, who can ever, in a future relationship with a "son" he has yet to meet, replace Malcolm.

The answer to why this outcome is not only possible but deeply probable in *The Bitterweed Path* can be found in Michael P. Bibler's reading of plantation social structures in *Cat on a Hot Tin Roof*. "The plantation must transfer from patriarch to patriarch," writes Bibler. "The patrilinear economy that ensures the perpetuation of the plantation as both an economic and cultural institution . . . privileges the notion of sameness, and is thus homosexual in nature . . . it flows not from father to oldest son so much as from same to same" (396, 397). In this sense, Malcolm and Darrell's love in *The Bitterweed Path* is anachronistic vis-à-vis the schema presented in Sedgwick's *Between Men*, which theorizes that male homosocial bonds are often camouflaged "within the structural context of triangular, heterosexual desire" (16). Just as the women in the English literature that Sedgwick reads in *Between Men* give a pair of ostensibly feuding men a reason to interact passionately with one another as a stage in reproducing that "patrilinear economy," it is the feminized but still male-identified Roger Pitt that originally gives Malcolm and Darrell a reason to interact. But while Malcolm and Darrell's relationship is initially triangular (with Roger serving as the third, ultimately excluded point), it ultimately involves neither actual women nor feminized male bodies. Thus Malcolm and Darrell's relationship conforms to what Sedgwick calls "classical [Spartan and Athenian] . . . models of virilizing male bonds, models in which the male homosocial institutions (education, political mentorship, brotherhood in arms) and the homosexual seemed to be fully continuous, and fully exclude the world of women" (207).

Perhaps it is for this very reason that Malcolm and Darrell's relationship can exist at all. According to Bibler's reading of race, gender, and sexuality on the plantation, elite white male homosexuality is permissible in this setting precisely because double patriarchs such as Jack Straw and Peter Ochello are, at the end of the day, still white male patriarchs. They love each other and not women, but ultimately this love does not threaten the plantation's social order; it does not question the places or roles that the plantation assigns to blacks or women. This argument of Bibler's can be applied very neatly to *The Bitterweed Path*. While Phillips makes a few hints towards Malcolm Pitt's progressive racial politics, he and Darrell are both plantation men who largely conform (with the exception of their sexuality) to the dominant social order. While Malcolm and Darrell's relationship is radical in the sense that it does open up one new space (for elite white male homosexuality) in southern culture, it is also reactionary in that it leaves a host of other (racialized and gendered) restrictions in place.

Tradition, Change & Accommodation

Towards the very end of *The Bitterweed Path*, Roger Pitt says to Darrell: "I never should have come back [to the plantation], but I wanted to be close to you. I wanted to be like you. Any day, any minute . . . I would trade with you . . . everything you are, I'd like to be" (311). While Roger—slightly effete, city-living, city-educated Roger who does all that is asked of him and still loses both a male lover and a father's love—undoubtedly feels completely alone at this moment in the text, I would suggest that he is hardly so. As I hope my readings of Williams and Phillips have shown, everything that Darrell Barclay is—white, working class but upwardly mobile, individualist, agrarian, and thus perceived as "normal" and "natural" even when behaving in ways that would usually be considered suspect or deviant—also happens to be everything that a great many southern men wanted to be. This is true in the fictional 1890s of *The Bitterweed Path* and the factual 1950s of its, and *Cat*'s, publication. After all, it is no accident that Phillips and Williams—two southern authors, both publishing in the 1950s and each wishing to re-imagine the southern sex/gender system in order to validate a type of same-sex desire—should ascribe the power to (imaginatively) rework masculinity to practitioners of good old boy masculinity.

For all that their work contradicts conventional views of same-sex desire in the fifties, Phillips and Williams are in fact part of a broader discourse addressing changes in masculinity in their time. Historians and literary critics interested in masculinity have repeatedly characterized the 1950s in America as a decade of intense "male panic," a phenomenon that James Gilbert describes as "a time when men self-consciously rebel against real or imagined 'feminization' developing within the workplace, public spheres and/or domestic relationships" (3). The second chapter of Gilbert's *Men in the Middle* contains a thorough overview of existing scholarship concerned with American masculinity. A great deal of this scholarship is characterized by, according to Gilbert, a "mood of crisis" that becomes particularly intense "during and after the 1890s [and becoming particularly intense in the 1950s], when the transformation of work and patterns of urbanization made it difficult to enact an older ideology of individualism, self-reliance, and manliness" (16). But Gilbert himself is skeptical about this sense of perpetual crisis in American masculinity and *Men in the Middl*e is devoted to highlighting the "accommodationist voices" of American men who welcomed the changes in sex, gender, and labor roles brought on by changes in labor (7).

The above readings of Phillips and Williams aim to demonstrate that both writers are, to varying degrees, "accommodationist" in regards to the changes in masculinity brought on by the shifting nature of work in the increasingly urbanizing American South post-1945. By this I mean that both Phillips and Williams attempt to bring some new kind of same-sex affective masculinity into both view and validation. *The Bitterweed Path* and *Cat on a Hot Tin Roof*, then, are two of what, if Gilbert is correct, were probably many "dissenting, clear voices" talking about masculinity in the 1950s, voices imagining "alternative constructions of gender" that might emerge out of the shifting masculine landscape (3). Viewed in this context, Phillips's novel seems more hopeful than Williams's play about the possibility of these "alternative constructions of gender" (and sexuality) being able to survive and replicate themselves, but this hopefulness is likely enabled by Phillips's decision to set the novel in the historically distant 1890s, a move that allows him to evade some of the particular pressures bearing down on all types of masculinity during the dawn of the 1950s, pressures that Williams takes on more directly in *Cat*. In particular, *The Bitterweed Path*'s 1890s setting allows Phillips (and his characters) to evade the ever-increasing hegemony of the homosexual/heterosexual binary wherein a man is assumed to have a quality known as a "sexuality"—determined by the gender of the man's sexual object choice—which in turn determines the rest of that man's identity. Williams, in turn, sets his work in the middle of the 1950s themselves, and concerns himself with dramatizing both the severe penalties that accompanied homosexual identification at the time[10] and the large and painful gap between the complex truth of Brick's lived experience (whatever that truth might be: homosexual, heterosexual, or something else altogether) and the restrictive binary assumptions that he and his culture operate under.

Both works are also "accommodationist" in the sense that they are at least cautiously optimistic about what changes to masculine identity in the 1950s might mean; each, in its own way, aims to re-imagine what masculinity might be and what those claiming it as part of their identity might be permitted to do. What both works prove *un*able to accommodate is an overly simplistic, dualistic homosexual/heterosexual binary, the very binary that was solidifying its claim to cultural hegemony in the decade of their publication. Although one of the works ends on a more hopeful note than the other, and one has achieved canonical status, the question of which work about same-sex desire in Mississippi is more progressive is not answerable in any neat and tidy way. The temptation to pass simple ideological judgments is ill-advised: Gilbert as well as Chauncey and Foucault all remind us in their work that all-or-nothing analysis is probably doomed to be overly simplistic. What could a simple ideological test make of the fact that both Phillips and Williams attempt to achieve their transformational, "accommodationist" goals by deploying more or less laudatory representations of good old boy masculinity, an agrarian type that any "accommodationist" worth his salt theoretically ought to be trying to leave behind?[11] Such a test would mistakenly see that strategy as a contradiction or incoherence in both authors' works. In fact, there is no such contradiction: the job of the artist is to imagine, and in the works discussed here, both Phillips and Williams use the tools of the known past and the available present in order to try and shape their own vision of a livable future for same-sex affective white men in the American South.

Notes

1. In referring to better known, more commercially successful southern literary work wherein men who love men come to bad endings, I am thinking primarily of the work of Carson McCullers and Tennessee Williams. For portraits of same-sex affective men whose story arc and/or lives end badly in McCullers's work, see John Singer, the suicide in *The Heart Is a Lonely Hunter* (1940), and the murderous Captain Penderton in *Reflections in a Golden Eye* (1941). For corresponding examples in Williams's work (in addition to *Cat On A Hot Tin Roof*'s Brick and Skipper), see Blanche DuBois's dead-by-suicide husband Allan Grey in *A Streetcar Named Desire* (1947) and poet/child predator/cannibalism victim Sebastian Venable in *Suddenly Last Summer* (1958). Still, it is worth noting that *The Bitterweed Path* is not the only exception to this mid-century southern literary trend of unhappy ending for homosexuals. Michael Bronski has in his anthology *Pulp Friction* iden-

tified three mid-century southern authors whose novels do not doom their gay male protagonists: Texans Lonnie Coleman (*Sam*, 1959) and Jay Little (*Maybe—Tomorrow*, 1952), and Georgian Calder Willingham. Significantly, Willingham's *End as a Man* (1947), the only such work put out by a major publisher, is the least progressive: in keeping with its satirical presentation of life for young military-college cadets, it presents one of its gay characters as an over-the-top caricature of a spoiled young southern aristocrat. For an overview on representations of gay men in southern literature (which, it should be noted, fails to mention Thomas Hal Phillips), see J. Randal Woodland's entry on "Gay Literature" in *The Companion to Southern Literature*, pages 289–92.

2. Desire here could certainly mean (homo)sexual desire, but the term could also be considered in the light of Eve Kosofsky Sedgwick, who uses it to mean not "a particular affective state or emotion" but the "affective or social force, the glue, even when its manifestation is hostility or hatred . . . that shapes an important relationship" (*Between Men* 2). Read in this way, the vast stakes of the issues in play here can be seen more clearly; after all, what man—gay or straight or anything else altogether—escapes having "an important relationship" with another man, especially in a patriarchal culture?

3. For historical evidence that an understanding of homosexuality that associated male-male desire with both effeminacy and criminality was circulating in Mississippi at least as early as the 1890s, see John Howard's "The Talk of the County: Revisiting Accusation, Murder, and Mississippi, 1895," in *Queer Studies: An Interdisciplinary Reader*. For more on discourses about homosexuality and gender insubordination in Mississippi from World War II forward, see Howard's *Men Like That*.

4. In addition to being paralyzed, Brick is also under siege. His wife and his father press him almost continually for the truth about his relationship with Skipper, and his brother and sister-in-law spy and circle like vultures in search of the same information. While it is easy enough for viewers/readers of *Cat* to hate the always snooping and eminently unlikable Mae and Gooper, John S. Bak deftly points out that Williams's play actually transforms audience members into the same kind of vultures: "we too become government spies and eavesdroppers during the private scene between father and son; and when we leave the theatre asking ourselves, as Walter Kerr did in 1955, 'Was Brick gay?' or 'Why didn't Williams just come out and say that Brick was gay instead of hiding behind all this "mystery" business?,' we are aligning ourselves more with the rumor-mongering Maggies and Maes of the world than we are with the victimized Bricks and Skippers. In other words, we too are guilty of determining a man's sexual nature based solely on our reading of his social identity, and thus forever marginalizing him socially, sexually, and politically in the process." (247).

5. David Savran praises Big Daddy's offer of tolerance as "an antihomophobic position" and "an attempt to neutralize Brick's self-hatred and forfend his 'queer' bashing." He also says that Big Daddy possesses "an unusual sensitivity to economic injustice" (101). Michael P. Bibler disagrees sharply with this reading and says that Savran fails "to search the text for any reason why we should accept his association of tolerance with something as decidedly oppressive and intolerant as the Southern plantation" (387). He then goes on to point out that "Big Daddy is not so isolated on the plantation as he claims because the plantation's success depends on the long-term settlement and control of a laboring black population kept in legal subordination" (389). I think that Bibler is right to point out that Big Daddy's power depends on the continued subordination of both blacks and women. But I fail to see why that makes his offer for tolerance for his son null and void. Must tolerance be universal to be sincere? I think not; it is entirely possible for Big Daddy to be both tolerant of his son's sexuality and intolerant towards the women and blacks considered beneath him on the social ladder.

6. In Williams's original draft of Act III, Mae mocks Brick on these very grounds, saying that he "never carried a thing in his life but a football or a highball" (149).

7. Phillips includes no overt time-stamps in the novel, so trying to date its events (or its characters' ages) precisely is an always-dicey proposition. Still, in the first chapter Malcolm Pitt reminds another man that the Civil War has "been over thirty years" and that they will both "soon be fifty years old" (10). Darrell is described as being in eighth grade in this first chapter, which would seem to make him thirteen or fourteen if we assume that today's school grade-to-age correspondences were the same in 1895. This would seem, however, to be an incorrect assumption, because when Darrell's father dies a few chapters (and some time) later Darrell feels "that he was no longer a child of twelve" (56).

8. Darrell's use of "another son" here refers to the fact that he has—during parts of the novel not covered in my reading here, married a woman named Emily. She and Darrell have twin sons and Emily dies while giving birth to a third, stillborn child. Rather than deflating the primacy of the Darrell-Roger-Malcolm homoerotic triangle, Darrell's heterosexual relationship only reasserts it. This is because Phillips suggests that Darrell only gets married because he wishes to be closer to both Malcolm and Roger, who at this point in the novel has already married a woman: "Darrell watched [Malcolm and Roger]: their tan faces, their muscled arms, their knowledged bodies. They were men with wives, he thought. A wall was between him and these two men. He could not talk to them now. But soon, very soon, he would be married to Emily; and the wall would be torn away" (194).

9. In what I can only read as a breathtaking understatement, Phillips admitted in a 1972 interview that "Yes, the father image is probably the dominant image in my writing" (Kelly 10).

10. For a useful overview of the homophobic atmosphere of America in the 1950s, see D'Emilio and Freedman, Chapter 12: "Redrawing the Boundaries," particularly pp. 288–300.

11. While Williams seems to use good old boy masculinity (in the character of Big Daddy) pretty much as he received it from white southern culture, Phillips clearly picks and chooses what he likes about the social type of the good old boy before he affirms it as an ideal. This is most clear in the case of Thad Barclay, Darrell's biological father. The elder Barclay's violent, ignorant (and ultimately fatal) racism is a character feature that Phillips clearly ascribes to Thad Barclay's class. It is also a feature which Phillips has Darrell leave behind as he enters the world of Malcolm Pitt, who is (relatively, for the time) racially progressive. Also, for all of his cruelty towards Roger around the issue of education, Malcolm does loan Darrell books from the big house library and encourage him to read them. Clearly, for Phillips, this does not make Malcolm any less admirable, or any less of a good old boy.

The Wrong Side of Town: *A Walk on the Wild Side* in an Age of Reaction

Ian Peddie

WHILE ATTENDING A forum on the role of the writer in America at the University of Michigan in 1962, Nelson Algren offered a rationale for writing that serves as a useful synopsis of his entire career and as a summary of what he felt was a civic duty: "I think that there is a vast multitude of Americans who are not recognized, who don't belong to American society," he contended, "and it's my particular self-appointed function to keep saying that they are there" ("The Role of the Writer in America" 23). Statements such as these not only form an interpretive context for Algren's fiction, but they are the core of his social vision. As early as 1934, for instance, in "If You Must Use Profanity," a short story that became part of *Somebody in Boots* (1935), Algren's debut novel, the author was already writing of the underclass, in this case railroad hoboes. Describing them as "bottom dogs," who drew a distinction between "themselves and those above," for the hoboes, as for so many of Algren's disaffected, the world was divided between "We and Them" (*American Mercury* 431). This "unabashed affection for the powerless" ("Foreword" x) as Russell Banks put it in 1989, Kurt Vonnegut saw as truly innovative, suggesting in his 1986 introduction to *Never Come Morning* that Algren "broke new ground by depicting persons said to be dehumanized by poverty and ignorance and injustice as being *genuinely* dehumanized" ("Introduction" xx). Yet ironically, in the light of his attempts to bring the excluded into mid-century fiction, Algren's affinity for the underclass was ultimately responsible for his own exclusion from the mainstream of U.S. literature, as he continued writing of class inequities well after that theme had become unfashionable among major artists and critics. With the last novel he published in his life, *A Walk on the Wild Side* (1956), he crashed directly into the pieties and shibboleths of 1950s America, in the process creating a harrowing critique of that era's values and a dark prophecy of conflicts to come.

Algren was born Nelson Ahlgren Abraham in Detroit in 1909, and in 1913 his family moved to the South Side of Chicago, the city which was later to provide the setting for his greatest literary successes. After graduating from the University of Illinois with a degree in journalism at the height of the Great Depression, Algren was unable to find a job and this, as much as anything, prompted him to begin writing. His first short story, "So Help Me," appeared in 1933 and two years later *Somebody in Boots* was published. To some degree or another, all of his subsequent works, among which are *Never Come Morning* (1942), *The Neon Wilderness* (1947), *The Man with the Golden Arm* (1949), *Chicago: City on the Make* (1951), *A Walk on the Wild Side* (1956), *The Last Carousel* (1973), and *The Devil's Stocking* (1983), are sympathetic to those who had "emerged from the wrong side of the billboards" (*The Man with the Golden Arm* 17). Active in the League of American Writers, which later brought him to the attention of the FBI, as a developing writer Algren—although never a *de facto* Communist—naturally sought the literary company of like-minded Left authors such as Jack Conroy and Richard Wright.[1]

If Algren's early predilection for Communism undoubtedly waned as the years progressed, his social vision of amelioration for the underclass never wavered. In one of many unguarded moments recorded in a notebook and never published, he confirmed his allegiance towards the truly disadvantaged, those "left with something to say and no one to say it," those who have to "win every round just to stay alive" (qtd. in Drew 112). But there was nothing new in such emotive statements. Algren had been making similar pronouncements for years and he would make many more before his death in 1981. What these articulations of the author's social vision reveal is a strength of conviction that fostered a lifelong vocation. For Algren not only used Walt Whitman's "I belong to those convicts and prostitutes myself— / And henceforth I will not deny them— / For how can I deny myself?" ("You Felons on Trial in Courts") as an epigraph, he actually tried to live the sentiments the verse embodied.

Unfortunately, nearly two decades before Algren made his Michigan pronouncement, critics had decided that such assessments were the province of the 1930s, a conclusion that revealed a political agenda designed to legitimize the prevailing status quo. Exorcising the ghosts of the red decade, however, meant far more than burying works of proletarian literature—a task at which critics were hard at work from the 1940s onwards—for much of the cultural criticism at that time harbored an unhealthy degree of uneasiness with social class that hinted at other worrying agendas. In "Ten Years in a Tunnel: Reflections on the Thirties," Irving Kristol gave a sense of what many felt was at stake when he concluded that "coming to terms with the thirties means coming to terms with the history and the prospects of American democracy itself" (6). To critics already peppered on a daily basis with the alleged evils of left-wing writers, the alarming ideologies attributed to the lingering affects of the "red decade" removed any remaining doubts. Because left writers were invariably codified as cultural fifth columnists and their work articulated as a threat to the very heart of democracy, intellectuals—and many of them were former fellow travelers—championed their censure. In his 1982 memoir *A Margin of Hope*, Irving Howe went further; after trivializing the left by admitting that what he called the "factional tournaments of the thirties" had taught him only "the skills of vicarious conquest" (56), he later admitted his collusion with *Partisan Review* editor Philip Rahv's agenda to "smash *them*" (130, italics added), a systematic program designed to banish left-wing writers once and for all.

Critics were helped in this enterprise by the fact that in the weeks and months after 1940, with the Moscow Trials and the Hitler-Stalin pact (1939) still fresh in its memory, the left was beginning to hemorrhage both members and credibility at an alarming rate. Why left-wing writers remained on the left when all available evidence seemed to suggest that it was no longer safe to do so became for their former associates an object of fascination. At stake here, once again, were critical attempts to tie the post-1939 literary left to its thirties predecessors, and as E. P. Thompson put it, to reduce the left to a "spoonful of Stalinist tar" ("Homage to Thomas McGrath" 113). Under the banner of "the God that failed," the "saved" began to issue charges of naiveté against "the damned" who persisted in their left-wing beliefs. Not surprisingly in the face of such pressure, at one stage apostasy became almost a genre in itself: Granville Hicks, Malcolm Cowley, Richard Wright, Sidney Hook, William Phillips, Philip Rahv, Irving Howe, and any number of other former fellow travelers recanted their previously held beliefs, and all went into print to explain their conversions.[1] "Never were so many people so fantastically wrong about so many things" (8), Irving Kristol wrote, and Granville Hicks agreed: "I had been wrong," Hicks submitted at the height of the Cold War. "To say this sounds self-righteous, as if I thought of myself as an innocent victim," Hicks continued, "perhaps I do" (*Where We Came Out* 8, 9). In fairness to Hicks, he also admitted that he had no right to think of himself as a victim, but the criticism that has grown up around the left has encouraged the notion that a number of intellectuals who flirted with the left did so chiefly because they had temporarily departed from reality—a position that allegedly deposited them at the mercy of an unscrupulous cadre seeking recruits at any cost.

The apologetics of the Cold War liberals provide an ideological framework through which we have inherited many of our interpretations of American literature. Manifestly, as the Cold War atmosphere began to shut down the old avenues of protest the near eclipse of class as a going concern in American literature paved the way for the reintroduction of the pervasive myth of classlessness that, as the 1950s approached, reappeared in American society. In this light, the closure in 1948 of the *New Masses*, perhaps the most important American radical journal of the twentieth century, now appears eerily symbolic, for the United States had been moving towards an idyll of classlessness at least since the sense of domestic unity engendered by the fight against the Axis powers, if not since Abraham Lincoln declared that all American workers were upwardly mobile (Seguin 1). From this perspective, "postwar prosperity is generally associated with a particular class," Andrew Hoberek points out, and "it is one that is traditionally understood in the United States as classless" (*The Twilight of the Middle Class* 3).

The myth of unity defined by a classless (read entirely middle class) consumerism was chiefly informed by a belief that just as divisions based on class distinctions were considered damaging to the war effort, so it followed that similar social discrepancies could be equally harmful in peacetime. Writing in 1957, journalist Max Lerner concluded that "the movement in America has not been from classlessness to class or from an open to a more rigid class system but from relatively clear divisions and modes of life to a situation where divisions have become more blurred, the stratification has become more subtle with shadings that are imprecise and elusive, and the modes of life have tended to converge in a large category of middle-class living" (*America as a Civilization* 471). This was the comfortable middle, the "imperial middle" as Benjamin DeMott calls it (*The Imperial Middle: Why American Can't Think Straight about Class*), a locus where class is a temporary staging post on the road to social mobility. Yes, there were classes, many critics agreed, but they were not static and fixed as they were in Europe; the growing middle class—and the alleged opportunities and benefits of belonging to it—ensured that polarized class relations could be presented as alien to the United States. This argument, which attempted to legitimize an autonomous and independent citizenry, proved remarkably appealing. As the critic Warren Susman asserted, it was a "fact" that "the story of American culture" was concomitant with "the enormous American middle class" (*Culture as History* 192).

All of these developments and initiatives, along with the arguments they spawned and the tensions they created, were part of the thinking underpinning the recasting of literary values that occurred after 1939. Among the literary power brokers, the growing insistence that class analysis was a worn seam was approaching the levels of implicit axiom by mid-century, and it ran hand in hand with critical convictions that left-wing writing was anachronistic. The die had been cast at least as early as 1937 in "Literature in a Political Decade," co-written by *Partisan Review* editors William Phillips and Philip Rahv. After articulating a contention that would run and run—that proletarian literature was rigidly formulaic—the essay went on to speak of "the sermons of proletarian writers" whose work they condemned as "as much imprisoned within a pragmatic mold as the average bourgeois novel" (175–76). Still more damning of proletarian literature was Rahv's now notorious 1939 postmortem into working class writing, "Proletarian Literature: A Political Autopsy," the implications of which reverberated throughout literary criticism for the next thirty or so years. While arguing that proletarian literature was formulaic, that its principal requirement was that "the writer should ally himself with the working class and recognize the class struggle as the central fact of modern life" (295), Rahv suggested that it always was, in fact, the literature of a party (Communist) masquerading as the literature of a class. Consequently, in the same essay Rahv was able to declare that "the period of the proletarian mystification of American letters is definitely over" (301).

For cultural arbiters of a similar persuasion to Rahv there were a legion of writers who could be condemned as literary dinosaurs, and no better example exists than Nelson Algren. In spite of the fact that Algren's novel *The Man with the Golden Arm* won the first National Book Award in 1949, his reputation as a "second-rate author," as one academic once described him to me, is undoubtedly attributable to critics' politically inspired denunciation of his work. Algren, as Leslie Fiedler's sweeping condemnation had it, "was made, unfortunately, once and for all in the early 1930's," and he has "stood still as our literature has moved on" ("Noble Savages" 43). Quite what "our literature" was Fiedler declined to say, but this typical attack affords a glimpse into how high the cultural stakes were at the time. As we have seen, what sustained those who shared the vision of Rahv, Fiedler, Norman Podhoretz, and others was a belief that what they were engaged in was a crusade to defend literature against would-be usurpers like Algren, whom they thought had been set adrift when the moorings that attached the "red decade" to American letters had been severed.

It was not only the political predilection of left-wing writers that rankled; left writers also wrote of subjects critics found unpalatable. In denouncing *A Walk on the Wild Side*, Norman Podhoretz asserted that Algren had produced "a lyrical rhapsody on the theme of bums and whores, hoboes and pimps, con men, and other social outcasts" ("The Man with the Golden Beef" 132). In a similar vein, Edmund Fuller went as far as to declare Algren one of the "destroyers of the social order" (*Man in Modern Fiction* 43). While criticism of this ilk was as unfair as it was wrong-headed, its proponents revealed that their idea of what constituted proletarian literature had moved not an inch since the end of the 1930s. In contrast, Algren was developing a much more sophisticated social vision than that of, say, Mike Gold, whose 1934 pronouncement that "there is NO RACE in the class war" ("A Word as to Uncle Tom" 136) now looks as one dimensional as the criticism Algren's work received. What Algren found baffling was that critics were unable to embrace his work as a developing and necessary social critique, fully concomitant with the times. Instead they saw it simply as a return to thirties proselytizing. But though *A Walk on the Wild Side* is set in the early thirties it is, *contra* Leslie Fiedler's condemnation of Algren, a novel that swings to a 1950s beat. In fact, for the people Algren wrote of throughout his entire career, the problems of the thirties were merely exacerbated by the attitudes of the 1950s; for the truly disadvantaged, any residual American dreams in which earlier generations had been schooled to believe had evaporated. Even those drawn to the individualist "ladder of success" realized that it was better to begin at the top and work downwards, "that route being faster" (117).

Critical hostility toward Algren's writing only strengthened his resolve. "There is no better way of recording the American saga than to study it from behind its billboards and comic strips, which tend to dwell upon the American dream [rather] than upon American reality," he told an interviewer ("Interview with Nelson Algren" 105). Despite Algren's insistence upon the ethical virtue of his social vision, however, he knew that this view of American society was rapidly losing ground. Vestigial memories of the 1930s, dominated by collectivism, poverty, and class, were being eroded in American letters, and to Algren the social climate, where timid conservatism prevailed, was being reproduced in literature. Authors in the fifties, Algren felt, had become "professional hallowers," extolling what now passed for American virtues. "Writers like Herman Wouk and Sloan Wilson," Algren contended, "are the spokesmen for the whole gadget-infested middle class" (qtd. in "Interview with Nelson Algren" 104).

The levels of despair these politically inspired observations elicited in Algren were compounded by concomitant changes in the literary establishment. Algren, who saw such changes as indicative of prevailing social ideologies, articulated them in terms of the social upheaval common to the inner-city populace that constituted his raw material. With anticommunist intellectuals dominating literary organs, "by the middle forties," he said of American letters, "new owners moved in." "They arrived directly from their respective campuses," he went on, "armed with blueprints to which the novel and the short story would have to conform, were a passing grade to be awarded" (Foreword to *Neon Wilderness*, 1960 ed). Algren concluded that the inspiration behind such attitudes were analogous to former left novelist Frank Yerby's contention that when he read *Anna Karenina* he found himself "skipping the peasant-in-relation-to-the-land parts [because] that sort of thing just isn't the novelist's job." But this prescription seemed to epitomize the problem. "How come," Algren wondered, "the Duke in relation to the Duchess, that sort of thing, is the novelist's job?" What was at stake Algren diagnosed as "the need not to be seen in shabby company" (*Noncomformity* 17–18). And by the time critics looked back at the thirties they found plenty of shabby company—which made it easier to attribute so many of the ills of American letters to the red decade.[3]

In their choice of anxieties to address,[4] popular fifties authors such as J. D. Salinger and David Riesman asserted a middle-class complacency that conveniently ignored the fact that *homo hierarchicus* still reigned and old inequalities remained. For Nelson Algren overturning the middle class's apparent denial of social reality was an essential preliminary to domestic amelioration. Amid the ambiguity and confusion at the heart of fifties America, a vague but nagging sense that for all its heralded successes the 1950s was not quite right persisted, and it was this that Algren exploited in *A Walk on the Wild Side*. Yet speaking in 1964, Algren averred that he "didn't make the least dent, because there is no way of convincing or making even the slightest impression on the American middle class that there are people who have no alternative, that there are people who live in horror, that there are people whose lives are nightmares" (qtd. in Donohue 94).

Algren, nonetheless, had no difficulty in deciding whether or not to go the way of the Cold War intellectuals and wring his hands over middle-class problems; he identified the characters he wrote of in *Wild Side* as "the accused, the underprivileged . . . people [who] are a little less lucky than most of us, but they're just as human" (qtd. in "Interview" 104, 105). Yet despite his insistence that society's interests were inextricably connected to such people, Algren was of the opinion that they were in most cases simply ignored or mollified by the panacea of the American dream. Accordingly, he argued that it was the rise of the middle class that had breathed new life into a problem he indicated in *Wild Side* was "ancestral" (108). Asserting that "the American middle class's faith in personal comfort as an end in itself is, in essence, a denial of life" (*Nonconformity* 20), in numerous interviews Algren admitted that since he had been a teenager he had held much of what he associated with the middle class in contempt. Such attitudes meant that he was on a collision course with the 1950s, not least because he framed his critique of American society in class terms, suggesting that middle-class values meant bourgeois values and a bourgeois country.

In the mid-fifties Algren articulated his idea of the middle class as the "Do-Right Daddies" of *Wild Side*, superficially respectable yet deeply corrupt. They were "the city fathers, Do-Right Daddies and all of that, Shriners, Kiwanians, Legionaires, Knights of this and Knights of that" (109), men who drank with outlaws and cavorted with prostitutes. It was the hypocrisy of it all that particularly rankled. For his transgressions a "Do-Right Daddy" needed to be ". . . purged of his guilt so he could sleep with his wife again. That was where the pulpit came in. There had to be something official like that to put the onus on the women. The preachers, reformers, priests and such did this work well. Some girls were just naturally bad, they explained. Others were made bad by bad men. In no case was it ever the fault of anyone who profited from the shows. Daddy, you can go home again" (109). As a comment on what Algren felt was the reality of power relations in the United States, this condemnation of institutionalized corruption and the scapegoating of the underclass must be read alongside the author's conclusion that the fundamentally inegalitarian nature of American society was congenital: "It was an ancestral treachery that all do-righters practice. When opening time was closing time and everyone was there, down where you lay your money down, where it's everything but square, where hungry young hustlers hustle dissatisfied old cats and ancient glass-eyed satyrs make passes at bandrats . . . when it's all bought and paid for then there's always one thing sure: it's some do-right Daddy-O running the whole show" (108–9). The rhythm jeers at the middle class in the same way that the exaggerated beatspeak mocks the idiom of the times. Like much of the writing Algren produced in the latter part of his career, this kind of satire had its own sharp edge, and it played an important part of a larger critique upon which the novel's foundations rested.

Algren saw defying the fifties drive towards conformity as a civic duty. In "Eggheads Are Rolling: The Rush to Conform," a 1953 commentary, part of which found its way into *Nonconformity*, Algren argues that "It no longer suffices to express our doubts privately. The out-loud kind of doubting which rescued American thought in the twenties from the files where the McCarthy's and the McCarrans and Jenners of that decade had locked it is what we most need in the timorous fifties" (306). Many of the most cherished articles of faith held dear by the "gadget-infested middle class" of Wouk and Wilson, Algren envisaged not merely as a middle-class malaise but as manifestations of social processes that reflected some of the worst aspects of capitalism. Conceived of in this way, the middle class that most cultural critics equated with America itself became a target of criticism and ridicule. The equation of the "imperial middle" with degenerate capitalism underpins *A Walk on the Wild Side*'s attempts to subvert the mid-century American dream. One of the core assumptions of the dream was a faith in the powers of consumerism that in *Wild Side* provides a stage for black comedy. Even in the middle of a depression, the narrator informs us, the housewife, conned into purchasing a "genuine French Dripolator" coffee machine she neither could afford nor needed, would often as not "sooner risk the black death than have her next-door neighbour own something she didn't" (123). While the pitiful one-upmanship lays bare how hollow consumerism could be, to Algren these and other similar episodes echoed lived realities that belied the American dream; in an interview the author condemned that large and increasingly influential body of American society unable to take solace "from [material] comforts" and for whom friends "are purely transient things where the main consideration . . . is whether they are in the same financial league" (*Interview with Donohue* 200, 310).

Notwithstanding the threats touted by the McCarthys and McCarrans, to Algren the irony was that in the 1950s the United States was a society where "the fear is not from monsters who walk abroad, but from monsters who walk in our own hearts" (*Nonconformity* 67). Nowhere are these "monsters" seen in more conspicuous relief than in *A Walk on the Wild Side*. Set in Texas and New Orleans, the novel uses satire and surrealism to frame a bawdy, knockabout story of the life and times of Dove Linkhorn, the youngest son of cesspool cleaner and religious zealot, Fitz Linkhorn, whose life is devoted to warning all who will listen of the "Papist Rapists" and their "international conspiracy against the Anglo-Saxon race" (10). Although the humorous tone with which the novel begins also foreshadows what will quickly become an open attack on the American dream, Algren heralds the direction *Wild Side* will take as early as the first page. Possessed of a "feeling of having been cheated—of having been cheated—that was it" (3), Fitz feels his unnamed loss "like some secret wound" (3). Not only do these sentiments initiate a subplot of frustrated power, they also outline the ambience of fraudulence and pretense through which Algren came to understand mid-century America.

The illiterate Dove's story begins in the dust of Arroyo and reaches its apex in New Orleans, where as the "Big Stingaree" he finds his true vocation playing the lead in live sex shows. As a kind of updated Nathanael West or inverted Horatio Alger, *Wild Side* is not what comes to mind when considering the typical fifties narrative.[2] Yet to Algren a parody of the American success story was entirely in keeping with the times: self-interest, which according to Algren is *the* dynamo at the heart of the American dream, in *Wild Side* often becomes the means through which social divisions are articulated. Thus he presented *Wild Side* as an assessment of some of the deep contradictions that blighted mid-century America; the novel was, Algren concluded, "an American fantasy, a poem written to an American beat as true as *Huckleberry Finn*" (qtd. in "A Talk on the Wild Side" 32). That this "American fantasy" begins in earnest when Dove has an affair with—and appears to rape—Terasina Vidavarri, a Mexican woman who runs a café, accentuates the sense of exploitation that Algren portrayed as endemic to the American dream. The sense of doom and victimhood is deepened by the story of the "tin soldier," which Vidavarri reads to Dove from her book of fairy tales. Like all fairy tales, this one too is allegorical: echoing the novel's obsession with thwarted autonomy, the tin soldier is eventually thrown into the fire "without rhyme or reason" (33), an event that extends beyond a comparison with Dove's own story, which will also end in tragedy as he is beaten blind in a barroom brawl. As James Giles points out, "the tin soldier story symbolically foreshadows the demise of another myth . . . the American dream of equal opportunity has become only a grim joke in the twentieth century" (*Confronting the Horror* 76).

Algren's parodic approach to the theme of self-interest creates some of the novel's most memorable passages, each itself a "grim joke" on the norms of the American success story. Thus when Dove stumbles into an eatery and sees "a Negro the size of Carnera, naked to the waist and shining with iron-colored sweat, decapitating snapping turtles" the ensuing allegory alludes to the ethics of class, of the American dream, and of American society: "Now the trouble with turtles is that they believe all things come to him who will but struggle," the narrator informs us.[3] "There's always room at the top for one more, they think. And in this strange faith the snapping kind is of all the most devout. For it's precisely that that makes them the snapping kind. Though the way be steep and bloody, that doesn't matter as long as you reach the top of the bleeding heap" (111–12). When one of the condemned turtles begins to speak, the allegory, which stretches over two and a half pages, promotes a sense of individual and collective complicity that parallels the harmonizing thread in Algren's critique of American society. After the turtle testifies that he "never knowingly harmed a fellow creature unless he got in [his] way," and that he "never took unfair advantage unless it profited [him]" (113), his final wish is that "gentle hearts" raise him so that he might "look one last time at the top of the heap" where he once "ruled so" (113). Not surprisingly, the ruthless social Darwinism to which this example points escapes Dove; as Bing Crosby's "I Aint Got Nobody" begins on the jukebox, Dove selects the "tarpon [terrapin] soup," still apparently blissfully unaware that "there was also room for one more at the bottom" (114). Both amusing and disturbing, underlying such allusive attacks on the middle class was Algren's conviction that resonates throughout *Wild Side*, that the prevailing zeitgeist, harbored a "sense of impending defeat" (110).

The remorselessness of the social critique *A Walk on the Wild Side* at times makes it a difficult book to read, as repeated allusions to the moral implications of class partition are as painful to the audience as they are to Dove Linkhorn. By the same token, Dove is as ill equipped to deal with the implications of the discourse of social apartheid as the reader is sensitive to them. Hence the amusement occasioned by Dove's naïve contention, made to a ship's captain whose vessel's mainmast a desperate Dove offers to paint in return for food, that "You got to work for nothing or you'll never get rich, that only stands to reason" (99) dissolves as his experience works to articulate a world Algren thought was being completely overlooked: "I feel like I been everywhere God got land," Dove thinks on the eve of his final brawl, "yet all I found was people with hard ways to go. All I found was troubles 'n degradation. All I found was that those with the hardest ways of all to go were quicker to help others than those with the easiest ways . . . poor bummies, poor tarts, all they were good for was to draw flies I was told. You could always treat one too good, it was said, but you could never treat one too bad" (332–33). The deep pessimism that lies behind these lines gestures not towards not the American dream but the real fate of those born "on the wrong side of a town that had only two sides, the wrong and the wronger" (35).

Here again, expressions of discontent are transmitted through textual allegory. Thus when Dove meets seventeen-year-old runaway Kitty Twist while riding the trains, her story supplies *Wild Side* with yet another context of despair. After admitting that her name is a pseudonym, and a sexually charged one at that, Twist confides: "I'm seventeen almost eighteen 'n I've run from five homes" (75). Though she has "never hustled" it emerges that "she knew the trade from older hands with whom she'd been institutionalized, and had run off with the prospect of going into business for herself" (77). Parodying the expectations of the "the affluent society" and the "new era of capitalism," such entrepreneurship calls into question the narratives of success by which many were encouraged to understand the postwar era. After ridiculing those populist schemas, Algren uses Kitty and Dove as a vector through which social attitudes can be symbolically examined. In this sense, when Kitty falls and hangs perilously while attempting to move between the railcars she and Dove are riding, his attempt to rescue her, where "he could not pull her up" and "he could not let her go" (73), is more than a transparent allegory of the plight awaiting those exiled from mainstream society. Transmitted thus, such examples illuminate the necessity of social obligation at the same time as they hint at the absence of a moral narrative that might supply the civic discourse Algren constantly expounds.

The humanism and compassion *Wild Side* implicitly longs for indicates its author's adherence to a belief that communal values are contingent upon moral responsibility. But the cultural narratives at work in the 1950s reconfigured collectivist ideologies of the thirties, turning them into what Thomas Hill Schaub calls a "liberal narrative" (*American Fiction in the Cold War* 3). This shift, conceived by Schaub as a "Blakean journey from innocence to experience, from the myopia of the utopian to the twenty-twenty vision of the realist" (5), incorporated the anticommunist fervor that cast out those associated with the 1930s left. In reality, far from being the clear-cut progression that some Cold War liberals would have liked, the 1950s was a bizarre mixture of sophistication and naiveté, of innocence and experience. From the Korean War to *Invasion of the Body Snatchers* (1956), from the Rosenbergs to Joseph McCarthy, from Sputnik to the prospect of asking a populace to "duck and cover" in the face of nuclear attack, perhaps it is not too surprising that American society in the 1950s was riven by the kind of fears that often manifest themselves as forms of social exclusion, in which the metaphor of expulsion has particular resonance.

In this respect, if the much-celebrated 1950s suburb masqueraded as a bastion of security against Cold War fears of nuclear Armageddon and Soviet "menace," then new suburbs also functioned to underscore racial divisions as non-whites were excluded and communities racially policed. In turn, as Leerom Medovoi points out, European immigrants living in "class-stratified enclaves in the cities [that] had encouraged a strong sense of themselves as ethnic groups" moved to the suburbs and found their former communal networks supplanted by "patterns of sociable consumption to be shared with new [white] neighbors" (*Rebels* 18). In this new milieu, Algren observed, self-worth came to be based upon the exclusion of others: "When we get more houses than we can live in, more cars than we can ride in, more food than we can eat ourselves, the only one way of getting richer is by cutting off those who don't have enough. If everybody had more than enough, what good is *my* more-than-enough? What good is a wide open meadow to everyone? It isn't until others are fenced out that the open pasture begins to have real value" (109–10). Predictably, in the recently built suburbs class consciousness was effectively suppressed. Algren interpreted the social consequences of these events as verification that deprivation was something the United States was quite prepared to tolerate. Here, the author felt, was confirmation that as the fifties moved further and further from any vestigial sense of social obligation, a vision where people contemplated "the world of their own needs alone" (*Wild Side* 233) became a normative principle.

Algren never ceased to articulate the many ways in which individual "success," as it was defined in the 1950s, was the negation of everything he stood for. He reserved particular vitriol for those "Brokers and buyers, efficiency experts with private means, personnel managers from banking families, men who had been born to ownership of ships and banks or mines or wells—the whole contented clan of white-collar foxes whose hearts were in their collars and their love locked in their files, who yet wanted to know of life—'What's the answer?' Without pausing once to wonder what was the question" (233). The comparison this passage invites, that these corporate Brahmins are as far removed from reality as is the American dream, constitutes an acknowledgment that social and moral visions have become unmoored from material life. Such abstraction had a more mundane corollary, however. For while Dove's admission that he wants "to make an honest dollar in a crooked sort of way" (164–65) was an Algrenesque assessment of the American economy, it was also indicative of a state of mind, a sensibility, which at mid-century the author thought more alarming than amusing.

As *Wild Side* unfolds, attacks upon the American dream and its constituent components are increasingly designed to shift the emphasis from the absurd, such as Dove's conclusion that unsalaried work is a logical avenue to success, to the grotesque, which is represented by the antics at the Perdido (lost) Street Brothel. Partaking of the very logic of exclusion that Algren sought to decry, Alfred Kazin singled out that aspect of the novel for condemnation: "It is not low life [Algren] is interested in but freaks; not tough people but grotesques; not the poor but the abnormal" (183). The conflation of the absurd and the grotesque, which lies at the heart of Algren's critique, also goes a good way toward explaining the estrangement of the "secret multitudes who belong to no world, no way of life, no particular time and place" (*Nonconformity* 36). In their imitative ways, then, the characters of *Wild Side* are caricatures of success. Among the most notorious examples in this respect are the violent pimp Oliver Finnerty, whose "talent lay in his limitless contempt for all things female" (198), and former abortionist Rhino Gross, who advises Dove to "look out for love, look out for trust, look out for *giving*" (181). The apogee of these parodies of American success occurs when Dove gets "work" at the brothel.

Even though it does not tackle large scale urban unrest, *Wild Side* is a study in the rage of the oppressed. The key figure in this regard is Achilles Schmidt, the legless cripple who wheels himself around on a wooden platform. According to Algren the inspiration for Schmidt, who also appears in the short story, "The Face on the Barroom Floor," came from a legless man he had previously met. Freddy "had lost both his legs working as a fireman on the Michigan Central years before, and must have been well over six feet before the accident," he told an interviewer. "Nobody, even when he was on his platform, thought of him as less," Algren continued, "I believe he was the strongest man I've ever known. I don't mean just in physical terms. He had a strength of *person* that dominated every scene he occupied" (qtd. in "A Talk" 83). In like manner, Schmidt, once billed in a carnie show as "the Birmingham strong boy" (266) before a Santa Fe freight train removed both of his legs, has a commanding sexual presence that is conveyed through his affair with Hallie Breedlove, a former schoolteacher forced into prostitution when school governors discover that she is black. Yet Schmidt's importance to the novel is more than another exercise on a theme of the virility of lower-class males. In this respect, James Giles is mistaken in characterizing Schmidt as "the personification of the lower classes" because it unfairly essentializes the working class though the persona of a man who, the same critic advances, is as "insane and dangerous as the corrupt economic system itself" (*Confronting the Horror* 81–82). A more fruitful approach to Schmidt's importance to the novel is to view it as a didactic meditation on the effects of ostracizing the lower classes, a view which encourages the conclusion that Schmidt's physical disempowerment is comparable to the economic crippling of a whole class.

Algren's use of grotesques as exemplars of capitalism's effects is evident in *A Walk on the Wild Side*'s exploration of several class-based stereotypes, one of which is the virility of the physically strong but mentally limited Dove. As the "Big Stingaree," Dove "seduces" prostitutes in front of an avid audience and this, his only real "success" in life, provides yet more material for Algren's parody of the American dream. But parody quickly gives way to mockery as the corollary of Dove's mantra, "'I don't know what kind of great I'm bound to be . . . all I know for certain is I'm a born world-shaker'" (56), operates to ensure that the homology of capitalist society and the grotesque is always at the forefront of the reader's mind. What "kind of great" he is about to be is revealed in the peep show scene, where a variety of viewers watch Dove go about his business; the sense Algren generates is that American society in the 1950s borders on the grotesque:

> Each watcher was affected differently. One paled slowly as he looked and, after a minute, left for good thinking how sad such things were so. Another laughed smugly deep as his liver, to see proven at last what he had long suspected: a man was a two-legged animal and a woman a four-legged one, nothing more. . . . Yet a third looked thoughtful, as at a demonstration in carpet weaving: see, there was still money to be made in small enterprise. Another felt stale lusts grow swift and bit his lip for lack of cash. . . . But the great cripple neither laughed nor paled. Only the lines of his heavy head hardened and he swung his torso on its tiny wheels and wheeled off down the hall, making a rolling thunder to hide his indignation. (249)

Lawrence Lipton has rightly identified this scene as representing "an attitude not only toward a peep show but toward the whole show, to the life of our time" (36). Algren's decision to offer as a synecdoche of society such a sordid episode was inspired by a growing belief that in the 1950s a "cold complacency [was] the coming thing." "Twenty years ago," Algren recalled, "people were asking, 'what is going to happen to man?' They used to talk like that, as if they were connected with one another" (qtd. "A Talk" 32). This bemoaning of the decline in communal sensibility in America in the fifties, it bears repeating, was a critique that emerged not only from the changing demography of American inner cities, which removed much of the raw material that had informed Algren's work, but also from the fact that the working class had been all but removed from the mainstream cultural discourse.

Thus when Algren drew a line separating himself from Sloan Wilson, Herman Wouk, and John O'Hara, decrying those novelists as suburban chroniclers who represented exclusively middle-class experience, he was bitterly aware that his concern for the lower classes placed him apart from most of his fellow novelists and from the temper of the times. There always was, he felt, more at stake than Maxwell Geismar's contention that "the real question for the novelist of this period is how to escape from the balm of moderation and the bane of normalcy" ("Against the Tide of Euphoria" 473). Algren made explicit his defiance of mainstream American writing's universalization of white middle-class experience in a 1959 interview when he washed his hands of the suburban middle class, declaring "I don't know about you!" (32).

In one sense *Wild Side* was prompted by that repudiation, for it presented a nightmare world where the ladder of success had been inverted. Inasmuch as the novel mocked American ideals of success, however, it simultaneously offered a grave warning. *Wild Side* saw the author return to his fear of the social consequences resulting from sealing off the lower classes from mainstream society; the novel is, then, a harbinger of the urban unrest that exploded in the 1960s. The savage fight between Schmidt and Dove that forms the novel's climax is the centerpiece of a nightmare to which the novel, and by implication the whole of the lower classes, is inexorably moving. But this is a passage towards the abyss not taken by choice. The brawl, where Dove is beaten blind and Schmidt subsequently killed by the watching crowd, suggests in microcosm the moral ramifications of economic and social injustice.

Notwithstanding these episodes borne of deprivation, amid the horrors the novel portrays, what emerges, ultimately, is an astonishing tenacity for self-preservation. As *A Walk on the Wild Side* records codes of behavior quite distinct from the legal system, it makes clear that those who live in the stews have not abandoned human virtue and this is what stops the novel from becoming a chronicle of complete despair. Important in this respect is the honesty and honor of Hallie Breedlove as she attempts to teach Dove to read, an altruistic act echoed through Schmidt's touching and genuine love for the former schoolteacher. While these virtues tend to become submerged under the weight of poverty and desperation, they constitute moments of moral and social reflection important to the novel's social trajectory. By their very poignancy, these moments only underscore Algren's conviction that postwar America was either no longer willing or was incapable of thinking seriously about its lower classes.

As early as 1952 the sophistication of Algren's social analysis was evident in "Spoon-Fed Universe," a review in which he concluded that Puerto Rican drug addicts living in American inner cities were inhabitants of "a double ghetto" of addiction and isolation, "walls within walls wherein useless children live out their useless hopes . . ." (35). In saying much the same thing four decades later, Irvine Welsh's novel *Trainspotting* would be hailed in some quarters as an important contribution to the understanding of drugs and poverty in Britain. But a sense of how advanced Algren's social vision was eluded most critics, who saw him as a relic of an age whose conflicts America had blissfully transcended. Given the perspective of dominant postwar American ideology, in social critiques designed to hit where it hurt, it made sense to emphasize not so much politics or hierarchies, classes or ranks, but the human cost of a society riven. This was the strategy Algren employed in an exposition part of which was originally delivered as a speech to the Missouri Writers Conference in 1952. Calling his essay "A Walk on the Wild Side"—only later would it become part of *Nonconformity*—Algren might have had his later novel of the same name in mind when he argued that "On the back streets and the boulevards of Palm Beach and Miami, on Fifth Avenue in New York and Canal Street in New Orleans, on North Clark Street in Chicago, on West Madison or South State or any street at all in Los Angeles: faces of the American Century, harassed and half-dehumanized, scoffing or debauched: so purposeless, unusable and useless faces, yet so smug, so self-satisfied yet so abject—for complacency struggles strangely there with guilt. Faces full of such immense irresponsibility toward themselves that they tell how high the human cost of our marvelous technological achievements really have been" (74).

Considered in relation to, say, Martin Luther King's 1968 "condition of America" question, posed just weeks before he was assassinated, which asked, "What good is it to be allowed to eat in a restaurant if you can't afford a hamburger?" ("Showdown for Non-Violence" 24), what becomes clear is that Algren's account announces a concern with inequality that connects the ideals of the old left with many of the issues with which the civil rights movement and New Left were preoccupied. Moreover, the connecting thread between the two, the matter of class and the conviction that class matters, links Algren to the New Left in such a way that it invites consideration of his social critique not as an anachronism left over from the "red decade," but as an important contribution to evolving left-wing opinion.

Algren, then, reiterated his concerns about the direction America was taking not because of some nebulous social appeal inspired by personal loyalty, but rather because he felt the necessity of recording the oppression visited upon those who suffered under a flagrantly unfair system. As Algren understood, if deprivation and destitution teach us anything it is that poverty is an awful business. Yet as we have seen, the universalizing of the middle-class at mid-century made this task especially onerous. In a year when Lionel Trilling wrote self-congratulatory pieces about how the existence of Nazis and Soviets validate Dickens's vision of "madness, absurdity, and malevolence" (*A Gathering of Fugitives* 44) and how opposition to those regimes confirms that novelist's view of goodness (evidently America is Little Dorrit), Algren took a very different tack on what we can learn from the novelists of the nineteenth century: "we live today in a laboratory of human suffering as vast and terrible as that in which Dickens and Dostoevsky wrote. The only real difference being that the England of Dickens and the Russia of Dostoevsky could not afford the soundscreens and the smokescreens with which we so ingeniously conceal our true condition from ourselves . . ." (*Nonconformity* 74). This articulation of the human side of the fifties records in powerful, polemical prose what *A Walk on the Wild Side* does in fiction.

To ignore what was evident in mid-century America, Algren felt, was tantamount to a denial of our responsibilities as humans. For Americans had "never lived so tidily as here amidst such psychological disorder. Never has any people lived so hygienically while daily dousing itself with the ritual slops of guilt," he continued. "Nowhere has any people set itself a moral code so rigid while applying it quite so flexibly. Never has any people possessed such a superfluity of physical luxuries companioned by such a dearth of emotional necessities. In no other country is such great wealth, acquired so purposefully, put to such small purpose" (75). While these insights provide a useful summary of the framework of *Wild Side*, they assume that the existence of an alienated "second-class citizenry" ("Spoon-fed Universe" 35) ought to be weighing on America's conscience. Working against a social grain that had in the postwar era internalized middle-class hegemony as the American way, Algren had to address how the propagation of monolithic values rooted in the premise of classless consumption all but elided the concept of class as he understood it. As the persistence and vigor of his testimonies reveal, the Chicago author knew instinctively that at stake here were not only those who lived on the margins but the ways and means by which they would be defined.

In the social climate that prevailed in mid-century America, where relations were increasingly conceived of in terms of competition rather than community, it is not difficult to see where a myth as powerful as the American dream might fit in. Nonetheless, that its claims to universality persisted in the face of overwhelming odds confirmed that it was largely a myth of individual assertion. For those who lived on the wild side, the American dream was an all but unattainable possibility that remained as the saying goes, "not for the likes of us." If the social cleavages these contentions belied suggested that the prospect of America sundered was always more complex than an "us and them" argument, Algren's insistence on claiming an "us" utterly at odds with the mainstream fifties "us" enabled him to articulate the moral insights that appear in *Nonconformity* and that are central to the closing of *A Walk on the Wild Side*. It is on such a negative note that the novel ends. As Dove Linkhorn returns to Arroyo, now blind and disfigured, his sexual prowess gone and his new-found ability to read removed, the "born world-shaker" becomes the embodiment of defeat. And it is the questions of moral responsibility raised by the vision of Dove alone and beaten that are at the heart of Algren's critique of 1950s America.

Notes

1. Regarding literary groups or cohorts, however, a point important to critical intimations that Algren was a Communist, this was about as far as it went, if only because Nelson Algren was always something of a lone wolf. But while he was probably never a card-carrying Communist—though the House of Un-American Activities Committee was later to prove such trivialities irrelevant—according to Bettina Drew the young Algren "worked actively and openly for the Communist movement, and he definitely considered himself a Communist" (*Nelson Algren: A Life on the Wild Side* 104).

2. Cold War conservatism and the pressure it was able to bring to bear on the literary left no doubt encouraged the public confessionals of a number of former Communist Party members. This *mea culpa* culture was perhaps most famously exemplified in the Richard Crossman's influential *The God That Failed* (1949). For other examples see Louis Budenz, *This Is My Story*; Elizabeth Bentley, *Out of Bondage*; Bella Dodd, *School of Darkness*; Hede Massing, *This Deception*; Julien Steinberg, *Verdict of Three Decades: From the Literature of Individual Revolt Against Soviet Communism, 1917–1950*.

3. Exactly how ingrained these ideas of what it may not be an exaggeration to call middle-class exceptionalism were is discernable in the thoughts of the writer Elizabeth Hardwick, a figure at the heart of the New York Intellectual circle. In the "easy days . . . right after the war," Hardwick conceded, "the therapy for all out moral discomforts was a daily recital of the sins of Communism and the Soviet Union and the subsequent healthy enjoyment of our own virtues." And this was, it bears repeating, a world in which according to Hardwick "nothing much was asked of us . . . no other sacrifice beyond reminding ourselves how good we were as a people and a system and that we did not need to suffer the infection of despairing self-criticism" (*A View of My Own* 126).

4. Timothy Melley has delved further into what underlay the era's middle-class anxieties, suggesting persuasively that the narratives upon which Riesman's *The Lonely Crowd*, William Whyte's *The Organization Man*, and Sloan Wilson's *The Man in the Grey Flannel Suit* are based constitute examples of "agency panic," a theme in which it was implied that a "new system of mass consumption was depriving Americans—and most vitally its men—of their hitherto distinctive autonomy, and thus diminishing the very value of freedom held to distinguish the first world from the second" (Medovoi, *Rebels* 21).

5. *Wild Side* includes rewrites of work Algren had already published. The short stories "Kewpie Doll," "The Face on the Barroom Floor," "Mr. Goodbuddy and the Mighty Dripolator," and "Lovers, Sec-fiends, Bugs in Flight" are all recycled in the novel. In the main, however, *Wild Side* is a reworking of *Somebody in Boots*, with the latter's Cass McKay transformed into Dove Linkhorn and much of the proselytizing of *Boots* removed too. Of the main similarities between the two novels, little more than the Texas origins of the main protagonists remain, and the changes Algren made reflect his own developing social vision. Important in this respect is the author's portrayal of Cass as a figure of oppression, his life at the mercy of the faceless authority that is somebody in boots. Dove, on the other

hand, whose life seems no less determined, nevertheless is a figure designed to illuminate how ridiculous the system is.

6. Primo Carnera (1906–1967) was an Italian boxer nicknamed "The Ambling Alp." Standing between six feet five and six feet seven inches tall, Carnera became world heavyweight champion by knocking out Jack Sharkey on June 29, 1933.

Postwar Left Feminism and Antifascist Resistance in the Cultural Work of Martha Dodd

Kathlene McDonald

Modern Day America with its policy of internal and external oppression, its brutal exploitation and calculated genocide has long been in the making; and also in the making have been the resistance, protest and fury which are now gathering forces in the country.
—Martha Dodd, Biographical note for *The Searching Light*

In her obituary of writer Martha Dodd, Katrina vanden Heuvel asserts, "In death, as in life, Martha [Dodd] Stern will be best remembered for her indictment on unproven espionage charges" and indeed, little has been written on Dodd that is not about her numerous affairs and her alleged espionage on behalf of the Soviet Union. In the 1930s, she supposedly had affairs with high-level French and German officials, including Rolf Diels, the head of the Gestapo, and with writers Thomas Wolfe and Carl Sandburg, and was seduced into spying for the Soviet Union after falling in love with the Soviet diplomat Boris Vinogradov (Brysac 141, 153–57). Historian Allen Weinstein and former KGB agent Alexander Vassiliev describe her as a "courtesan, agent, and student of communism," willing to sleep with "leading Nazis and other notables" in order to assist the Soviets (53, 50). While the evidence in recent works of Dodd's espionage and promiscuity would seem to be damning, the accuracy of the materials on which these works are based is questionable, and thus Dodd's reputation continues to be the subject of much debate, even after her death in 1990.[1]

My purpose in this essay is neither to refute nor defend the charges against Dodd. Rather, I seek to examine her literary career, which has been obscured by the controversy surrounding her. A committed antifascist, Dodd wrote two novels to call attention to the dangers of fascist control: *Sowing the Wind* (1945), about the rise of fascism in Germany, and *The Searching Light* (1955), about the rise of McCarthyism in the U.S. In these two novels, as well as her short story "Maria," she uses female activists to challenge some of the conventions about femininity in the immediate postwar era. Dodd's work is distinctive among novels from this period; she presents women not simply as domestic goddesses or morality police but as actors in their own right. Yet at present, no scholarly work has been done on Dodd as a literary figure.[2] This essay, which draws heavily on documents from the Martha Eccles Dodd Papers at the Library of Congress, aims to establish the connections between Dodd's writings and an emergent Left Feminism during World War II and the postwar era.[3] Several important recent historical studies, most notably by Kate Weigand, Rebecca Hill, and Daniel Horowitz, have shown the extent to which much of the second-wave women's movement was shaped by ideas that were formulated by women in the Old Left. However, like Dodd herself, this connection has been red-baited out of history. In resurrecting Dodd's literary career and connecting her works to the Left feminist ideas of the 1940s and '50s, I aim to show a continuous thread of ideas—and a continuous tradition of resistance—between women in the Old and New Lefts.

Dodd was involved in the antifascist resistance movement connected to the Communist Party in the U.S., and many of Dodd's writings reflect the changes in the Party's approach to the "Woman Question" during World War II and the postwar era.[4] In its early years, the Party viewed gender oppression as secondary to class oppression. However, as women swelled the Party ranks during World War II, gender issues became more of a priority. During World War II, over 15,000 Party men enlisted, leaving women to take over the vacant leadership roles within the Party. By 1943, women made up almost half of the Party's membership, compared to 10 percent in 1930. When peacetime reconversion sent Rosie the Riveter back to the home, women fought to hold on to their roles within the Party. As a result of their influence, the Party's official position on the Woman Question changed dramatically. Whereas previously, the Party had considered women's oppression as secondary to economic oppression, many Party leaders began to acknowledge that women were oppressed not only as workers but also as women. In addition to making connections between gender, race, and class oppression and challenging male supremacy (both within its ranks and larger society), Party officials made efforts to recruit and train women activists and supported issues such as the unionization of domestic workers, equal pay and job training for women, workplace discrimination, daycare, and national health insurance. Women activists started independent women's organizations such as the Congress of American Women, taught classes on the Woman Question at the Jefferson School of Social Science, and encouraged debate on women's issues in Party publications such as *Masses and Mainstream*, the *Daily Worker*, *Political Affairs*, and *Freedom*. Perhaps one of the most dramatic shifts in Party policy, though, was the willingness to consider the role of culture and ideology in women's oppression.

According to historian Rebecca Hill, during World War II, American Communist women "attacked the ideology of domesticity as an element of fascism" and used the idea of the "fascist triple K," based on the Nazi slogan of *Kinder, Kuche, Kirche*, or "children, kitchen, church," which mandated that women should be defined by their roles as wives and mothers, to describe this ideology. As an alternative to women's role under fascism, they promoted images of "model anti-fascist women warriors" (Hill 76). Many women writing in the *Daily Worker* called attention to women's oppression under fascism. As one writer noted in a 1945 editorial, the battle against Nazism had also been about ending women's oppression: "The enemy, fascism, is dedicated to the enslavement of women, making them prisoners of breeding and baking" ("Woman's"). After the war, Party women were quick to point out that the emerging domestic ideology in the U.S. bore a striking resemblance to that of Hitler's Germany. In "Hitler's 3 K's for Women: An American Rehash" (1947), Party leader Elizabeth Gurley Flynn critiqued the ideas in *Modern Woman: The Lost Sex* (1947), a best-selling book that urged American women to return to the home for the good of their country and to find fulfillment in marriage and childcare. Throughout the article, she juxtaposes statements from the book with statements from Hitler, and she ends by warning readers that this book is not the only culprit: "There is a veritable flood of such books and articles attacking the American modern woman. The stench of fascism arises from them. This happened in Germany when Hitler came to power. Back to the kitchen, the brothel, the menial tasks, breed the master race—are the degrading concepts of women inherent in fascism" (208). This book frequently came under attack by Party women and was dissected by Party chair William Foster in an essay in which he outlined the Party's new approach to the Woman Question.

As an alternative to women's role under fascism, many Party writers championed images of women as militant activists, fighting to challenge fascism and oppression, both in the U.S. and internationally. In her columns in Paul Robeson's *Freedom*, Lorraine Hansberry linked women's activism in the U.S. to women's roles in colonial struggles worldwide. The *Daily Worker* published articles contrasting women's position under capitalism in the U.S. to that of women in socialist societies. One *Worker* column describes social services for working mothers in Czechoslovakia, including free maternity care and paid maternal leave, childcare facilities, housecleaning and cooking cooperatives, and health insurance. The column concludes that these services have enabled women "to participate fully in the life of the community and the country" ("What"). A *Masses and Mainstream* article declares, "In its provision for the care of mothers and children a socialist society exemplifies its regard for all human life" and addresses the need for "a comprehensive Marxist treatment of the woman question on the American scene" to build a similar society (Epstein 93–94).

Yet while the Party made great strides in dealing with sex discrimination and male chauvinism within its ranks during this era, the Party's official position did not necessarily filter down to the rank-and-file membership. Men still wrote letters to the *Worker* declaring women's rights "impractical" and protesting women's political involvement (B.). Often, female activists were relegated to secretarial tasks or treated as "Party wives," rather than as members in their own right. And Party women did not necessarily experience the effects of this changed approach to women's issues in their personal relationships. When I interviewed writer and former Party member Dorothy Sterling, she remembered discussing theoretical essays on the Woman Question at Party meetings but said that the theory rarely trickled down to personal relationships. As screenwriter Jean Rouverol Butler put it, "The American Left male articulated a very good position on women's rights. But he didn't live it in his own domestic relationships. There were very few exceptions" (McGilligan 164). The 1954 film *Salt of the Earth*, based on a true story in which women play an integral role in a mining strike, shows this gap between theory and lived reality by poking fun at the sexism of the union men and male organizers. In one scene, organizer Frank Barnes tells the workers, "We can't think of them just as housewives—but as allies." His wife (played by the wife of the real-life organizer), however, takes him to task for not living his politics in his relationship. She snorts in reply, "Look who's talking! The Great White Father, and World's Champion of Women's Rights. [. . .] when Dr. Barnes gives you his cure all for female troubles, ask him if he's tried it at home" (Wilson 43–44).

In real life as well, many women activists refused to acquiesce to the sexism of their male counterparts. Many Party women held their ground and fought for their rights both within the Party and larger society. For every letter to the *Worker* protesting women's political involvement, there were several more, from men and women, arguing that men and women needed to work together to create more cooperative relationships. Hill claims that Left feminists from this era "challenged patriarchy, not on the basis of women's moral superiority, not with the concept of women as a class, but by identifying and attacking the idealized image of the 'essential' woman in American popular culture and replacing her with new models of women's agency and liberation" (90). Literary works by writers such as Dodd, Alice Childress, Lorraine Hansberry, Sanora Babb, Beth McHenry, and others not only present such "new models" but also offer glimpses into the difficulties, challenges, and tensions of being a woman on the Left during this era.

Much of Dodd's work reflects Communist women's line on the connections between domestic ideology and fascism. In her two novels, she showed how fascism oppressed women and offered images of activist women to counter what she saw as the fascist domestic ideology of both Germany and the U.S. *Sowing the Wind* shows the damaging effects of fascism on German women and highlights the role of women in antifascist resistance movements; *The Searching Light* makes connections between fascism and political repression in the U.S. during the McCarthy era. In *The Searching Light*, Dodd portrays resistance not as un-American but as the means necessary to achieve American ideals. The novel suggests that women best exemplified the American spirit when they participated in the struggle against fascism rather than remaining confined to the home and teaching children Cold War values. In both novels, Dodd contrasts the domesticity and self-sacrifice of older generations of women with the freedom and rebellion of youth; young women serve not only as the consciences of other characters but also as the chief representatives of resistance and liberation.

Both novels also reflect the ways in which women activists were marginalized, as Dodd puts white men at the center of both novels. However, these men falter and fail precisely because they do not listen to the more radical voices of the white female activists, who insist on the need for coalitions with other antifascist, antiracist, and labor groups. In her shorter works, too, Dodd explores some of the obstacles that hindered women's activism. Her 1950 short story "Maria" describes the development of political consciousness in a black, working-class Cuban woman who learns to break out of her shell of passivity and to challenge the class, race, and gender roles she is expected to fulfill. While maintaining a focus on the importance of women's activism, these works of fiction further illuminate some of the tensions and obstacles faced by women on the Left in the postwar era.

Like Maria, Dodd took some time to achieve the conviction that a woman's place was in the collective struggle against fascism. In order to explain her commitment to antifascist resistance, an account of her process of coming to political consciousness is necessary. Dodd was born on October 8, 1908, in Ashland, Virginia, but her family moved to Chicago shortly after her birth. Her father, William E. Dodd, Sr., chaired the History Department at the University of Chicago. Dodd's father encouraged critical thinking and the exchange of free ideas both in the classroom and at home; Dodd writes that one of her father's main objectives and ideals was the "triumph of democracy in the modern world" ("Biography"). While her father did his best to instill the values of democracy in his children, Martha Dodd developed little concern for social problems.

As a young woman, Dodd worked as assistant literary editor for the *Chicago Tribune*. While working for the *Tribune*, she began writing short stories, hoping to make the shift from literary critic to author. Robert Morss Lovett, a professor of English literature and composition at the University of Chicago, tried to make her see the impossibility of living and working in isolation from economic inequality and other forms of injustice. But these concerns, she writes, "only touched the surface" of her mind. Despite her respect for Lovett, she continued to believe that artists and writers should remain unaffected by society. And although she shared a close creative and personal relationship with socialist poet Carl Sandburg, he, too, failed to develop her social consciousness. She remembers, "He revealed the profoundest contempt for the aloof, the objective spirit," but that she "fought against his ideas, reviled radicals and their ilk, and resented the emphasis that he put upon the simple man" (*Through Embassy Eyes* 6, 8). Dodd resisted these efforts to politicize her, holding fast to her belief that books and politics should not interfere with each other.[5]

Dodd's political apathy changed in 1933, when Franklin Delano Roosevelt appointed her father ambassador to Germany and she decided to accompany her family to Berlin. In her 1939 memoir *Through Embassy Eyes*, written shortly after her return from Germany, she claims that she could not pass up the opportunity to experience German society as an ambassador's daughter and so she left her job at the *Tribune* and moved to Berlin with her family. However, she was also leaving behind what Brysac refers to as her "dark secret," a failed marriage to George Roberts, a New York banker (138).[6] When she first arrived in Germany, she was seduced by what she saw as the efficiency and success of the Nazi party. But she quickly recognized the brutality and insanity of the Nazi program. The numerous atrocities she witnessed and the suppression of free ideas clashed with the liberal ideals she had come to expect as a basic right in the U.S. and made her realize that she could not remain neutral. In an unpublished essay, she later referred to Nazi Germany as her "political baptism of fire" ("Biographical"). During the four and a half years she spent living under Nazi power, she developed a profound awareness of and hatred for the destructiveness of fascism and became involved in the pro-Soviet antifascist resistance movement, as she saw the Soviet Union as an important ally in the war against Hitler.

Upon her return to the U.S. in the winter of 1937, she became involved in the growing antifascist movement connected to the American Communist Party. In an interview for the *New York World Telegram*, she made one of her first public statements on the subject: "When I went to Berlin with my father four and a half years ago I wasn't much concerned about Fascism. I had been the assistant literary editor of the Chicago *Tribune* for two years, and was mainly interested in writing short stories. . . . I thought that writing was the be all and end all. . . . I saw a lot of Fascism, and I made up my mind about it. I am opposed to Fascism in all the forms it takes. . . . Cultural life has disintegrated in Germany. There are no good writers left, except those in the concentration camps. The good ones are in exile" (Press). In publicly professing her opposition to fascism, she asserted that good literature could not survive in an atmosphere of political repression, making the connection between culture and politics that she theorized and practiced for the remainder of her life. Rather than being a writer completely removed from society, she now wanted to be a writer who changed it.

In 1938, Dodd married Alfred K. Stern, a public housing expert who had recently been appointed to Mayor La Guardia's Committee on Property Improvement. While most accounts of Dodd's alleged espionage include accounts of her numerous affairs, letters in her correspondence files suggest that in Stern, she found a partner who shared her political commitments. The two were involved in numerous Left causes, including public housing, health care, racial justice, labor rights, and antifascist struggles, and were active in the American Labor Party, a pro-Communist party on whose ticket Stern ran (unsuccessfully) for Congress in 1940.[7]

Shortly after returning to the U.S., Dodd became involved in the American Writers' Congress, a conference established in 1935 by the Communist Party with the goal of creating a revolutionary literature in America. While the original Congress focused on the role of the worker, the political agenda in the second and third Congresses had shifted to the battle against fascism.[8] Although male authors dominated the first two congresses, women began to play a more active role by the third. In 1939, Dodd attended the third Congress and was elected to the National Board, along with Lillian Hellman, Genevieve Taggard, and six other women and seventeen men. Writer and literary critic Dorothy Parker and union activist-songwriter Aunt Molly Jackson also took part in the proceedings. At the fourth Congress in 1941, Dodd was reelected to the National Board, along with Taggard, Joy Davidman, Muriel Draper, Eleanor Flexner, Ruth McKenney, Myra Page, Tess Slessinger, and six other women, plus twenty-three men ("Women"; Wald, *Exiles* 259).

Dodd's first novel, *Sowing the Wind,* contributes to the project of using literature in the service of antifascist resistance. It also reflects Party women's position on connections between domestic ideology and fascism. *Sowing the Wind* tells a chilling tale of the rise of Nazi power and its corrupting influence on Eric Landt, a brash young pilot and respected war hero with a deep and unflagging love for his country. The novel centers on Landt's transformation from a good-hearted individual to a degenerate and inhuman Nazi general, and Dodd uses him to show the appeal of fascism and its power to seduce even those who question it. Even though Landt disapproves of many Nazi actions, he is willing to work with the Nazis because he believes that they have the best interests of Germany at heart. Hitler, as Dodd represents him in the novel, possesses the shrewd ability to play on Landt's intense patriotism, and Landt proves unable to resist. Although he makes a few efforts to challenge some of the more repressive aspects of the regime, he lacks the courage to renounce all ties to Germany or to abandon the wealth and power he enjoys as a Nazi officer. As the story progresses, he becomes more and more unable to recognize the evils of National Socialism, and he grows blind to the consequences of his own actions.

Dodd based her representations of fascist violence and repression on her own experiences living in Germany. At the same time, her treatment of women's oppression reflects the position of the U.S. Communist Party on the relationship between sexism and fascism. *Sowing the Wind* shows German women's role in resistance to the Nazi regime, despite a national ideology that strove to keep them powerless. Dodd places a man at the center of her novel, but she gives the strongest voice of antifascist resistance to a woman. While the novel focuses primarily on Landt's moral decline under fascism, the main female character, Lina, attempts to get him involved in fighting against Nazi power. At the beginning of the novel, Lina acts as Landt's conscience, cautioning him against further involvement with the Nazis and forcing him to see the corrupting and reprehensible actions that he would rather overlook. Lina is an avowed feminist and anti-Nazi, and Dodd presents her as a foil to Landt's blind patriotism and need for power. Landt is drawn to her from their first meeting, and for a while, she provides him with the courage to rebel against Nazi influence, giving him the strength to resist that he does not have on his own. She provides the sole voice of critique throughout the novel, pointing out injustices and encouraging Landt to take action, yet she feels powerless to act herself. When Landt challenges Lina to work with him to oppose Nazi policy, she responds by asking, "What can a woman do today in Germany" (127)?

Lina's recognition of women's lack of power in Nazi society leads her to believe that women cannot resist the roles thrust upon them. The few scenes between Gertrud and Wolfgang Von Richter, an aristocratic couple loyal to the Nazi regime, depict these roles with brutal clarity. As Gertrud tells herself after Wolfgang insults her, "It was a woman's role [. . .] to accept the arrogance and abuse of her husband, to enjoy her subservience, to obey her husband's whim to the last letter. [. . .] it was good, it was instinctive and a part of National Socialist ideology to recognize the superiority of men" (46). According to this ideology, women are valued for their femininity, their skill in maintaining the home, and their ability to bear children for the Third Reich. Lina, who wears her hair short and thrives on intellectual exchange, manages to maintain a sense of independence, but she obviously feels thwarted by such an environment. Gertrud, who accepts this role unquestioningly, eventually sees the emptiness of her life. She commits suicide, believing she has no other options for escape.

While women, as Lina acknowledges, have almost no power under National Socialism, they nonetheless represent the few possibilities for resistance in the book. Lina eventually comes to see the cowardice in her failure to act, recognizing that she had "tried to evade responsibility on the grounds of being a woman," and joins the German underground (130). Her courageous actions for the underground movement demonstrate the importance of women's refusing to accept their position in a fascist society. Her actions with the underground mirror many of the stories told in the pages of the *Daily Worker* during the war, stories that featured the heroism of female antifascist fighters in the Soviet Union and Germany.

Dodd also shows how individual groups of women found ways to resist fascism outside of the organized resistance movement. One of the most powerful scenes in the novel depicts a group of working women waiting in line at a butter shop. Frustrated by their lack of access to basic necessities, such as food and clothing, they begin criticizing the Nazi regime. After one woman is arrested for speaking out too loudly, each of the remaining women places her hand on the shoulder of the woman in front of her in line, forming "a curious living chain of strength, pity and resolution" (150). Their silent gesture of defiance affirms both their solidarity and their refusal to submit to repression. In standing together, they create, at least for a few moments, a space in which Nazi power cannot touch them.

Dodd suggests that no successful resistance movement evolved in Germany because of a failure to unite these isolated pockets of resistance. The Nazis' multiple forms of oppression—their suppression of working-class agency, their commitment to maintaining racial purity, their treatment of women, and their use of homophobic, xenophobic, and anti-Communist rhetoric to divide the opposition—work effectively to consolidate their power. Lina, in refusing her disenfranchised place in society and rebelling with other victimized groups, acts courageously, as do the women at the butter shop, but the actions of a few courageous souls are insufficient to challenge the breadth of Nazi power. The novel's tragic ending demonstrates the devastating consequences of failing to work with others in the fight against fascism. Landt succumbs completely to fascism; he deteriorates into a fat, miserable drunk who perpetuates the violence he once condemned. Lina's actions in the underground, without the numbers of a mass resistance movement to support them, result in her life sentence in a concentration camp.

Dodd's novel was widely reviewed and highly acclaimed. It received high praise from Thomas Mann and other exiled German writers for its effectiveness at capturing the repression of Nazi Germany. But in her 1945 review of *Sowing the Wind*, Eleanor Roosevelt expresses uneasiness with the novel's ending. She writes, "It left me with a sense of emptiness and hopelessness," and indeed, the novel's final image of "an enormous white tomb erected over the ravished land" (311) contributes to a feeling of the pervasive destructiveness of the Nazi regime and its ability to annihilate the spirit of a people. Read in the context of Dodd's other work, though, the novel can be seen less as a statement that fascism will always triumph and more of a warning against the danger that results when a critical mass of people accept its horror. If Lina and the women at the butter shop had connections to a broader movement, Dodd suggests, they might have been able to do more in the battle against fascism.

Within a few years of *The Searching Light*'s publication, Dodd saw a frighteningly repressive climate emerging in the U.S. In her writings, she often made connections between the fascism she witnessed in Nazi Germany and the political repression in the U.S during the McCarthy era. As she wrote in 1958 for a German edition of *Sowing the Wind*, "The reader will certainly recognize that the plot and the events described in the novel, are of an appalling verisimilitude today. He has only to read his morning newspaper to know that similar occurrences are taking place" (Postscript to German). The similarities she saw between the repression of the McCarthy era and the fascism she witnessed in Nazi Germany haunted her, especially as she herself became a victim of McCarthyite repression.

Throughout the 1940s, Dodd and her husband were accused of being Soviet agents, harassed by the FBI, and vilified by the media. Due to their outspoken antifascist politics (and their generous contributions to the American Communist Party), she and Stern suffered vicious character attacks and custody threats regarding their adopted son, Bobby. By 1953, the persecution had become so intense that they fled with Bobby to Mexico City in order to escape the slanderous attacks against them. Sources close to the Sterns believe that the couple was also trying to escape FBI threats regarding their son. According to several friends and relatives, the FBI contacted Bobby's birth mother and forced her to sue the Sterns for custody of the child on the grounds that their Communist involvement made them unfit parents. Rather than risk losing their son, they left the country.[9] Several years later, Dodd claimed that they were attacked for two reasons: "First, because we were, and are, committed anti-fascists and learned a long time ago that the end of war and exploitation of man can only be achieved with the destruction of big capital, and, second, because our names and our case could have been very useful to further the hysteria of fear and other ends of the cold war in the Unites States" (Postscript to German).

In 1957, a federal grand jury indicted Dodd and Stern *in absentia* on espionage charges after Boris Morros, a former Hollywood producer and U.S. counterspy, identified Dodd as a Soviet agent in his House Un-American Activities Committee (HUAC) testimony. His testimony clearly established both Sterns "as part of the Soviet apparatus"; he claimed he met them through a Soviet official and that Stern advanced him $130,000 for a business to be used as "an espionage cover" ("Morros"). Morros, who was later proven to be a spy for both the Soviet Union and the U.S., was not considered to be a credible witness by many journalists of the time, and the Sterns denied all charges. In a press release issued in September 1957, they decried Morros's accusations as "fantastic inventions" and described their persecution as a "vicious technique Morros and the agencies of the U.S. government and Committees of Congress are employing to try to destroy or silence those people who dare to dissent." Despite their repeated assertions of innocence, they were forced to alter their lives irrevocably in order to escape the continued attacks against them. They never returned to the United States, spending the rest of their lives in Mexico, Cuba, and Prague.

In 1951, Dodd began working on her second novel, *The Searching Light*, as a response to the insidious attacks against her. She intended for her novel to educate people about the dangers of McCarthyism and the necessity of collective resistance to it. The novel tells the story of the battle by Professor John Minot and several of his colleagues against the imposition of a faculty loyalty oath. Dodd portrays the fight against the loyalty oath as primarily a white, middle-class male struggle; but she again makes women the heroes of the novel. While the female characters might lurk at the edges of the novel's central plot, they are by no means spectators. Instead, their voices provide the strongest call for collective resistance in the book, and they encourage the men to develop an awareness of the need for coalitions with other victimized groups.

Given her reputation and the novel's subject matter, she had difficulty finding a publisher. Harcourt, Brace and Company, which had published *Sowing the Wind* and *Through Embassy Eyes*, rejected *The Searching Light*, even though these first two books were widely reviewed and very well received.[10] Citadel Press accepted the novel for publication in 1955, and it was eventually published in England, Italy, Czechoslovakia, Poland, Germany, and the Soviet Union. It was generally favorably received, both in Left and mainstream presses, as a novel possessing both political relevance and aesthetic value.[11] Within the Left, writers and activists such as W. E. B. Du Bois, Albert Maltz, and Annette Rubinstein recognized the novel's value for resistance movements, and it was circulated at Left book clubs.[12] Albert Einstein, who publicly defended academic freedom, wrote Dodd that he had read her novel "with great interest," as it "shed light on the whole morbid and fantastic process of which we are witnesses." He went on to say, "Your work merits, in my opinion, the attention of all reasonable people who are interested in the social problems of our day."

The novel takes place over the course of an academic year at the fictional Penfield University, a small, liberal arts college nestled in the Appalachian Mountains of Virginia. In a letter to a friend, Dodd claimed she based Penfield on "a composite of universities leaning heavily on the University of California" (Letter to D. N. Pritt). In 1949, as part of their campaign to eliminate Communism in education, the UC Regents began requiring all faculty members to sign loyalty oaths stating that they were not members of the Communist Party. Over thirty professors refused to sign and were subsequently fired, even though none of them were—or had ever been—Party members. Following in California's footsteps, other universities, both public and private, began pressuring faculty members to sign similar oaths. The imposition of these oaths was generally the first step toward the regents' asserting control over classroom content (Schrecker, *No* 116).

Dodd traces the repression on Penfield's campus from a supposed effort to eradicate Communism to a thorough surveillance of speech and classroom content. The witch-hunt at Penfield begins under the pretense of eradicating Communism on campus in order to protect the value of American education, but the persecution shifts gradually to those who refuse to sign the oath. Most of the non-signers supported the integration of Penfield's campus, striking workers, immigrant rights, and the anti-fascist movement in Spain. As Minot tells his wife, Julia, "They're not after Communists here, they're after nonconformists of any shade of political opinion" (167). And Blackwell, Penfield's president, affirms Minot's suspicions. Referring to the non-signers, he says, "They've been active in all the campus ruckuses and they cooperate not only with their colleagues but with the students! This university needs a real house cleaning" (94). Like other writers on the Left, Dodd represents the crusade against Communism as a means of establishing complete control over educational and cultural institutions, rather than a strategy that was necessary to protect the U.S. from a violent takeover. She tried to show that the events on which she based her novel were not isolated or unique incidents. As Minot's daughter, Lucy, points out to her father, "there's nothing special about the case at Penfield. It's the trend all over the country" (119).[13]

Dodd portrays the crusade against Communism as un-American, equating the climate of repression that develops on Penfield's campus with the early stages of fascist control. She saw this climate as building toward a level of intolerance and surveillance similar to the one she experienced in Nazi Germany, and her book can be seen as a warning against allowing this repression to remain unchecked. Origano, an Italian artist whose father was killed for refusing to sign a loyalty oath, fears that the U.S. is headed on a similar path as the Italian fascist regime. He claims, "My youth was ruined by oaths. I thought there'd be some security in America, in a democracy" (133, 135). Eventually, he commits suicide rather than go through the repression he experienced in Italy. As Origano tells his colleagues when they doubt the loyalty oath will be imposed, "It happened in Italy, it happened in Germany, why shouldn't it happen here" (21)? In looking beyond the repressive acts to examine the effects of this repression on American culture, *The Searching Light* helped expose the hypocrisy of McCarthyism.

But as important as her denunciation of the Red Scare's effect on men's lives and work is Dodd's critique of the ways in which the domestic ideology of the era limited women. As in *Sowing the Wind*, this novel's treatment of domestic ideology was in keeping with the Party's postwar position on the connections between fascism and male chauvinism. While during the war, Communist women provided alternate images of antifascist fighters in other countries, in the postwar era they championed images of American women activists. Accordingly, Dodd constructs two strong female activists who challenge the domestic ideology embodied in some of the other women in the story.

In many ways, Minot's wife Julia exemplifies that domestic ideology. She has a "strong sense of her duty as a wife" and has sacrificed her life for her family, but Dodd presents her life as rather empty. Dodd afflicts Julia with a serious heart condition, suggesting that this kind of life is deathly for women. Even with this illness, Julia has trouble stepping outside her role of wife and mother. When Lucy tells her she should not work so hard to do things for her, Julia replies by asking, "What would my life be worth if I couldn't do for my family?" (172, 11, 35). She defines herself through serving her husband and daughter: her identity exists only within the domestic sphere. As John's wife, she views his success as her own. She helps edit and type John's books and articles, providing support for his work but not producing anything on her own. She has no independent identity in the outside world.

As the book progresses, however, Julia comes to see the emptiness of her life and wishes she had "learned some profession, or developed a youthful talent which could have filled the empty years when her family grew beyond her" (61). She regrets some of her decisions, regrets sacrificing herself for her marriage and family: "Instead of an ailing and querulous woman she would have been a wife whom John could lean on, respecting her equal courage" (259). By the end of the novel, she wants "to live bravely and well, for myself too" (330). After this realization, Dodd lets her begin to get well, suggesting that only through breaking free from these roles can women be healthy.

Throughout the book, Julia tries to encourage her daughter to fulfill her proper role as a woman and worries that Lucy will be so wrapped up in her career that she will fail to get married. Lucy, however, rejects her mother's values, telling Julia, "I like my life—but maybe it won't be just like yours" (29–30, 14). And the life Lucy chooses is one in which she will create politically meaningful art in the tradition of 1930s artists and the Mexican muralists.[14] Furthermore, as an outsider to the events at Penfield—she lives and works in New York City—she is able to see the oath in a wider context. She continually reminds her father and the other professors that Penfield's situation is not unique and warns them that they cannot see the situation on their campus as separate from other instances of McCarthyism. While her mother suffers for her adherence to the domestic ideology, Lucy's rejection of these values enables her to become a valuable part of the professors' struggle. As Origano tells her shortly before he kills himself, she is "the best of America" (257).

Like Lucy, Alice Aiken calls attention to the need for the professors to look at their situation beyond Penfield's campus. Alice, a young student activist, warns the professors of the dangers of intellectual isolation, urging them to see their struggle as linked to labor and antiracism struggles. In many ways, hers is the most courageous and uncompromising voice in the book. Dodd's choice to give this voice to a woman was clearly intentional; Alice has a twin brother who shares her politics but rarely speaks. Throughout the novel, Alice holds Minot and the other professors accountable for their compromises and their failure to act. She helps organize student protests, and she remains loyal to the professors' cause even after the other students abandon it. The novel's final scene takes place at the graduation ceremony, which occurs after all the professors have signed the oath or been fired. Alice refuses her diploma, and in an impassioned speech, she announces that Penfield has corrupted American education and avows her allegiance to the fired professors. Even though she acts alone, the importance of her act is recognized by the audience. The book ends with the lines: "The clapping started at first slowly, strong but not boisterous. Then a dozen more people joined in, and gradually the applause scattered through the hall . . ." (345). By ending her novel with a round of applause for the female activist and then trailing off with an ellipsis, Dodd leaves open possibilities for other people to join Alice in her struggle.

As in *Sowing the Wind*, Dodd highlights the necessity of collective resistance. The professors lose their battle against the oath, Dodd implies, because of their failure to form coalitions with other groups victimized by the crusade against Communism. In a postscript written for the Czech edition of the novel, Dodd compares Penfield's climate to the fascism she witnessed in Nazi Germany: "Unfortunately, a great number of Americans, like a great number of Germans before them under Hitler, plagued by anxieties about their economic security and their future in this atomic age, have been psychologically prepared to blame any minority, like the Communists, the Jews or the Negroes for their sterile uncertain life and therefore fall easy prey to the vicious propaganda of the hate-mongers who are now in control of national life." In linking anticommunism to racism, economic exploitation, and gender inequality, Dodd shows how they are all elements of fascist control. Thus, both books stand as a call to form coalitions between these exploited groups as the only effective response to political repression and incipient fascism.

While both of Dodd's novels use female radicals who encourage the male characters to become more politically active, these works do not address the process by which women themselves become politically conscious. She explores this process in her short story "Maria," published in *Masses and Mainstream* in 1950. The story describes the development of class and race consciousness in a black, working-class Cuban woman whose husband organizes the cane workers on a sugar plantation. It appeared in *Masses and Mainstream* in the same issue as Alice Childress's one-act play *Florence*, which deals with the political awakening of a black, working-class woman in the American South, suggesting that the Party wanted to raise awareness of the obstacles to women becoming politically active.

When the story begins, Maria's husband Jose has recently been killed by the plantation overseer for his organizing work. At first, Maria's actions are limited to grieving over her husband's death and worrying about their young child, Josefina. Even these actions are always guided by what her husband would have wanted. After his death, she moves to live with her sister's family in the city, because his fellow workers tell her that "Jose would have wanted her to go." Once in the city, she refuses to accept charity to feed her daughter, because Jose "could not have endured the sight of his wife begging with his daughter looking on" (21, 20). Although she desires to provide a better life for Josefina, she adheres to his wishes nonetheless. Her actions represent her lack of agency, her inability to make decisions for herself.

At this point in the story, she does not understand why Jose would have wanted her to refuse charity. She does not yet have the awareness of the Cuban class structure that keeps people like herself in a permanent underclass. When people offer her coins, she regrets her inability to support her daughter on her own and thinks about how hard it was "to be proud when you had nothing, absolutely nothing." Jose, she knows, "would have risen angrily from the bench and cursed the givers," but "she was not like that." She lacks the angry pride that her husband recognizes as a necessity for someone in their class position. Jose repeatedly told her "that to have no anger or to have anger and keep it inside, was a bad thing," but she clings to her gentle ways (20).

As a male worker, Jose had recourse to his male comrades in the sugar fields, whom he taught to "help one another like brothers" (21). And they respond by standing in solidarity after Jose's death. But Maria has no such "sisters" on whom to rely, and thus she has difficulty learning the value of solidarity and resistance. Through her role as a mother, though, she gains the courage to stand up to an attempt to remind her of her place in society. Not wanting Josefina to be subject to humiliation, she refuses to accept the offer of a grapefruit for her child, rolled across the street and into the gutter by a woman who clearly reeks of class privilege. Maria recognizes the woman, in her silk stockings and fur coat, as "that 'certain kind' of *blanco*, predatory and rich, the Cuban of the sugar plantation." She cannot accept a gesture of charity from a woman who represents the power of the sugar plantation responsible for her husband's death. When the woman yells at Josefina to pick it up, Maria, who up until that moment believed herself incapable of hatred, decides to act: "With the dignity of a slow gathering but inevitable rebellion Maria stood up slowly, gave the woman a long hateful look, cleared her throat as loud as she could and spat hard and full at the golden fruit in the gutter, and then kicked it savagely across the street again. Trembling with rage she sat down and moved close to the child on the bench" (23–24). For the first time, she recognizes that hatred against those who have power over her can be empowering.

And her action has direct results: the woman becomes frightened and flees the scene. In standing her ground, Maria retains her dignity and gains the satisfaction of triumphing over someone more powerful. Additionally, she gains the respect of others. The fruit vendor clasps his hands over a head in a sign of victory, telling her, "*Bien, bien*, my friend. Well done! That is the way, all right" (24). But more importantly, she learns the power of anger and resistance. While she does not take on the role of male revolutionary leader that Jose played, she finds her own way of resisting the Cuban power structure. While at the beginning of the story, Maria believed that she was defined by her role as wife and mother, by the end of the story she has learned that women can and do play a role in resisting race and class oppression.

Although Dodd's work clearly reflects what today would be referred to as feminist consciousness, like many female activists in the 1930s, '40s and '50s, she shied away from using the term "feminist." Yet, although she preferred to be known for her antifascist work, she did not want to ignore the issue of women's oppression. In her laudatory memoir of radical writer Agnes Smedley, she explains how Smedley saw possibilities for transforming gender relations through socialism. This 1960 essay, entitled "Daughter of Earth" (or "*Hija de la Tierra*," as it was titled when published in the Cuban *El Mundo*), provides some insight into

Dodd's own Left feminist ideals. In it Dodd discusses the lessons Smedley's work provides in regards to the possibilities that socialism offered for women: "Agnes Smedley was wrongly called a 'feminist.' What she really wanted and fought for all her life was the revolutionary power of the working class, and full legal, sexual and economic equality for women. [. . . she was convinced that] an honest and equal relationship between men and women would be possible only after revolution, and even then would be slow in evolving. 'Property relationships must change, and also the habits of men!'" (2–3). Like Smedley and other women writers on the Left, Dodd gave the struggle against fascism and racial and economic exploitation primacy over women's issues, but both women made sure that women's issues did not get silenced on behalf of any greater struggle. In a 1981 letter to a friend, she referred to herself as "a woman liberationist [. . .] from the old days," acknowledging the importance that she placed on women's issues (Letter to David Klopfer).

Dodd believed that women could not enjoy full equality under fascism or capitalism, and she often wrote about the possibilities that socialism offered for women. After leaving the U.S., she continued to maintain connections to Communist organizations in China, Prague, the Soviet Union, and the U.S. While living in Mexico, Dodd was part of an exile community of blacklisted artists, including several members of the Hollywood Ten. Her papers include correspondence with Jack Lawson, who wrote about sexist images of women in films in "Degradation of Women," a section in *Film in the Battle of Ideas*, his 1953 study of Marxist film criticism. She also exchanged letters with Paul Jarrico, the producer of *Salt of the Earth*, and the actress Gale Sondergaard (wife of *Salt* director Herbert Biberman), who performed a one-woman Marxist-feminist show in the 1950s. Many of these people remember participating in discussion groups and seminars that focused on the connections between gender, race, and class oppression, and many of them were working to incorporate representations of women's activism into their cultural works. Given her efforts to address women's activism in her writings, Dodd more than likely would have been part of such discussions.[15]

Many of Dodd's essays from the late 1950s and 1960s address the benefits of living in a socialist society, such as attention to child welfare, affordable food and housing, efficient public transportation, shared community facilities, and readily available health care. These essays (published primarily in foreign periodicals) are similar to ones published in the *Daily Worker* during this time, comparing women's experiences in socialist societies to women living under capitalism. Dodd described the services available to improve women's lives in socialist societies. In articles such as "Hoyerswerda: Socialist New Town" (1960), she interviewed women in the German Democratic Republic about the advantages that socialism provided for women, including facilities and support to "relieve woman of household drudgery, and the excessive hours and worries connected with childcare" ("Hoyerswerda" 108). In "Waiting at Poprad, CSSR" (1961), she describes the childcare services a small town in Slovakia had established for women who lived and worked in the town. Although useful historical documents, these later writings presented an idealized and uncritical view of the liberatory possibilities socialism promised women and do not reflect the contradictions and obstacles that her earlier work illuminates. These nonfiction works reflect an uncritical belief that socialism would relieve women of their domestic duties, yet her fiction shows that achieving equality for women was not so easy.

Taken together, Dodd's cultural work provides what Constance Coiner refers to as "a wedge into history" (11) a glimpse of some of the contradictions and tensions for women on the Left in this era that has heretofore been unavailable. Her work also bolsters the recent historical studies that have shown that feminism did not die out in the years between the first- and second-wave women's movement. As shown in Kate Weigand's *Red Feminism: American Communism and the Making of Women's Liberation* (2001) and Rebecca Hill's "Fosterites and Feminists, Or 1950s Ultra-Leftists and the Invention of AmeriKKKa" (1998), many of the ideas debated and discussed by Dodd and other Left feminists of the postwar era anticipate ideas generally attributed to the second-wave women's movement.

Perhaps the most striking example of the relationship between postwar Left feminism and the modern feminist movement can be seen in Betty Friedan's *The Feminine Mystique* (1963). Friedan is widely recognized as one of the founding mothers of feminism's second-wave. Her presentation of herself as an unhappy homemaker, bored with her domestic suburban lifestyle, tapped into the feelings of discontent shared by many white, middle-class women throughout the U.S. Friedan's work has come under attack as focusing too narrowly on the concerns of white, middle-class, married women and ignoring the struggles of working-class women and women of color.[16] It is surprising, then, to learn that she had previously had connections to groups committed to women's rights in the context of struggles against racial oppression and economic exploitation. In *Betty Friedan and the Making of* The Feminine Mystique: *The American Left, the Cold War, and Modern Feminism* (1998), historian Daniel Horowitz carefully traces Friedan's roots as a Left activist and radical labor journalist in the 1940s and early 1950s. From 1946–52, she wrote for *UE News*, the official publication for the United Electrical, Radio and Machine Workers of America (UE), one of the most radical unions in the postwar era. Her 1952 pamphlet, *UE Fights for Women Workers*, argued for the need to improve women's pay and working conditions and challenged stereotypical assumptions about women's roles in American society. In 1953, she published *Women Fight for a Better Life! UE Picture Story of Women's Role in American History*, a pamphlet that championed the role of black, working-class, and activist women in struggles for peace and justice (121, 138–39). While Friedan completely disavows this radical past and reinvents herself as a middle-class housewife in *The Feminine Mystique*, many of the ideas in this work are deeply rooted in the Left's critique of domestic ideology in the 1940s and '50s. In one section, Friedan uses the concept of the fascist triple K to describe the domestic ideology championed by women's magazines. Her critiques of books and magazines bear a strong resemblance to those in the *Worker* and *Masses and Mainstream*. And she devotes a significant amount of space to discussing *Modern Woman: The Lost Sex*, using language that echoes the 1940s critiques of Party leaders Elizabeth Gurley Flynn and William Foster.

Although Friedan sought to deny it, these similarities are not coincidental; they can be directly traced to Friedan's involvement in the Old Left. While many feminist historians credit *The Feminine Mystique* with starting the modern feminist movement, Horowitz's work makes a powerful case for this movement, and Friedan's book, being rooted in the ideas and struggles of the Old Left. As he puts it, "social movements and their leaders do not . . . come out of nowhere. They have histories that powerfully shape their destinies" (245). While understanding Friedan's past provides an entirely new lens through which to view the modern women's movement, Friedan made every effort to distance herself from Horowitz's findings. After finding out that he intended to write about her Left past, she refused to cooperate with Horowitz, to allow him interviews, or to grant him permission to publish anything from her unpublished papers. In the final years of her life, rather than acknowledging the source of many of the ideas in her groundbreaking book, she attempted to maintain the image of herself that she constructed in *The Feminine Mystique*.[17]

In contrast to Friedan, historian Gerda Lerner chose to embrace her Left past in *Fireweed: A Political Autobiography* (2002). Lerner, a pioneering scholar of women's history, is candid about her involvement with the Communist Party and claims that her attention to race, class, and gender as a historian "comes directly out of my life and experience." She writes, "I could never have written and edited *Black Women in White America: A Documentary History* (1972) . . . if it had not been for my experiences in the Congress of American Women, in the interracial housing struggles in Astoria, in living in an interracial community" (371). By being unrepentant about her Left history, Lerner acknowledges the debt that she and other feminists owe to the Old Left. Works like Lerner's, as well as those of Horowitz, Hill, and Weigand, help to rewrite the history of feminism in the U.S. in a way that acknowledges a continuous tradition of resistance, a tradition that has largely been erased by the red-baiting of the McCarthy era and by revisionists such as Friedan.

The blacklists, the HUAC interrogations, and FBI harassment damaged the Left not only as a political force but also as a cultural one. McCarthyism severely hampered the careers of hundreds of Left cultural workers, relegating many of them to obscurity. In a 1959 letter to *Mainstream* editor Charles Humboldt, written shortly after she and her husband moved to Prague, Dodd wrote, "There is no way of conveying the excitement a writer feels over here, at last to write and be published!" In the rest of her letter, she describes the vibrant cultural community there and the prospects it provided for artists and writers. While she felt energized by this group, other letters reflect a desire to return to the U.S. Although she built ties to resistance movements in Prague, China, Cuba, Mexico, and the Soviet Union, her writing was her only means of remaining connected with the Left in the U.S. Purged from literary and feminist history, Dodd's work addresses ideals of alliance-building and consciousness-raising that remain relevant to an understanding of feminism. In rescuing Dodd from her Cold War exile, this essay contributes to the projects of writing the cultural history of Left writers from the McCarthy era and establishing links between postwar Left feminism and the second-wave women's movement in the U.S.

Notes

1. While Dodd and her husband were cleared on all counts in 1979, due to lack of evidence, various sources have since contended that there was some truth to the charges. Weinstein and Vassiliev's *The Haunted Wood: Soviet Espionage in America—the Stalin Era* (1999) charges that Dodd was most definitely spying for the Soviet Union, based on Weinstein's temporary and exclusive access to the Stalin-era files of the NKVD (the Soviet intelligence agency and predecessor to the KGB). Further, in *Venona: Decoding Soviet Espionage in America* (1999), John Earl Haynes and Harvey Klehr indict Dodd (along with several hundred other Americans) as a Soviet spy, based on the Venona files, a series of Soviet cables intercepted and decoded by U.S. intelligence agents in the 1930s and '40s. However, many historians have argued that the content of both the NKVD and Venona files is unverifiable; and their usefulness is in doubt for identifying specific individuals whose complicity in espionage is not supported by other evidence. Weinstein has come under fire for his failure to follow the accepted scholarly standards of openness. His publisher paid for exclusive access to the NKVD files, and Weinstein has not allowed anyone else to see the archival materials he and Vassiliev draw on in *The Haunted Wood*. When Weinstein was nominated to be the archivist of the United States (a position he currently holds), nineteen organizations, including the Society of American Archivists and the Organization of American Historians, issued a joint statement expressing concern about his nomination on ethical grounds. Even those who agree with his conclusions, such as Whittaker Chambers's biographer Sam Tanenhaus, have been critical of Weinstein's methods, particularly his failure to document his archival sources. Moreover, the intercepted cables use code names to refer to the individuals involved, which government employees in subsequent years have associated with specific individuals, sometimes on the basis of speculation or in the face of contradictory evidence. Klehr and Haynes rely on these uncorroborated attributions as proof; additionally, they leave out evidence that might challenge their inferences. As historian Ellen Schrecker writes in *Many Are the Crimes: McCarthyism in America* (1998), "There are too many gaps in the record to use these materials with complete confidence" (xvii–xviii). Similarly, Victor Navasky argues, "thus far Venona has been used as much to distort as to expand our understanding of the cold war."

2. Alan Wald has acknowledged that Dodd's life and work would make her an "excellent candidate for revival," but otherwise, cultural histories of both feminism and the Left fail to include her. See Wald, *Writing* 21. However, with the recent publication of a German edition of Dodd's memoir, *Through Embassy Eyes*, by Frankfurt-based publisher Eichborn Verlag, it is possible that her literary works will begin to receive more attention.

3. Although the term "Left" has been used to describe various groups and ideologies, in this study I use it to refer to a political position aligned with the Communist Party in the U.S. From the 1930s to the early 1960s, numerous organizations worked in tandem with the Party because they saw Communists as their best allies against fascism, sexism, racism, workplace exploitation, and colonialism. Whether as card-carrying members or as fellow travelers, people who were part of what Ellen Schrecker refers to as the Communist "movement" shared a vision of a more egalitarian world that could be achieved through socialism. I use the term "Left feminist" to connote more an activist position than a theoretical one. Amy Swerdlow describes this position as believing that "the attainment of genuine equality for women required the mobilization of the 'masses'—for equality and social justice for all" (299).

4. In *Women and the American Left: A Guide to Sources*, Mari Jo Buhle defines the Woman Question as "how could women make claims on behalf of the liberation of their sex and simultaneously, with equal commitment, advance the struggles of the working class? In other words, what was the categorical relationship of class and gender in theories, strategies, and practices of social change" (viii)?

5. Dodd came to appreciate both men's integrity and their sense of the need for artists to be concerned with injustice. She dedicated her first novel to Lovett (and her husband) and continued to turn to him for creative advice.

6. According to press clippings in the Dodd papers, she had been secretly engaged before marrying Roberts but had broken off the marriage.

7. Officially a party from 1936–56, the American Labor Party originally forwarded a pro-Left but non-Socialist platform. Communists quickly gained control of the Party and, by 1941, had driven away the liberal Left wing. While clearly a party that fought for working-class interests, the ALP also prioritized antiracism and antifascism. See Isserman, *Which Side*; Meyer, "American."

8. See Aaron, Denning, Foley, and Wald, *Exiles*.

9. Sylvia Crane tells this story in her comments at Alfred's memorial service in 1986. When the Sterns were charged with espionage, Crane was among those interviewed by the FBI about the Sterns' Communist involvement and was later subpoenaed by HUAC to testify about their activities.

10. *Through Embassy Eyes* was a best-seller upon its publication and was reprinted on the day it was issued; it went through four printings in its first month.

11. The *New York Times* describes it as "challenging to the mind" (Mitgang); the *St. Louis Post Dispatch* claims that "by spreading understanding about the real threat to the democratic way of life" represented by "the shameful incidents" in the novel, it "may help to prevent their recurrence" (Aldridge); the *Nation* described it as "a true mirror image of the United States today," based on "an honest commitment to freedom and truth" (Feuchtwanger); the *National Guardian* reviewer wrote that *The Searching Light*'s "powerful lessons" make it "one of the very important novels of 1955," one that "deserves the widest reading" (Citron).

12. Maltz, the radical novelist and dramatist and member of the Hollywood Ten, described the novel as "a substantial contribution to the literature of the American scene in the era of the Cold War." Annette Rubinstein (Vice-chair of the New York Peace Association) wrote that *The Searching Light* is not only a "good novel," but one that can "deepen the understanding and strengthen the determination of those who [. . .] already know that nothing which is happening in the world about us is truly apart from themselves" (63).

13. In a 1949 article on university loyalty oaths, published in *Masses and Mainstream*, Samuel Sillen discusses several cases in which professors with otherwise unblemished academic records were fired. While a few of these professors belonged to the Communist Party, he argues that most were targeted because of their association with antiracist or antifascist struggles ("Behind").

14. Dodd was an admirer of the work of David Alfara Siqueiros, a revolutionary Mexican painter whose artwork and activism prioritized the plight of the worker and the inevitability of Revolution, and the Communist muralist Diego Rivera. Siqueiros was jailed in Mexico City for his activities as an organizer of workers, artists, and intellectuals. Dodd tried to raise awareness of his plight in her 1961 article, "Imprison a Flame," published in the Sunday *Worker* and in China, Cuba, and several European newspapers. In drawing attention to Siqueiros's situation in this essay and in "Prisoner #4678860" (published two years later in the *Worker*), Dodd calls attention to the growing threat of anticommunism for political activists and cultural workers throughout the world. Siqueiros became a hero of sorts to the Left. Pablo Neruda wrote a poem about him, and Lorraine Hansberry signed a petition calling for his release.

15. For information on the Left feminist politics of the Hollywood Left, see Rosenfelt, Commentary 107, 159. Dodd's letters also indicate close friendships with Ring Lardner, Albert Maltz, and Dalton Trumbo.

16. See hooks, Tong, Boucher.

17. The majority of obituaries printed after her death would suggest that she was largely successful in upholding this image. For example, Margalit Fox's obituary in the *New York Times* makes no mention of Friedan's radical past.

Anybody's Protest Novel: Chester Himes and the Prison of Authenticity

Stephanie Brown

> The "protest" novel, so far from being disturbing, is an accepted and comforting aspect of the American scene, ramifying that framework we believe to be so necessary. . . . The failure of the protest novel lies in its rejection of life, the human being, the denial of his beauty, dread, power, in its insistence that it is his categorization alone which is real and which cannot be transcended.
> —James Baldwin, "Everybody's Protest Novel"

Literary critics and historians have in recent years begun the important work of reexamining and often exploding the assumptions that underpin "the fifties" both as historical and cultural construct and as literary and artistic era. In the process, a startling array of texts have been recovered and reconsidered, even generically reclassified. Yet in the center of this important activity, a strange lacuna in work focusing on African American literature has persisted, out of which the postwar era in African American novels emerges, by default, as the space *between* Richard Wright's *Native Son* and the Black Arts movement, a generally homogenous period of unremarkable literary output punctuated only by the "anomalous" masterpiece of Ralph Ellison's *Invisible Man*.[1] The critical truism, only slightly generalized, holds that with the publication of *Native Son* in 1940, Wright ushered in a new type of African American fiction, the gritty, urban social realist novel, which redefined African American literature and provided a template for "authentic" work by black writers for the next twenty years.[2] It further contends that the lone exception, Ellison's *Invisible Man*, hailed in 1952 as a modernist masterpiece, supports Ellison's famous, largely unchallenged, dictum that Wright was no literary ancestor of his, but merely a "relative"; though it continues to be argued that "there has been a tendency to peg *Invisible Man*—against Ellison's express wishes—as a 'black protest novel'" (Stephens 125), it seems to me that such a claim cannot be substantiated by more than a small fraction of the massive amount of Ellison scholarship, past and present.[3] It does no disservice to Ellison's achievement to suggest out that, although both he and James Baldwin, whose well known 1955 essay obviously inspired this paper's title, repeatedly asserted the dominance of the protest novel genre in postwar African American belles-lettres while simultaneously disparaging it as a "failure" within whose strictures they refused to write, scrupulous critical attention should nevertheless be paid to the texts actually being produced by black writers during the period in question in evaluating the validity of these remarks. Such attention, to writers including Wright, Ellison, and Baldwin's contemporary Chester Himes, forces us to refine and complicate our received notions of the attributes of postwar black fiction.

Both the progression from *Native Son*'s celebrated role as the progenitor of the black protest novel (as black social realism came quickly to be known) to the dismissal and obscurity of Wright's later work and that of his contemporaries, and the elevation of *Invisible Man* to canonical status, are critical narratives tailor-made to fit the expectations of a postwar literary critical establishment not only heavily invested in New Critical paradigms but, more importantly for my purposes here, firmly under the sway of broader cultural notions of racial authenticity and its literary manifestations. Writing in 1953, Carl Milton Hughes observed in the introduction to his survey of African American literature of the preceding decade that "the art of telling a story well has not eluded the Negro writer. In fact, it has always been characteristic of some Negroes. Whether a Negro relates incidents of ribaldry and earthiness because of impoverishment or isolation or whether he subscribes to urbanity with its attendant sophistication, there seems to emanate always from a certain type of Negro with the least provocation a spritely [*sic*] story" (19). Nevertheless, by the end of his study, he felt constrained to remark that despite this natural aptitude for storytelling, the Negro novelist had a considerable way to go before being able to join the ranks of truly great American writers, allowing only that "[e]ven though Negro novels are defective, they are not without positive virtues." Chief among these virtues is what Hughes ultimately identifies as the only major contribution of African Americans to American letters: their "authentic interpretation of Negro life and the Negro world from experiences inside the restricted and isolated Negro world" (267).

From the vantage point of the twenty-first century, Hughes's remarks might be construed as at best quaintly essentialist and at worst openly racist, but they were neither novel nor representative only of views outside the African American literary community. Indeed, Hughes provides little more than a recapitulation of the then nearly thirty-year-old views of critic William Stanley Braithwaite, whose 1925 essay "The Negro in American Literature" boldly argued that "[i]ndeed the Negro novel is one of the great potentialities of American literature." Braithwaite asks only rhetorically if this masterpiece "must . . . be written by a Negro," quoting W. E. B. Du Bois at length in response: "The white writer seems to stand baffled before the enigma [of the Negro novel] and so expends all his energies on dialect and in general on the Negro's minstrel characteristics. . . . We shall have to look to the Negro himself to go all the way. It is quite likely that no white man can do it" (qtd. in Mitchell, 42). Similarly, Nick Aaron Ford writes, in his 1936 *The Contemporary Negro Novel: A Study in Race Relations*, that "in spite of the faithful representation and sympathetic treatment of the race by [white] authors, they cannot think the thoughts of their characters, nor can they see the world through their eyes" (14). Indeed, letting African Americans "speak for themselves" is so important that Hugh M. Gloster asserts that in his 1947 survey *Negro Voices in American Fiction*, "the author has tried to permit no theory—economic, political, social or philosophical—to influence his approach. As far as possible, he has let Negro writers of fiction speak for themselves. . . . [Although] some of the best transcripts of Negro experience have been made by white authors . . . [t]his volume, undertak[es] to present the Negro as his own interpreter [and] furnishes first-hand evidence of [the true African American experience] . . ." (Introduction, viii).

This identification of the authenticity of the African American novel with the authenticity of its black author has, of course, a long history beginning with the authentication of the slave narrative[4] and continuing through the New Negro Renaissance fascination with the concept of the folk.[5] In the ongoing quest to articulate what Henry Louis Gates, Jr. has termed the "signifying black difference," African American fiction finds itself in a complex position vis-à-vis African American identity. Forced not merely to grapple with the weight of an oral and written tradition but also to participate in the construction of this "signifying difference," the black novel carries the particularly heavy burden of interpreting "blackness" textually. The focus of the text can become the issue of, as Joel Williamson puts it, "not whether to be or not to be . . . but of how to be" black (164).

I submit that these problematic questions of how to communicate the experience of the racialized self, how to "write black," reach a new high point in the postwar period, in what I would argue has been erroneously dismissed as nothing more than the golden age of the black novel of protest. As white American intellectuals of this period began increasingly to see themselves as victims of a postwar society "spoiled by success" (as Warren Susman puts it), the African American "experience" began to be cast as simultaneously vitally important and inscrutable to white culture, a locus of authenticity in an increasingly standardized and corporatized postwar U.S. The vehicle for the communication of this authenticity, widely identified with a simplicity of self indistinguishable from primitivism, was the African American protest novel, itself cast as a primitive (and thus, more real) version of the novel form itself. The protest novel, as it was understood by white and black critics alike, sought not artistic innovation or philosophical complexity, but rather simply the expression of the "black experience." Yet the strictures of the protest novel form confine and constrain the "experience" whose representation they purport to enable, and ultimately serve only to reify the black identity most useful for white intellectuals seeking a space to articulate their dissatisfaction with their own postwar whiteness. It is in this context that I explore the work of Chester Himes, identified by Hughes as a "realist" of the Richard Wright school but now best known for his Harlem cycle detective fiction, whose arguably earnest first and clearly parodic last "protest" novels, *If He Hollers Let Him Go* (1945) and *The End of a Primitive* (1956)[6] frame the period under consideration. While *If He Hollers Let Him Go* hewed sufficiently close to critical expectations for black protest fiction to be at the time noteworthy only for its vehemence, Himes's use of black humor and metatextual strategies in the latter novel unmistakably suggest a parodic reworking of this conventionalized form, allowing for a reconsideration of the construction of the black identity as "protest"-oriented and demanding a reevaluation of his own early contribution to the genre. Furthermore, *The End of a Primitive* savagely attacks the notion of an authentic African American self and undermines the positioning of this identity by (predominantly white) intellectuals in the 1950s, revisiting, through the inclusion of semi-autobiographical detail, Himes's own reception in the U.S.

By the 1950s, questions of what constituted the authentic, not merely in the racialized subject but in a far more inclusive sense, had gained new resonance. A constellation of factors, some if not most of them unique to the decade immediately following the Second World War, combined to make the period one which clung desperately to notions of the real. In his perceptive essay "Hip and the Long Front of Color," Andrew Ross speaks of a Cold War–era desire to rediscover "useful history," grounded in local and vernacular practices, overwhelmingly identified with both a racialized other and/or a working class romanticized to the point of unrecognizability. Even as the Cold War era rejoiced in its technological advances and standardization of the trappings of middle class affluence (poverty would not be "discovered" until 1962, with the advent of Michael Harrington's *The Other America*, and few questioned the general belief in the accumulation of household accoutrements, to which Nixon alluded in his famous 1959 "kitchen debate" with Khruschev, as synecdoche for and symbol of the triumph of capitalism in the West), concerns about the homogenization of American culture preoccupied more than a suspicious and alienated few. Fears of a creeping sameness identified closely with modern advances had long characterized a distinct strain of American literature[7]; however, the quest for the "authentic" intensified exponentially after World War II. Television was one contributing factor in this new suspicion of mass mediation. At the same time that television broadcast the ideal family and diminished previously broad differences in accent, it allowed for the division of the lives of others into short, discrete segments, bringing previously exotic realities into the living room and effecting a radical change in the ways in which viewers experienced visual media.[8] Film had of course for many years offered this opportunity to usurp another's reality, yet television was qualitatively different, partly in its emphasis on the molding of the everyday into set patterns, partly in its ubiquity. Although television had first been offered to the American public in 1939, it did not gain popularity until after the war, when the number of television sets per capita soared. In 1947, there were approximately 170,000 television sets in American homes; by 1952, a year after Jack Kerouac wrote *On the Road*, there were over a million.

Not everyone accepted with equanimity the televised mediation of lived experience, the discovery that, as Don DeLillo puts it in *White Noise*, "everything was on television last night" (268). As Andrew Ross has pointed out, the quest of postwar intellectuals was for heroes more "authentic than the plastic icons on television" (122). By the time *On the Road* at last appeared in 1957, Kerouac's articulation of the desire to discover "the real America" before it was lost altogether in an ever-widening sea of simulacra, struck a chord for many reviewers, including Gilbert Millstein of the *New York Times*, who hailed the novel as "an authentic work of art." Although this, too, is a longstanding trope in American fiction (Twain's *Roughing It* is but one example of a nineteenth-century text exploring the difficulty of finding new ways to represent an already thoroughly "discovered" West), in Kerouac's work (as well as that of John Clellon Holmes and others) urgency crucially underpins the narrative. *On the Road* continually filters Sal Paradise's perceptions of events and people through the filmic and literary equivalents which precede them in his mind; the narrator variously invokes Hemingway, Steinbeck, and London in characterizing a nostalgic West, while his first impression of Dean Moriarty is that of "a young Gene Autry—trim, thin-hipped, blue-eyed, with a real Oklahoma accent—a sideburned hero of the snowy West" (5).

In his desperate search for the "real," Sal endlessly congratulates himself on what he hopes is the completeness of his immersion into unfamiliar situations and milieux. In order to take on these multiple personalities, of course, he must erase whatever has passed before for his own subject position, a feat he accomplishes in an anonymous Midwestern hotel room with no conscious effort at all: "I woke up as the sun was reddening; and that was the one distinct moment in my life, the strangest moment of all, when I didn't really know who I was—I was far away from home, haunted and tired with travel, in a cheap hotel room I'd never seen, hearing the hiss of the steam outside, and the creak of the old wood of the hotel, and footsteps upstairs, and all the sad sounds, and I looked at the cracked high ceiling and really didn't know who I was . . ." (17). His delusions perhaps reach their apogee with his observation, during his brief stint as a "Mexican" cotton picker, that he is "sighing like an old Negro sharecropper" as he reflects on his duty to the "family" he helps support until his aunt sends him the last of many checks that have "saved [his] lazy butt again" (101).

However, and this is a crucial point, the narrative makes a distinction between Sal's miming of race and his yearning to experience it authentically. As much as Sal may be able to make of his self an empty vessel into which other class- and ethnicity-based identity options may be poured, there is an authenticity so pure in the black experience that he cannot approach it except as an inauthentic outsider: "At lilac evening I walked with every muscle aching among the lights of 27th and Welton in the Denver colored section, wishing I were a Negro, feeling that the best the white world had offered was not enough ecstasy for me, not enough life, joy, kicks, darkness, music, not enough night . . . I wished I were . . . anything but what I was so drearily, a 'white man' disillusioned. . . . I was only myself, Sal Paradise, sad, strolling in this violet dark, this unbearably sweet night, wishing I could exchange words with the happy, true-hearted, ecstatic Negroes of America" (180). Sal's giddy depiction of "ecstatic" black life is based entirely on his perceptions as an outsider, since, as he readily admits, he cannot even talk to the blacks he meets, let alone really get to know them. African-Americanness is the one quality Sal Paradise and most of his companions cannot acquire[9]: though Dean Moriarty boasts that he can "go anywhere in America; it's all the same, I know the people" and Sal prides himself on his chameleon-like ability to pass for a down-on-his-luck hobo one day and a middle-class college student the next, nevertheless he is easily identified (even in the dark) as a white man: "A gang of colored women came by, and one of the young ones detached herself from motherlike elders and came to me fast—'Hello, Joe!'—and suddenly saw it wasn't Joe, and ran back, blushing. I wished I were Joe" (180).

It is, of course, entirely possible that Joe might also wish he were Sal, but as a "happy, true-hearted Negro" he has access to only one identity at a time. While Sal suffers as a "'white' man disillusioned" from a lack of stable selfhood, his momentary black doppelganger, Joe, has so much authenticity that his life is both immediately readable and entirely inaccessible. An ungenerous reader might call him stereotypical.[10] Sal's unstable white identity, an only slightly *avant la lettre* postmodern self, is both performative and radically contingent, and while its fluidity allows him a freedom of subject position not unlike the freedom of movement his aunt's money provides, he yearns for an essential self firmly rooted in biological difference and local practice.[11]

However, reductionist or not, *On the Road*'s depictions of African Americans provide important insight into the role played by blackness in the alternative scene following the Second World War. Sal's characterization of the authentic African American self insists on its pleasure in the bodily (its unfettered access to the "kicks" Sal and his cronies endlessly seek), its simplicity and, perhaps most significantly, its perceptions that are curiously out of sync with "modern" (white) America: "There was an old Negro couple in the field with us. They picked cotton with the same God-blessed patience their grandfathers had practiced in antebellum Alabama . . ." (96).[12] Pierre Bourdieu has written that "the purely ethical pursuit of 'authenticity' is the privilege of those who have the leisure to think and can afford to dispense with the economy of thought that 'inauthentic' conduct allows" (291). To this one might add that the projection of "authenticity" also requires the perception of the Other as being outside that economy of thought and, in the postwar era, to being outside the capitalist economy as well.

Kerouac's contemporary, Norman Mailer, makes a perhaps still more explicit identification of African Americans with this kind of allochronic authenticity, and explicitly takes the important step of identifying this modern primitive with protest against the American status quo. For Mailer, the survivalist modus operandi of the African American living in a racist America provides a blueprint for the redemption of the "white man disillusioned." In his controversial essay "The White Negro," which appeared in *Dissent* in the summer of 1957, a few months before *On the Road*, Mailer famously designates black experience coterminous (when not synonymous) with (a now specifically sexualized) primitivism: "Knowing in the cells of his existence that life was war, nothing but war, the Negro (all exceptions admitted) could rarely afford the sophisticated inhibitions of civilization, and so he kept for his survival the art of the primitive, he lived in the enormous present, he subsisted for his Saturday night kicks, relinquishing the pleasures of the mind for the more obligatory pleasures of the body, and in his music he gave voice to the character and quality of his existence, to his rage and the infinite variations of joy, lust, languor, growl, cramp, pinch, scream and despair of his orgasm" (341).

Of course for Mailer sexuality (that is, the "good" orgasm, rather than the "bad") is the mark of engagement with the real; it goes without saying that such sexuality is closely linked to violence.[13] In a *Village Voice* column written a year earlier, Mailer outlines his differentiation between "the hip and the square" through a discussion of "artistic" rape; as literary critic and Mailer biographer Mary Dearborn writes, "[s]exual expression, the more transgressive the better, was at the heart of Hip . . . so too was violence . . . only outside the law, where our darkest instincts hold sway . . . is there real vitality" (114). However, in "The White Negro," the racialization of Hip is well delineated. To be white is to be, with rare exceptions, "Square," to value what Kerouac describes as "white ambitions." In this formulation, blacks are spared the fate of the corporate man, allowed no access to Riesman's "lonely crowd." As white America perceives itself as progressively more conformist, the African American finds himself[14] positioned as the repository of all that technological advances and material gain have stripped, in the name of progress and the Cold War, from white American men.

Mailer's point, of course, is that in fact it is possible for whites to get back in touch with their more primitive instincts (this is the job of the psychopath or the hipster), but it is important to note that hipsters approach the primitive from the exalted position of the alienated existentialist, co-opting and recuperating the primitive as a stance deliberately outside the narrow confines of "square" consciousness. "For Hip," Mailer pronounces, "is the sophistication of the wise primitive in a giant jungle, and so its appeal is still beyond the civilized man" (343).[15] Lest this wise primitivism be construed to be the province exclusively of whites, Mailer pays lip service to the trope of the inscrutable Negro, yet the apparent idiot savant turns out, upon closer inspection, to be merely a keen observer and careful mimic: "I remember once hearing a Negro friend have an intellectual discussion for half an hour with a white girl who was a few years out of college. The Negro literally could not read or write, but . . . as the girl spoke, he would detect the particular formal uncertainties in her argument, and . . . would respond to one or another facet of her doubts. . . . Of course, he was not learning anything about the merits and demerits of the argument, but he was learning a great deal about a type of girl he had never met before, and that was what he wanted. Being unable to read or write, he could hardly be interested in ideas nearly so much as in lifesmanship . . ." (350).

Mailer's "Negro friend" is a natural artist, able to perform as an "intellectual" without even the ability to read in the same way that the jazz musicians Kerouac extols in *On the Road* can play brilliant music despite their lack of formal training; in both cases, the untutored, "spontaneous" quality of their skill arises from their experience as blacks in a white world that forces them to express their oppression as art. The overlap between black life and black art, between autobiography and "protest fiction," is worth noting. There isn't an especially great logical gap between Mailer's insistence on the African American as a specialist in "lifesmanship" and C. M. Hughes's belief that the African American novel is valuable primarily for what it communicates about authentic African-Americanness. Again, the black writer can take as his subject only the writing of black life, a subject whose central thrust is always predetermined by its emphasis on "protest." Mailer's insistence that black existence can be "war, nothing but war" suggests the essential homogeneity of black experience as resistance. The "protest novel" is to Hughes and his contemporaries the only real postwar African American literary form; yet, as Hughes makes clear, it is a curiously stunted and incomplete one: "[v]aried as it is and inclusive of American interests, Negro writing concentrates on one weakness of American society [the "unhappy fact" of the inequality of races] rather than its virtues. . . . Variations on the same theme are hardly conducive to producing a great literature" (250–51). The African American novel is cast as a primitive form of the genre, in the sense in which Freud used the term: like the "primitive" society evolving toward greater complexity,[16] black fiction has yet to mature fully, to take its place among the more technically sophisticated and intellectually demanding novels of white postwar writers.

It is useful to define what it is we mean when we talk about African American fiction in the "era of protest." The novel of protest itself is generically well defined by George Goodin, whose 1985 book *The Poetics of Protest: Literary Form and Political Implication in the Victim of Society Novel* seeks to lay out an anatomy of protest fiction generally. Goodin refers of course not exclusively to the African American protest novel, preferring to categorize his chosen texts (which are fairly wide-ranging) according to the type of victim each features: the "innocent" victim, the "virtuous" victim, the "flawed" victim, and the "pseudo" victim. However,

Goodin can scarcely help using *Native Son* (whose hero is classified as "flawed," for obvious reasons) as his single example of a protest novel written by an African American. It is probably impossible to exaggerate the extent to which *Native Son* is the touchstone for criticism of African American writing that postdates the novel itself by as much as thirty years. In the opening line of *From Apology to Protest: The Black American Novel*, Noel Schraufnagel announces that "[t]he birth of the modern Negro novel is marked by the publication of Richard Wright's *Native Son* in 1940, in the same way that the modern English novel is dated by the 1740 edition of Samuel Richardson's *Pamela*" (ix). According to Schraufnagel, writing in 1973, all African American fiction after Wright is some variety of protest fiction, whether it be "apologetic" or "accommodationist."[17] It is worth noting that the substance of the bulk of his evaluations can be found in more subtle formulations throughout the more critically alert 1980s and 1990s. As Madelyn Jablon puts it, "[a]s a result [of advocating literature by blacks as distinct from white literature] an aversion to formal innovation became rooted in the sociohistorical approach to African American literature. Within this context, black writers who demonstrated an interest in artistic concerns such as those suggested by literary self-consciousness or metafiction were criticized for undercutting the most important justification for the study of black literature: content that expressed the need for political reform" (16).

It is in the context I have outlined above that I wish to examine the manipulation of the protest novel form by Chester Himes. Himes's debut novel was identified by critics (including Hughes) not merely as a work of protest belonging to the Wrightian school but, as Himes himself recalls it, as a "series of epithets punctuated by spit" (*The Quality of Hurt*, 77). *If He Hollers Let Him Go*, which appeared in 1945, is the story of the anonymously named Bob Jones, a shipyard worker in wartime Los Angeles, who finds himself accused of rape by a white female coworker, Madge, and subsequently is severely beaten by his white male coworkers, jailed, and ultimately forced into the army as a condition for the dismissal of the trumped-up charges against him. Contemporary reviewers praised the book for being "effective in defining sharply the inner turmoil of an intelligent Negro" (*American Mercury*, 249) and a "ruthless analysis of an emotionally unstable Negro" (Tracy 110). "Since Himes is a realist," writes Hughes, whose discussion of *Native Son* segues into that of *If He Hollers Let Him Go* and thus emphasizes their perceived similarities, "he finds the situation and its outlook for Negroes . . . hopeless" (210). Ultimately Bob Jones's fate, while obviously less tragic than that of his predecessor Bigger Thomas, does seem (over-)determined by events that originate in racist societal conditions beyond his control.

Despite generally favorable reviews, however, *If He Hollers Let Him Go* was often misinterpreted. Critics dwelled on the biographical similarities between Himes and his character, stressing that Himes (who held, by his own reckoning, twenty-three different jobs in the first three years of World War II, "all in essential industries" [*The Quality of Hurt*, 74]), had experienced the wartime workplace racism that destroys Bob Jones's life firsthand and could testify that its depiction was "authentic." Even the novel's lack of a conclusive ending could be read as a reflection of Himes's own divided consciousness, his lack of solutions to the "Negro problem" he describes and his rage. *If He Hollers Let Him Go*, opined Earl Conrad in a review in the *Chicago Defender*, "is at war with itself, as is Jones, as is Himes, as is the American Negro."[18] This conflation of Himes's life and his work underscores not only reviewers' investment in, and narrowly defined criteria for determining, the novel's authenticity, but also the apparently willfully myopic readings this conflation entailed. Ultimately, as Himes biographers Michel Fabre and Edward Margolies have noted, "critics dwelled on its sociological implications, often ignoring its wit and sardonic humor" (56)[19] as well as its complexity.

An attentive reading of *If He Hollers Let Him Go* reveals not only the wit and humor to which Fabre and Margolies rightly allude, but also the novel's keen interest in foregrounding issues of presumed authenticity and the presentation of narrative. Bob offers a cutting evaluation of the racial authenticity of those he sees around him, brutally dissecting the behavior of Alice, his successful, extremely light-skinned girlfriend, and her well-off parents while simultaneously distancing himself from the clichéd mannerisms and modes of expression of his fellow workers, who are less educated than he is and hail from the rural South. Significantly, however, Bob does not restrict his analysis to his fellow African Americans, noting instead the performative aspects of race among the whites he encounters as well, a phenomenon he employs a series of metaphors to describe. (For example, he observes wryly that "the white folks had sure brought their white to work with them that morning," and wonders later "when white people started getting white," neatly encapsulating his view of whiteness as a series of behaviors, rather than some essential quantity.) Crucially, this knowledge of the role played by performance in interracial interaction informs Bob's reading, in medias res, of his encounters with Madge, the white woman who is finally his downfall. Encountering her for a second time at work, Bob knows before a word is exchanged between them what will happen: "I knew the instant I recognized her that she was going to perform then—we would both perform" (27).

This conception of identity and the actions that manifest it as scripted beforehand lends Bob an uncanny knack for knowing what is going to happen before it actually does. The compactly structured plot unfolds over a period of four days, each of which begins with a dream Bob has reflecting (accurately, if sometimes sketchily) the coming day's events. Workplace humiliations are thus preceded by a dream in which Bob is forced to ask two white men for a job only to hear their excuse that he doesn't have the right tools and their mocking laughter; an encounter with a racist policeman who labels Bob and Alice "coons" is foretold by a dream about being taken away in a squad car. In one of his more symbolically laden, yet obvious, dreams, Bob imagines Alice being killed by white women affecting sympathy for her: "I saw what at first looked like a little rag doll, but when I turned it over I saw it was Alice . . . her body had shrunk until it was no more than a foot long and she was dead. . . . [T[here were millions of white women . . . looking at me, giving me the most sympathetic smiles I ever saw" (101). It is not just Bob's dreams that mirror the events in his life, however; while at a bar with a predominantly black clientele, Bob also witnesses the manipulation of two black men by a white "Arkansas slick chick" who flirts with them in an attempt to start a fight: "All she's got to do now, I thought, is start performing. She could get everybody in the joint into trouble . . . [. . .] All of a sudden, I thought of Madge; the two of 'em were just alike" (76).

Yet despite multiple warnings that contact with Madge will destroy him, Bob cannot stop himself from going to her hotel room, even as he laments the consequences he knows must follow. "All of a sudden," he announces, "I knew I was getting ready to go back and see Madge. Getting my gauge up to be a damn fool about a white woman, to blow my simple top, maybe get into serious trouble. . . . It was crazy; I knew it was crazy." (142). From the moment Madge opens her door to Bob, the novel begins its ineluctable descent into the specific tragedy associated with the presence of a black man and a white woman in an intimate space. Although Bob does not kill (or even harm) Madge, his doom is nevertheless sealed as inexorably as Bigger Thomas's. The narrative is inescapable, the mandates of the genre too strong. Allowed to question the utility of the trajectory of the protest novel, Bob is nevertheless confined to its conclusions, unable to conjure up an alternative narrative for himself. As he observes early in the novel, when forced into a conversation about Wright's book with one of his girlfriend Alice's "liberal" white friends, the Wrightian protest novel has its limits: "You couldn't pick a better person than Bigger Thomas to prove the point [of the oppressed status of African Americans]. But after you prove it, then what?" (88).

Then what, indeed. Just over ten years later, Himes, by this time an expatriate who believed with some justification that he had found a more appreciative and sophisticated audience in Europe, again took on the theme of interracial sex and violence in *The End of a Primitive*, an ambitious novel he praised in interviews as his "favorite book."[20] As the title suggests, *The End of a Primitive* confronts head-on the idea of the African American as the final repository of the bestial in technologized postwar society. At the same time, however, it interrogates the ways in which black writers of protest fiction are complicit in this narrativizing of blacks as primitives through their insistence on the importance of race as an organizing principle for writing by African Americans, a strategy which could only result in the "blueprint" of which Wright spoke in an influential 1937 essay. Wright argues that "reduced to its simplest and most general terms, theme for Negro writers will rise from understanding the meaning of their being transplanted from a 'savage' to a 'civilized' culture in all its social, political economic and emotional implications . . . when they [black writers] have begun to feel the meaning of the history of their race as though they in one lifetime had lived it themselves throughout all the long centuries" (rpt. in Mitchell, 104–5).

In *The End of a Primitive,* Himes rips off and riffs on the prototype that provides the narrative for the black protest novel, rewriting the central event of narratives from *Othello* to *Native Son*: the "rape" and murder of a white woman by a hapless black protagonist invariably doomed to suffer white vengeance. In so doing, he also suggests that the dominance of specific narratives of African-Americanness spills over into the lived experience of the creators of stories as well as the characters who inhabit them[21]; the novelist protagonist of *The End of a Primitive* is both a character and a creator of characters. Moreover, in this novel, Himes deliberately elides the distinction between autobiography and fiction by building into *The End of a Primitive* stories and events that are easily recognizable as having been lifted directly from his own writing career, suggesting most clearly that the novel provides a corrective lens through which to read interpretations of his earlier work, especially *If He Hollers Let Him Go*. Himes's parodic revision and subversion of the African American protest novel must be read as a searing critique of a postwar theoretical-critical apparatus, endorsed by African American writers themselves in the interest of strategic essentialism, that allows Hughes to state with certainty that "*since* Himes is a realist" he must find "the outlook for Negroes . . . hopeless."

The End of a Primitive is the story of the encounter with "civilization" of the latest in a series of primitivized Othellos, Jesse Robinson, a black novelist who kills his white female lover in an alcohol-induced blackout. Although the story is ultimately tragic, it relies heavily on humor for its effect. This is unsurprising, given Himes's characteristic fondness for jokes. Even a relatively cursory look at his work reveals an almost obsessive fascination with the power of the joke: to exclude outsiders from an "in" group, as when, for example, the white supervisor Kelly in *If He Hollers Let Him Go* deliberately tells a racist joke within earshot of Bob Jones, but also to subvert, to tolerate, to rationalize, and to comprehend. For the most part, Himes's humor partakes of the gallows genus, wringing bitter amusement from situations that can hardly be less hilarious. As Joe, the main character in Himes's 1937 short story, "A Nigger," tells himself as he hides in a closet listening to his black girlfriend Fay trying to seduce her elderly white lover, "If I can only get it funny. . . . It is funny! Funny as hell!" (*Collected Stories* 32). In this example, the joke functions, as most theorists of humor among marginalized groups have argued, to render oppression bearable.[22] But there is another sense in which Himes's particular brand of humor participates not merely in the tradition of African American black humor, but also in the postwar project of "black humor," usually identified with "American Surrealist" Nathanael West and with Vonnegut, Heller, and Pynchon. Himes's work operates at the crossroads of these two modes of understanding "the black joke." His "black joking" constitutes a disruption, both ideologically and narratologically, and thus resists the established narrative of the "protest novel," and indeed of the novel form generally. Although Himes obviously belongs among those writers identified by Bruce Janoff, in an early attempt to codify the tenets of "black humor," as having a perspective existing "in a terrain of terrifying candor concerning the most extreme situations" (Janoff 37), he also must be recognized not only as a writer of parody, but also as a deeply subversive satirist in the sense that his work is, as Steven Weisenburger has written of Ishmael Reed, "a revolt against . . . the fictions of power" (Weisenburger 162). Himes makes clear that the protest novel form is, like any narrative, a structure dedicated to the support of other structures, some if not all of which work to select, restrict and maintain access to avenues of knowledge and power.

African American humor has always provided outlets for the articulation of sentiments which had otherwise to be suppressed, and has thus traditionally functioned as a progressive and even liberating force. As Lawrence Levine suggests, in *Black Culture and Black Consciousness: Afro-American Folk Thought from Slavery to Freedom*, African American humor is "closely related to the humor of absurdity . . . which reveal[s] the gap between appearance and actuality and perform[s] what Anton Zijderveld has called 'the unmasking function,'" (312) here of the absurdity of American racism. Mel Watkins, writing of the "creative resourcefulness involved in reversing an accepted joke and turning it to one's own advantage," cites Ralph Ellison's remark that " [African Americans] couldn't escape, so we developed a style of humor which recognized the basic artificiality, the irrationality, of the actual arrangement" (Watkins 33). Such a kind of humor allows the black jokester to make use of a situation in which, as Henri Bergson suggested nearly a century ago in his widely known essay "Laughter," a black face is ipso facto comedic: "Why does one laugh at a Negro? . . . [A] black face, in our imagination, is one daubed over with ink or soot . . . [a]nd we see that the notion of disguise has passed on something of its comic quality to instances in which there actually is no disguise" (86). The notion of the disguise, or of the mask, is of course central to an understanding of the potential for subversion inherent in blackface humor, which historians have in recent years come to recognize and redeem as a vehicle for satire.[23]

A humor based on the ironized playing of societally designated roles necessarily foregrounds the parodic and performative aspects of identity construction, but Himes allows his black jokes a still more aggressive punch line, using a specific brand of parodic impulse, one that refuses to relinquish the most two-dimensional of stereotypes, to question realistic form altogether, as well as the limits and conventions of narrative. In his Harlem detective fiction, for example, the unremitting barrage of blaxploitative language (combined with an exquisitely detailed catalogue of grotesquerie and violence) both establishes the characters as brutal caricatures and creates a knowing metacommentary on "realist" African

American fiction, an effect which is only heightened by the quasi-bowdlerizing behind such terms as the awkward yet omnipresent "mother-raper."[24] Abandoning the terms and conditions of "realistic" representation allows Himes to foreground the issues which concern him, specifically the sense in which African American identity, no matter how inherent and "authentic" it might be romanticized as being, exists only in and through representation, inescapable, except insofar as its grip can be loosened through parodic revision.

In *The End of a Primitive*, the narrativized quality of experience and identity construction is emphasized by the narrator's own obsession with writing his life. Jesse Robinson, who is, as I have suggested, a not-very-well-disguised Himes stand-in, is the author of twelve published novels pigeonholed both by reviewers and by his own editor as "typical protest" fiction, a genre understood here to preclude any interpretations that are not entirely sanctimonious. The opening of *The End of a Primitive* finds Jesse, recently separated from his wife, living in a room in a Harlem apartment with two older men, one of whom makes constant advances toward him, and a pair of spoiled and superannuated Pomeranians. Like so many of Himes's characters, Jesse tells himself jokes, generally centering around his playing the role of one modern primitive or another,[25] in dire circumstances; in jail for recklessly allowing a white woman to hit his car with her own, he feels "laughter . . . welling up from the depths of his despair. 'You should have stayed in that tree, son,' he thought" (*EP* 93). Here, the black joke performs the function Lawrence Levine identifies for it, springing from "the desire to place the situation in which we find ourselves into perspective; to exert some degree of control over our circumstances" (*Black Culture* 300). Echoing Joe of the previously mentioned early story, Jesse observes, as he examines his haggard, hungover reflection in a mirror, that white hegemony is "'funny, really. Funny as hell if you just get the handle to the joke. . . . No point in being mad, son. Better get your black ass glad.' . . . He raised the glass to his reflection. 'Smile'" (*EP* 123).

Jesse's jokes have no place in the white establishment's understanding of his actions or of his writing; comedy is the province of the white writer, whose novels are not valuable primarily for what they communicate about "experiences inside the restricted and isolated Negro world" and who can afford the luxury of humorous and thus "inauthentic" representation. At the same time, however, the protest genre confines and limits him. Jesse recalls "an editor who'd rejected his second novel," asking why "you fellows . . . don't try writing about people, just people?":

> "What I really ought to have told the son of a bitch," he thought, "is why don't you read the Old Testament? Or even Rabelais for that matter. That's how I should have started the damn book. . . . The nigger woke, sat up, scratched at the lice, stood up, farted, pissed, crapped, gargled, harked, spat, sat down, ate a dishpan of stewed chitterlings, drank a gallon of lightning, hated the white folks for an hour, went out and stole some chickens, raped a white woman, got

> lynched by a mob, scratched his kinky head and said boss, Ah's tahd uh gittin' lynched . . . and the Boss said Go on home and sleep nigger, that's all you niggers is good for. So he went back to his shanty, stealing a watermelon along the way, ate the watermelon rind and all, lay down on his pallet, blinked, yawned and went to sleep hating the white folks." "We can't print this crap," the editor would have said. (*EP* 55)

Indeed, Jesse later does have the opportunity to invoke Rabelais in his own defense when his latest editor puts the institutional kibosh on Jesse's new work, which he says sounds too much like "fictional autobiography." The lack of differentiation between the events Jesse hallucinates and those which "really" take place in the narrative emphasizes the fundamental inescapability of stories, the interdependence of fiction and "life"; furthermore, the mis-identification of Jesse's novel as "autobiography" suggests that the narrative framework into which his identity will be made to fit is largely dependent on the expectations of the reader. Jesse's editor, felicitously named Pope, demonstrates not just the faith in the enlightened, universal, and rational that his name implies, but also a fundamental inability to recognize the black jokes in Jesse's novel:

> "Funny!" Pope stared at him incredulously.
>
> "That part where the parents wear evening clothes to the older son's funeral," Jesse said, watching Pope's expression and thinking, "What could be more funny than some niggers in evening clothes? I bet you laugh like hell at Amos and Andy on television."
>
> "That made me cry," Pope accused solemnly. (*EP* 117)

Here Himes, as Robert O'Meally has written of Ralph Ellison, "brilliantly exploits the tension over black/white humor," by calling attention to the dynamics of the joke self-reflexively, providing both joke and white reader, and by making it incumbent upon the actual white reader to participate in a perhaps incomprehensible discourse in which he or she wants desperately not to find anything funny. Destabilizing the reader/text relationship by rupturing the seamlessness of the narrative with a metatextual prod, the black joke here is a weapon, not merely against the stereotyping impulse of minstrelsy, but also against the subtler oppression of white liberal guilt that demands a "success story," replacing one tale of blackface with another. "Why don't you write a black success novel?" Pope asks Jesse. "I don't have that much imagination," Jesse responds. "How about yourself?" Pope insists further, unable to stop conflating Jesse's autobiography and his fiction. "You're certainly a success story." The unspoken joke, of course, is that Jesse's life is evidently *not* a success story, as the preceding conversation makes clear.

Pope's dismissal of Jesse begins Jesse's spiral downward into the long joke of the book, that his life and his art really will be forced willy-nilly into the preestablished parameters of the protest genre. Wandering in a drink-induced blackout, Jesse decides to embark upon a compulsive binge weekend in the company of an alcoholic, sex- and narcotics-addicted white ex-lover, Kriss Cummings. Kriss is driven by different demons than is Jesse, but is similarly obsessed by the narrative of her own life, which she reviews often and ever more lugubriously. (The target of her constant refrain, "you ruined me, you son of a bitch," is generally unclear.) Despite her insistence that she is "tired of listening to . . . blacks whining" (62), Kriss is a self-proclaimed "Negrophile," most of whose friends and lovers are black. Invited to her Gramercy Park apartment for what he assumes is a weekend of non-stop sex, Jesse finds Kriss desperately unhappy and dangerously rage-filled; the book proceeds inexorably toward its final conclusion, in which Jesse emerges from another booze-induced stupor to discover that he has "unknowingly" stabbed to death the woman whom he initially believes to be sleeping peacefully in the next room. The conclusion is so heavily foreshadowed (before killing Kriss, Jesse sinks a knife into both his own manuscript and uncooked dinner rolls described as resembling "mutilated mammoth white testicles [157]) that only the most resistant reader could doubt its inevitability, but this is really the point.[26] From the moment in which Jesse exclaims that "the bitch wants to die," the novel unfolds as horrific and ineluctable parody, highlighted by Jesse's metatextual musings on the process of writing the black joke as he "amus[es] himself with this parody on a fine novel written by a fellow black author":

> —Ah likes chiddlins, do you like chiddlins?
> —Ah likes chiddlins.
> —Chiddlins is good.
> —Ah likes de big gut, do you likes de big gut?
> —Ah likes de big gut.
> —De big gut is good. (*EP* 90)

The point of the novel is its grotesque inevitability stemming from a kind of narrative certitude, a sense that only a limited number of stories can be realized, and that all "reality" must succumb to the Procrustean bed of fiction. Walking aimlessly through Times Square, Jesse muses that it's a "good thing you like movies, son. . . . Otherwise you'd believe all that crap about your country you experience every day" (*EP* 42). The feeling of being trapped in, or at least in the audience of, the wrong film never leaves him; much later, during a heated argument with Walter, a friend of his and Kriss's and the editor of a successful black picture magazine, Jesse observes with amusement that "it was as if he were watching, with impersonal interest, some vaguely valid but not very novel exhibition of idiocy, like a Hollywood treatment of a Negro theme" (*EP* 184). The final moments of the novel are heavily mediated by this pre-scripting of events; Jesse learns of his crime while watching television the morning after it has happened, during a news report by a talking chimpanzee (chimpanzees are cast throughout the novel as fellow primitives—Jesse considers writing a novel about chimps only to dismiss the idea because "some white woman" would no doubt object that she had once been "leered at in a zoo") whose commentary takes in not merely current events but also imminent ones: "defense will allege that he was completely blotto all during this time . . . —will dismiss the insanity plea . . . and Robinson will be electrocuted in Sing Sing prison, December 9th . . ." (*EP* 193).[27]

Returning to the bedroom, Jesse discovers Kriss's dead body between the sheets, and "when the full realization of what he had done penetrated his intelligence, his mind turned inward and became sealed within a sardonic, self-lacerating humor." He assesses his situation in a fiercely condensed summary that both acknowledges and seems to mock the existentialist overtones of the final chapters of *Native Son*: "End product of the impact of Americanization on one Jesse Robinson—black man. Your answer, son . . . BLACK MAN KILLS WHITE WOMAN. . . . Proof beyond all doubt. Jesse Robinson joins the human race" (*EP* 199). His words recall the encounter with Walter, in which Jesse, in a flash of inebriated insight, outlines the ironic conditions under which black men are allowed to "join the human race," suggesting that only by performing the identity they are assigned, especially vis-à-vis white women, can African Americans hope to be recognized as "people." As Walter, both his sexual interest and his fury aroused through Kriss's machinations, tries to attack Jesse with a knife, only to be restrained by his (black) wife,[28] Jesse muses that "the bitch has got us niggers killing off each other . . . now I really do believe the sonofabitch has joined the human race . . . right attitude . . . good nigger . . . footsteps of tradition . . . no wonder they let the nigger join" (*EP* 184). As Jesse congratulates himself on his "successful" entry into humanity, the language degenerates into a sick commercial, the discourse of the media completely suffusing the narrative: "[The non-human status of black men is the] best thing they [white Americans] ever had for all their social ills . . . Be Happy—Go Nappy . . . Feel Low? Lynch Negro! . . . Can't Fuck? Shoot a Buck!" (*EP* 199). Picking up the telephone to turn himself in to the police, Jesse, determined to have the last laugh (and underlining the vicious circle his life has become by echoing his own earlier remarks), comments that it's a "damn good thing [he] read[s] detective stories; wouldn't know what to do otherwise" (*EP* 201).

This insistence on the articulation of African American identity as both pre-narrativized and performative lends plausibility to the claim that Himes must be considered a postmodern satirist, one whose satire is directed less at the societal conditions surrounding the novel's production and more at the form of the novel itself. Though his satire might be construed to have a "real" external target, whether that target is black/white relations or Cold War–era domestic policy (the other major subject of the chimpanzee's commentaries), it is impossible to say that a traditional definition of satire can begin to encompass so self-contained a narrative as this one, particularly if that definition chooses to suggest that satirists write "in order to benefit society as a whole" (Highet, qtd. in Weisenburger 19). Instead, Himes's narrative worries less about inspiring righteous anger against the political and social oppression that supposedly inspires the protest novel than about wreaking havoc on the oppressive structure of the protest novel itself.

Thus, in *The End of a Primitive*, Himes's parodic reworking of the central event of the "classic" protest novel (the alleged "rape" and murder of a white woman followed by the inexorable punishment of the black protagonist) allows the narrative to regain a measure of control over events whose absurdist momentum would otherwise spiral out of control. By eliding the fictions of Jesse Robinson's novels and of his life, Himes creates a multilayered commentary on the strictures which result from the conceptualizing of African American writing as "protest"; by giving Jesse the role of parodically reworking his self as fiction, Himes allows for a space outside the pre-scripted identity construction so closely linked to the novel form itself. Himes's metatextual and postmodern version of Ellison's "change the joke and slip the yoke" strategy combines with what Weisenburger calls the "violence" and "suspicion of all structures, including those of perceiving, representing and transforming" of the black humorist degenerative satire to create a form which is paradoxically hyperreal in its refusal to surrender stereotype and obsessively formal in its challenge to traditional narrative and mimesis. Extending a long tradition of African American humor as resistance to white hegemony, while reflecting suspiciously on the ways in which meaning can be made, Himes's primitive refuses to let pass unremarked the fact that he joins Wright's "civilized culture" only "under protest."

Notes

1. Critical reassessments of the culture of 1950s have proliferated since roughly the end of the Cold War; early contributions to the field include Lary May's pioneering collection, *Recasting America: Culture and Politics in the Age of Cold War* (1988), Stephen J. Whitfield's *The Culture of the Cold War* (1990), and W. T. Lhamon's recently reissued cultural history *Deliberate Speed: The Origins of a Cultural Style in the American 1950s* (1990, 2002). Almost without exception, however, the focus has been on the work of white writers, while black musicians and (more rarely) visual artists have stood in for the cultural production of African Americans more generally. Ralph Ellison provides, as might be expected, the single exception; furthermore, readings of *Invisible Man* that highlight the now durable comparison between its aesthetic and that of a symphonic jazz composition and thus blur the boundaries between music and writing serve to marginalize even Ellison. Alan Nadel's *Containment Culture: American Narrative, Postmodernism and the Atomic Age* offers a refreshing shift from Ellison to John A. Williams and Alice Walker as representative Cold War African American novelists, but the fact that the works he discusses date from the mid-sixties and mid-seventies respectively underscores the absence of black writing of the 1950s.

2. Jeff Karem's recent book, *The Romance of Authenticity: The Cultural Politics of Regional and Ethnic Literatures*, offers a useful analysis of the shift that *Native Son* is presumed to have inaugurated and encapsulated. As scholars such as J. Martin Favor have established, with "authenticity" in African American writing before 1940, even that produced

in the urban north, was overwhelmingly identified with rural, vernacular and geographically delimited practices which "privilege[d] the African American folk and its cultural forms" and excluded the "non-folk" (Favor 4). Karem writes that that assumption both limited Richard Wright and paradoxically made it possible for him to establish his credibility as a black urban observer; although *Native Son* defied readers' expectations for another regional portrait of black life like the earlier *Uncle Tom's Children*, most were willing to trust Wright's knowledge of black life because of his Southern provenance.

3. Stephens quotes Ellison's introduction to the 1981 edition of *Invisible Man*, in which Ellison recalls that he "was trying to avoid writing what might turn out to be nothing more than another novel of racial protest" (Ellison xviii); however, it is worth noting that even contemporary reviewers of *Invisible Man* tended to concur with Saul Bellow, who wrote in his own review in *Commentary* that "Mr. Ellison has not adopted a minority tone" (609). Later critics, beginning with Irving Howe in 1963, in fact criticized Ellison for his novel's *lack* of protest; for an overview of this trend, see Ernest Kaiser's "A Critical Look at Ellison's Fiction and at Social and Literary Criticism by and about the Author" in *Black World* (December 1970).

4. Authors of slave narratives often found themselves at the mercy of white prefatory authenticators who attested to the credibility of their stories, even when they admitted to having made changes in the original manuscript, as Lydia Maria Child did in her introduction to Harriet Jacobs's *Incidents in the Life of a Slave Girl* (1861). See the introduction to Andrews's and Gates's *Civitas Anthology of African American Slave Narratives* for an explanation of the necessity of white legitimization of the African American writer.

5. J. Martin Favor has written persuasively of the influence of a persistent identification of racial authenticity in the 1920s with rural, vernacular and geographically delimited practices on subsequent formulations of race identity which "privilege the African American folk and its cultural forms" and exclude the "non-folk" (4).

6. *The End of a Primitive* was published under that title at this time only in France; in the edition copyrighted by the New American Library, it was edited substantially for "obscenity" and retitled *The Primitive*. References here are to the 1990 restored version, which makes Himes's revision of the protest novel form clearer than previous editions.

7. In the aftermath of the Civil War, the work of local colorists implicitly defended regional dialects and practices fading away before the onslaught of industrialization, while naturalist fiction writers after the turn of the century looked, with Jacob Riis, to an impoverished immigrant class for difference, for exotic others to people a new, urban frontier. Most modernist writers between the wars openly feared the standardization of human perception and sought to use formal innovations to shock readers out of their complacency by disrupting their reading practices. Despite high modernist radical experimentation with language, there remained a desire to leave behind the artificiality of the imposed narrative structures and devices characteristic of the nineteenth century and to map lived experience as it was—fragmented, chaotic, without a comfortable unified perspective from which to witness events. Obviously this desire took for granted that representation was not merely possible, but imperative, and that the real had merely been straitjacketed in artifice so long that readers, like the first viewers of cubist paintings, had lost the ability to differentiate between what they "saw" and what they expected to see, due to long exposure to given narrative forms. The implicit corollary to this belief in the authenticity of perception was a staunch faith in the necessity of observation and personal experience to "real" fiction, especially for the writer whose subject matter was "alien" to him or her. For an exhaustive exploration of the shift from a nineteenth-century aesthetic of imitation to the twentieth-century fascination with the authentic, see Miles Orvell's *The Real Thing: Imitation and Authenticity in American Culture, 1880–1940*.

8. It is my argument that television enabled viewers to naturalize the process of suturing themselves into the subject positions demanded of them in a way film did not; be-

cause watching television was less the public event than going to the movies was, the idea of "borrowing" a variety of realities while sitting in one's own living room, became deceptively mundane, blurring the boundaries between viewer and object far more effectively than film had ever done. The influence of television on quotidian perceptions was perceived as pernicious by some (see Robin R. Means Coleman's discussion of contemporary condemnations of Amos 'n' Andy in *African American Viewers and the Black Situation Comedy*) and as an opportunity for cultural legitimation by others (see Donald Weber's account of the mainstreaming of Jewish culture in "The Goldbergs." Clearly, television was widely regarded, in the 1951 words of *Pittsburgh Courier* columnist J. Bibb, as "destined to become a dynamic and far-reaching method of propaganda" (quoted in Means Coleman, 64).

9. It is worth noting that Sal does allow for the possibility that certain specific types of white men may find black identity more accessible than he does. Allowing blackness to be a constituent part of a white man's identity is only possible, however, when the white man is himself a dropout from modern America, one who has clearly abdicated his position in contemporary American society in favor of a liminality marked by anachronism or outright criminality (as in the case of Elmer Hassel, the "New York dope addict" to whom Gene is also compared), and when the blackness in question is a kind of "old-fashioned," pre-contemporary construction of African American identity.

10. I am only one of many such ungenerous readers (among a far larger number of more obliging ones). Mark Richardson's recent "Peasant Dreams: Reading *On the Road*," which baldly links Kerouac's real-life racist diatribes to his fiction "across a spectrum running from embarrassing, to bad, to abominable" (231), is perhaps the sharpest critique Kerouac has undergone since James Baldwin offered his in "The Black Boy Looks at the White Boy" (1961).

11. In this sense, Kerouac anticipates one of the central issues in the ongoing debate over the political viability of the decentered, deconstructed postmodern subject, namely the uncomfortable fit between it and (potentially more politically expedient) raced identity. While a growing chorus of critics has argued that the practices of marginalized groups constitute a de facto deployment of postmodern identity (Craig Owens provided one early model with "The Discourse of Others: Feminism and Postmodernism" in 1983, though critics of African American literature, including Mae Gwendolyn Henderson and Barbara Johnson, have made the most persuasive cases by far), many voice deep reservations about letting go of what Gayatri Spivak and Diana Fuss have termed "strategic" essentialism. Furthermore, they argue, the emphasis on the postmodern subject further reifies the mutual exclusiveness of race, politics, and theory in favor of a postmodernism that, as Walter Benn Michaels asserts, employs a socially constructed version of race in ways that are "incoherent" without essentialism. As Glenn Jordan observed in remarks following a 1998 talk called "Can the Postmodern Subject be Black?": "I don't know why anybody in the world would want to think of him- or herself as a postmodern subject anyway." (For two widely divergent but detailed discussions of postmodern subjectivity, essentialism, and race, see bell hooks's "Postmodern Blackness" and Walter Benn Michaels's "Race into Culture: A Critical Genealogy of Cultural Identity.")

12. Such characterizations of the "fellaheen" are variations on the practice Mary Louise Pratt has memorably dubbed the "timeless present," a characteristic feature of frontier literature that sought to "codify difference, to fix the Other in a timeless present in where all 'his' actions are repetitions of 'his' normal habits" (121).

13. Ascribing both "primitive" sexuality and a kind of peacetime combat mentality to African American men was really nothing new. In fact, Mailer's words strongly echo those of Margaret Halsey, whose popular 1946 book *Color Blind: The White Woman Looks at the Negro* had argued both that African Americans had "more freedom from inhibition and greater sexual potency" than whites and that "No white person, even when he wants

to, can understand what it means to be a Negro living in the United States of America, any more than a non-combatant can understand what it means to be in action. The constant danger which enshadows the Negro American all his life—danger of small and great indignities, and of actual physical harm or outright destruction—is something that cannot be conveyed to those who have not lived through it, any more than the feelings and sensations of being in combat can be shared with those to whom it did not happen" (113, 116). Unlike Halsey, however, Mailer does not see the future of American civilization in the assimilation of blacks into mainstream white culture; rather, his conclusions are essentially the obverse.

14. That this blackness is primarily masculine is perhaps obvious. Cheryl Wall has argued that despite significant contributions to the vernacular voice, women have perhaps been left out of formulations of "authentic blackness" because women have traditionally lacked access to the signifying practices so central to the development of African American identity. Yet there is a sense in which the representation of African-Americanness in the postwar period centers even more noticeably on men than women; as Nellie McKay observes in her introduction to *The Third Door*, the 1955 autobiography of Ellen Tarry, "to many readers . . . stories of powerful black male anger command more immediate attention than texts less overtly hostile to the dominant culture" (xxiv). This "powerful black male anger" provided, I would (perhaps cynically) suggest, a convenient space in which white males, increasingly self-perceived as a disempowered, emasculated group of suburban-dwelling capitalist tools, could explore the selfhood they felt "Square" white culture, filled with what Michael Kimmel identifies as "emasculating demands and humiliating [workplace] hierarchies" (241), denied them.

15. James Baldwin, who also offered a searing critique of Kerouac, both demystified Mailer's romance with his constructed image of blackness and reinscribed some of its fundamental beliefs when he wrote in the 1961 *Esquire* article "The Black Boy Looks at the White Boy" that "Negro jazz musicians, among whom we sometimes found ourselves, who really liked Norman, did not for an instant consider him remotely 'hip.' . . . They thought he was a real sweet little ofay cat, but a little frantic" (quoted in Dearborn 121).

16. For an incisive critique of Freud's view that the primitive is a "necessary state of development through which every race has passed," see Marianna Torgovnick's *Gone Primitive: Savage Intellects, Modern Lives.*

17. By contrast, African American novelists writing before 1940, from William Wells Brown to Zora Neale Hurston, are lumped together in a single chapter under the rubric "Before *Native Son.*"

18. Himes's response to such critics appeared in "The Author Talks Back," a special feature in the *Saturday Review of Books*; describing it in *The Quality of Hurt*, he notes that "to those who had complained that I offered no solution for the problem my book presented, I wrote that I belonged to a nation which . . . had learned to split the atom as a weapon more powerful than could be conceived by the average intelligence, and to ask me, an incidental black writer with a limited education and no status whatsoever, to solve its internal race problem was preposterous. Let the white people solve it their own goddamn selves" (77).

19. Although *If He Hollers Let Him Go* continues to enjoy a reputation as a "novel of social rage" (as Eileen Boris classifies it [1998]), it has also recently been recast by critics interested in intersections between working-class literature and African American criticism, such as Bill V. Mullen (2001), as a "labor classic."

20. Himes also considered *The End of a Primitive* to be his most honest book. Contrasting it to *The Third Generation* (his most "dishonest book,") Himes told John A. Williams that "I wrote that [*EP*] out of a completely free state of mind from beginning to end, where I saw all the nuances of every word I put down . . ." (Williams, "My Man Himes"; rpt. in *Conversations with Chester Himes*, Michel Fabre and Robert Skinner, eds.).

21. Himes's attitude toward Wright's influence was obviously ambivalent. Although

he considered "Dick" a friend and *Native Son* a "great book," he also remarked in a 1972 interview that if he were asked to assemble a list of required reading for children in the ghetto, he might not include it. "I don't know if it would affect a ghetto kid's mind the right way. . . . I think it would have an adverse effect" (quoted in Fabre 109).

22. Much of the pioneering theory in this area of inquiry has focused, unsurprisingly perhaps, on Jewish humor. One can easily recognize the argument behind the political strategy of parodistically recuperating the racist (or sexist or homophobic) insult so as to strip it of its power in Martin Grotjahn's summary of the logic behind Jews telling anti-Semitic jokes: "It is as if the Jew tells his enemies: You do not need to attack us. We can do that ourselves—and even better. But we can take it and we will come out all right" (25).

23. Bergson's "disguise" is related, of course, to W. E. B. Du Bois's notion of the "veil." Du Bois's suggestion that African Americans live "behind the Veil" and as such experience a "double consciousness" which enables them to see themselves both through their own eyes and as they are perceived by others, provides one of the main paradigms for understanding black identity.

24. Consider, for example, the exaggerated treatment of the use of so-called "vernacular" language in the following description of T-Bone, a short-lived character in Himes's last (and easily most brutal) detective novel, *Plan B*:

> T-Bone was clad only in a pair of greasy black pants. . . . His long, narrow face was hinged on a mouth with lips the size of automobile tires. . . . He had his bare black feet propped up on a kitchen table with the white soles toward the television screen. He was white-mouthed from hunger but was laughing like an idiot at two black-faced white minstrels on the television screen who earned a fortune by blacking their faces and acting just as foolish as T-Bone had done for free all his life.
>
> In between laughing, he was trying to get his old lady, Tang, to go down to Central Park and trick with some white man so they could eat.
>
> "Go on, baby, you can be back in an hour with 'nuff bread so we can scoff."
>
> "I'se tired as you are," she said with an evil glance. "Go sell yo' own ass to whitey, you luvs him so much" (*Plan B* 4).

25. Himes leans fairly hard on the idea of Jesse as hypersexualized ur-primitive, giving him a steady diet of Scotch and raw eggs, which the alcoholic Jesse believes will enhance his virility. His status as non-modern is also emphasized by the contrast between his living arrangements and those of his erstwhile white lover, Kriss; Jesse's communal apartment is crammed with old-fashioned furniture and outmoded junk, while Kriss's Gramercy Park flat is decorated in coolly modern pastels and sleek furniture of fifties' functionalist design.

26. In addition to being an obvious reworking of the crucial scene in *Native Son*, in which Bigger Thomas accidentally kills the daughter of his white employer as she lies drunk in bed, the final pages of *The End of a Primitive* also reference the death of Desdemona at the hand of Othello. As Jacquelyn McLendon has pointed out, Jesse's attempts to rouse Kriss from what he assumes to be a deep sleep, presumably for sex, suggestively recapitulate Othello's much-analyzed words before killing Desdemona: "I will kill thee / And love thee after." Jesse himself remarks at the outset of his encounter with Kriss that "I'm going to have you whether you like it or not"; his last words before discovering that she is not ignoring him, but rather is dead echo this initial vow: "You know, Kriss baby, you can be a very unpleasant bitch . . . and whether you like it or not . . ." (68, 197).

27. Temporal differentiation obviously collapses here, but the narrative has played fast and loose with the conventions of linearity from the outset, using Jesse's blackouts to structure a narrative filled with lacunae the details of which are never supplied. Here, however, the joke shifts, taking aim at the conventions of the realistic novel form itself;

Jesse is abruptly interpellated into a surreal three-way conversation with the chimp and the newscaster Gloucester (which ends when the chimp is reminded by Jesse of a joke about Generalissimo Franco).

28. According to Himes's biographers, Edward Margolies and Michel Fabre, Walter and his wife are modeled on Ralph and Rose Ellison (186).

Rewriting Patriarchal Paradigms of Retardation in Elizabeth Spencer's *The Light in the Piazza*

Ladislava Khailova

To THOSE FAMILIAR with the literary scene of the late 1950s and early 1960s, the incorporation of an analysis of Elizabeth Spencer's *The Light in the Piazza* in a critical collection focused on noncanonical fiction may come as a surprise. Upon its publication in 1960—first in the *New Yorker* and shortly after as a separate book—the novella quickly became the author's most acclaimed work. With some minor exceptions, it was very positively received by its numerous reviewers both in the United States and abroad,[1] and brought Spencer considerable financial success. It became a bestseller and won the author the $10,000 McGraw-Hill Fiction Award for 1960 as well as a movie contract with Metro-Goldwyn-Mayer. As Spencer has repeatedly told her interviewers, she did not expect such popularity from a text which she wrote "as a sort of an amusement in six weeks" (Haley 53), and which she initially considered "a rather crazy story [she] was writing to get down a lot of impressions" (Broughton 105). She even found it troublesome that this speedily composed novella was her best-known work (Bunting 449); as she intimated, "to have people come up to me, as they do, and gush about *The Light in the Piazza*, and be totally ignorant that I ever turned a hand at anything else, is . . . upsetting" (Phillips 139). However, the popular and critical interest in this slim novella, as well as in Spencer's fiction in general, gradually began to fade. Critics have attributed the author's loss of popularity to the publication of *Knights and Dragons* (1965), her second Italian work, which was criticized severely by most reviewers, as were her later novels *No Place for an Angel* (1967) and *The Snare* (1972) (Winchell 583). As Terry Roberts points out in "This Crooked Narrative Way," Spencer's fame has been on the rise again since the early 1980s, partly because of the success of her collection *The Stories of Elizabeth Spencer*, which appeared in 1981 (61). Unfortunately, the attention *The Light in the Piazza* enjoyed shortly after its publication has yet to be fully revived.[2] Currently, the MLA Bibliography lists only a handful of critical studies devoted to it, indicating that the novella has fallen out of canon.

If the noncanonicity of *The Light in the Piazza* can be partially attributed to this southern text's loss of popularity among the general as well as critical readership, it stems primarily from the novella's revision of prevailing interpretations of mental retardation, as those intersect with patriarchal constructs of female sexuality.[3] I argue that Spencer challenges the fifties' nationwide alarm over increasing female socioeconomic independence by rewriting the eugenic paradigm of female retardation as a sexual menace, instead presenting the disability as a possibly regenerative, liberating force. Initially, the author seems to follow the established patriarchal stereotypes because she configures her cognitively disabled character, Clara, as the abject that threatens to explode the boundaries between human and animal identity through socially transgressive, promiscuous behavior, and offers such conservative plot resolutions as a traditional marriage. Nevertheless, Spencer ultimately counters the fifties' misogynist discourse by showing the positive aspects of Clara's unconventionality, while pointing out the often absurd and always protean character of all paradigms of femininity both in the United States and internationally. She presents the spontaneity of the retarded woman and her resulting individuation (even though limited and short-lived) both as a challenge to the patriarchy in the South, a region where gender polarities have been the hardest to overcome, and as the potential for intersubjective connections, an alternative model of the traditional community. In this way, *The Light in the Piazza* shows one way in which the fifties, conventionally considered a decade of conformism, served in fact as a germination period for the liberation movements of the late 1960s and 1970s.

The Light in the Piazza's use of retardation offers a complex response to historical changes in societal attitudes towards mental particularity in its gendered variants. Poststructuralist and disability studies theorists demonstrate that with the transformation of feudal societies into industrial, urban capitalist domains, which occurred in the United States in the nineteenth century—during the Progressive years in the South—human beings began to be viewed instrumentally. Michel Foucault shows in *Madness and Civilization* that the capitalist economy produced dichotomous classifications of bodies/minds into healthy (normal) and pathological (abnormal). As a consequence, those perceived as unproductive—beggars, the poor, the sick, the insane, and the retarded—were assigned to hospitals to be segregated from the productive others and disciplined. Many disability studies scholars expand on Foucault's theories of the origins of the punitive, normative system by linking them even more explicitly to capitalist economy. For example, Lennard Davis in *Enforcing Normalcy* attributes the emergence of the *homo moyen*, the average man, to eighteenth- and nineteenth-century industrialization and ideological consolidation of the bourgeoisie and its power, which was accompanied by the developments of statistics as scientific justification for moderation and middle-class ideology and of eugenics as an attempt to eliminate deviations from the norm (23–49). Rosemarie Garland Thomson in *Extraordinary Bodies* recasts these pro-normalizing patterns in uniquely American terms. Situating the disabled body within the ideology of liberal individualism, she explains that the construct of the "American Ideal," a four-part self-concept constituted by self-government, self-determination, autonomy, and progress, assigns the bearers of difference the role of ultimate "not me" figures that subvert the ideal cultural self but also absorb its disavowed elements (41–44). She adds that the double function of people with disabilities becomes even more distinct in relation to the concept of production, in which the abstract principles of the ideal American self are manifested most completely (46). In her words, "Labor, the definitive creed of Puritan through contemporary America, transforms necessity into virtue and equates productive work with moral worth, idleness with depravity" (46–47).

As for cognitive disabilities specifically, these new pro-capitalist attitudes resulted in a change from concern for caring about those who are mentally retarded to one of protecting the public from them (Beirne-Smith, Ittenbach, and Patton 36). The existence of retarded individuals was increasingly perceived not only as an economic burden, but also as a threat. Leo Kanner describes the revised prevailing perceptions of this minority group as follows: "The mental defectives were viewed as a menace to civilization, incorrigible at home, burdens to the school, sexually promiscuous, breeders of feebleminded offspring, victims and spreaders of poverty, degeneracy, crime, and disease. Consequently, there was a cry for the segregation of all mental defectives, with the aim of purifying society, of erecting a solid wall between it and its contaminators" (85). As the quoted passage indicates, a substantial fear-causing factor in relation to mental retardation was the belief that the condition was hereditary—in Kanner's words, "mental defectives" were considered to be "breeders of feebleminded offspring" (85). These theories culminated in the American eugenics movement of the early 1900s, mentioned above in relation to Davis's study, which set as its goal the elimination of individuals who are retarded and other "defectives" through selective breeding. Correspondingly, a committee of the American Breeder's Association, formed in 1911, stipulated that "segregation for life or at least during the reproductive years must . . . be the principal agent used by society in cutting off its supply of defectives" (Kanner 136). As an added measure of protection against the procreation of these "unfits," institutions strictly separated male and female inmates or sterilized them (Beirne-Smith, Ittenbach, and Patton 37).

The eugenicists' practices occasionally find reflection in the early works of the Southern Renascence movement, such as William Faulkner's *The Sound and the Fury* (1929). The novel encodes Benjy, its mentally retarded character, as an amalgam of a holy innocent and a degenerate, concepts that originate in the pre-Enlightenment era and in the eugenics movement, respectively. Accordingly, Benjy's extraordinary insight is linked to his unusual olfactory capabilities, suggesting that he displays divine as well as animalistic characteristics. In accord with the discourse of eugenics, one form of these animalistic features is Benjy's potentially dangerous sex drive. For instance, Dilsey considers it unsafe for Caddy to continue sleeping with her prepubescent retarded brother (Stewart and Backus 451). Likewise, Benjy attempts to "rape (or simply embrace?) [my translation]" a schoolgirl whom he mistakes for Caddy (Tumanov 143). Based on these incidents, Mr. Compson decides to restrict Benjy's sexuality by having him castrated. Mr. Compson's action is easier to understand in the context of the narrative's repeated emphasis on the hereditability of negative traits, codified as the Compson (bad) blood (103, 243). Reflecting the eugenic stereotypes, the novel presents retardation as a culmination of this hereditary negativity in the Compson family (103), while linking it to the collapse of the Southern patriarchal system.[4]

When analyzing *The Light in the Piazza*'s use of mental particularity in view of the eugenics paradigms and their reflection in the works of Spencer's southern predecessors, it is important to keep in mind that gender has traditionally played a significant role in the eugenicists' fears of the sexuality of those who are retarded. If retardation of people of either gender represented a genetic threat that had to be controlled, the retarded woman was often singled out as a symbol of the menace of the category of cognitive disability as a whole. According to Licia Carlson, at the end of the nineteenth century, a "feebleminded woman" emerged as "a distinctly gendered class of 'mental defectives'" (126). Apart from the belief that retardation was hereditary, Carlson attributes the origin of this gendered category to a number of other related factors, mainly the prevailing stereotypes of women as vulnerable procreators, which made them seem particularly dangerous, and the emergence of moral imbecility as a subcategory of retardation (Carlson 127). To support her arguments, Carlson quotes Walter Fernald, the superintendent for the Massachusetts School for the Feebleminded from 1887 to 1924. His speeches show that by 1912, the "feebleminded woman" was considered to be almost invariably promiscuous, the carrier of venereal diseases, "twice as prolific as the normal woman," and as such a bad mother of illegitimate children who were as defective as herself (Carlson 127). This logic worked in both directions: if "feebleminded women" were automatically viewed as promiscuous, the sexually transgressive behavior of women became a sign of their mental retardation (Carlson 128). As Peter Tyor puts it, "nineteenth-century sexual norms and gender roles encouraged physicians to treat deviant female sexual behavior as evidence of mental retardation which warranted stringent measures of social control" (473). Thus, the creation of the category of "feebleminded woman" served a dual function: it represented an attempt at the elimination of retardation through genetic control and reinforcement of dominant patriarchal stereotypes of ideal womanhood.

Steven Noll seconds Carlson's and Tyor's opinions, while documenting that the nationwide growth of involuntary sterilization as one of the solutions to the problem of retardation also revealed the gendered bias. As Noll demonstrates, superintendents of mental institutions much more frequently authorized sterilization for females—especially those from lower-class backgrounds—than males (75). For example, in North Carolina, women formed nearly 80 percent of the 858 persons who were sterilized between 1929 and 1940, and in Virginia, they constituted almost 60 percent of the 3,453 persons sterilized from 1928 to 1940 (75). In accordance with the stereotypes of mentally retarded women's sexuality described by Carlson, Noll mentions that Bell and A. S. Priddy, superintendents at Virginia's Lynchburg State Colony for the Feeble-Minded, justified the fact that mainly females were sterilized by interpreting them as "more dangerous eugenically than the male" (76). They based this claim on their belief that women tend to be "an easy prey to the sexual aggressions of males of superior intellect as well as to those of [their] own mental level," and are prone to be sexually immoral, which they thought applied especially to "the high-grade moron women of the anti-social class" (76).

The 1925–1927 *Buck v. Bell* case, serving as a test case for the state of Virginia and for many other southern states that used the Virginia sterilization law as its explicit model (Noll 71), illustrates the social uses of this construct. Carrie Buck, an eighteen-year-old white inmate of the Lynchburg State Colony for the Feeble-Minded, was selected by the Virginia courts as a perfect example of the alleged connection between heredity, retardation, and immorality. Her mother was a mentally retarded resident of the same institution, and Carrie gave birth to an illegitimate female child who was also labeled feebleminded (Noll 69–70). Based on the seeming hereditability of the trait of retardation, Justice Oliver Wendell Holmes supported his decision to apply the Virginia sterilization statute to Buck's case by stating, "We have seen more than once that the public welfare may call upon the best citizens for their lives. It would be strange if it could not call upon those who already sap the strength of the State for these lesser sacrifices, often felt to be much by those concerned, in order to prevent our being swamped with incompetence. It is better for all the world, if instead of waiting to execute degenerate offspring for crime, or to let them starve for their imbecility, society can prevent those who are manifestly unfit from continuing their kind. The principle that sustains compulsory vaccination is broad enough to cover cutting the Fallopian tubes. . . . Three generations of imbeciles are enough" (qtd. in Beirne-Smith, Ittenbach, and Patton 39). However, the research of sociologists who later analyzed the case shows that there were no "three generations of imbeciles" in Buck's family. Carrie's daughter was labeled feebleminded when less than a year old, and it was discovered that she developed into a brighter-than-average child until she died of smallpox in the second grade (Macklin and Gaylin 67).

The general attitudes towards retardation started changing again in the early 1930s, this time in a more favorable direction: they shifted "from fear and revulsion to tolerance and compassion" (Beirne-Smith, Ittenbach, and Patton 43). The authors of *Mental Retardation* explain this turn in terms of the economic crisis of the 1930s and Roosevelt's New Deal philosophy, which encouraged the country to assume responsibility for those in need (41–42). More importantly, they indicate that with the development of the science of genetics and the corresponding reassessment of prior research studies on retardation, earlier opinions that retardation was genetically transmittable were found wanting (Beirne-Smith, Ittenbach, and Patton 41).

In the fifties the process of redefining mental particularity was further accelerated by Americans' increased sense of vulnerability in the aftermath of World War II and by the nation's booming economy, which allowed for more resources to be spent on progress in the area of disabilities. As a result, several important policies supportive of the needs of people with disabilities emerged. Beirne-Smith, Ittenbach, and Patton mention that by 1952, forty-six states enacted laws for educating students with mild forms of mental retardation (43). In addition, in 1954 Congress passed the Cooperative Research Act, providing funds for research focused on retardation (43). In correlation with these legislative measures, a new view of mental particularity—one which took into account social and cultural variables in disability definitions—was forming (43).

Nevertheless, society scarcely ever transitions smoothly from one paradigm of a minority to another; echoes of earlier interpretations continue to survive in their later modes. Spencer's *The Light in the Piazza* reveals that, in spite of the positive redefinitions of disability in the 1930s through the 1950s, the nexus of femininity, retardation, and illicit sexuality continued to have a strong presence in literary representations of cognitive disabilities. The conflicting trends are easier to understand with a view to the decade's definitions of womanhood. The fifties had a problematic relationship with female sexuality in general. While the sexual revolution that started in the 1920s continued to gain ground in the decades that followed, it was considerably slowed down during the 1950s by the opposing messages that women were receiving regarding sexual freedom (Coontz 196–97). If the media glorified sexuality and women were encouraged to be passionate, erotic mates, they were simultaneously submitted to very narrow sexual norms and faced the danger of social stigma should they violate the accepted regulations (Breines 86–87, May 123). Often likened to atomic energy, female sexuality was perceived as beneficial only if "contained and domesticated" (May 112). Therefore, women were expected to give in to flirtation—which often included petting and necking—with their dates but held solely responsible for putting on the brakes to retain their virginity until marriage, when they were supposed to compete figuratively with "bad" women to satisfy their spouses (Coontz 27, 39–40, May 101–2, 116, 127–28). As Wini Breines poignantly puts it, "the sexual double standard meant that white, middle-class girls had to walk a tightrope of respectability, never going (or never appearing) to go too far sexually, but giving just enough of their bodies to keep boys interested" with the goal of getting married (125, 107).

The Light in the Piazza shows that, in the fifties' suspension between sexual permissiveness and punitiveness, mentally retarded women continued to be perceived as emblematic of the threat of uncontained female sexuality. Spencer's text revolves around the actions of its central consciousness, Margaret Johnson, a middle-aged, well-to-do Southern woman from Winston-Salem, North Carolina, who feels compelled to police the sexuality of her mentally retarded daughter, Clara. Margaret's husband, Noel Johnson, has accepted the fact that Clara suffered a childhood accident which left her with the mind of a ten-year-old as an "ugly finality," something that "happened . . . which he was powerless to do anything about" (81), and wants to dispose of his daughter by putting her "in a sort of 'school' for 'people like her'" (74). In contrast, for Margaret, Clara's cognitive disability has always represented a problem that needed to and could be removed. She nurtures her dream that one day, her daughter will "be perfectly well" (61), and carries out trials to that end. In the past, the most significant of these was perhaps the school experiment, in which she got Clara enrolled at an educational institution in a different section of town, hoping that her daughter would become like others. When the experiment failed, Margaret's resistance almost vanished: from that moment, she too was inclined to accept the "realities" of life (63). However, her desire to have control over Clara's development has been rekindled by her daughter's physical maturity.

In more specific terms, Margaret demonstrates a strong resistance to any indications that Clara is a sexual being—in that aspect, she likes to perceive her daughter as a perpetual child. In the opening chapter of the novella, she draws the readers' attention to Clara's "innocent smile" (14), and mentions her tendency to explain Clara's condition to young men as follows: "Every mother in some way wants a little girl who never grows up. Taken in that light, I do often feel fortunate. She is remarkably sweet, you see, and I find her a great satisfaction" (15). The argument is aimed at protecting Clara from these men, indicating that she is mentally a juvenile who should not be viewed as a sexual object. Accordingly, Margaret becomes quite alarmed at her daughter's clear demonstration of her interest in the opposite sex by flinging her arms around a grocery boy in Winston-Salem; she decides to take her daughter to Italy. Reversing the intentions that prompted her school experiment, she starts plotting to repress Clara's social involvement, hoping that the change in geographic space will make Clara regress to the prepubescent stage. However, as the courtship of a young Italian man, Fabrizio Naccarelli, soon makes Margaret realize, Italy won't make her daughter give up her sexuality. The romance seems platonic at first: making pyramids, triangles, and squares from coins together, Fabrizio and Clara look to Margaret "like two children" (21), with Clara "smil[ing] sweetly and laugh[ing] innocently" (20). Nevertheless, the sexual context of the relationship is soon to unfold for Margaret. Watching Fabrizio and Clara chasing each other in the pool, she feels compelled to compare them to "endlessly energetic" butterflies, with the difference that butterflies "do not really think very much about sex" (25). Her previous perceptions of Clara and Fabrizio's courtship as a pastoral idyll vanish;

she becomes fearful of the consequences that this love affair could have. In correspondence with these feelings, Margaret, meeting Clara unexpectedly in the street and, noticing her almost Italian sex appeal, views her daughter's attractiveness with "an added sense of displeasure, almost of disgust" (51). Margaret simply refuses to grant Clara her right to her own sexuality.

Clara's father Noel is similarly fearful of his retarded daughter's sexual maturation. Much later, when Margaret calls him from Florence to inform him about Clara's Italian romance and prepare him for the possibility of their daughter's marriage to Fabrizio, he gets extremely upset at Margaret's claim that she is "only trying to let things take their natural course" (73). "*Natural* course!," Noel exclaims, making his wife "jump . . . even at such a distance" (73; emphasis Spencer). Margaret's response to Noel's angry words implies that he took the phrase "natural course" to refer to sexual activities: Margaret attempts to calm him down by assuring him that the lovers are closely watched by her as Clara's guardian. "I am with her constantly, Noel. I don't mean they're left to themselves" (73), she asserts. Clearly, if Clara's parents disagree on whether she can become a part of the mainstream society, they both assume that any sexual liaisons of their daughter should be strictly prevented.

In any androcentric society, such fears of women whose sexuality is potentially unrestricted by their reason, and the corresponding efforts to restrain those women, can be explained by the desire of a patriarchal power structure to preserve the status quo in which female bodies are treated as a property acquired by men through the institution of marriage. As Luce Irigaray explains, in a patriarchy, a husband regards his wife as a possession and attempts to immobilize her to control her better (28). The fifties' culture with its misogynistic tendencies subscribed to this practice, advocating the containment of women in a marriage with traditional gender roles because they were gaining sexual and economic independence. The cultural ideal was a matrimony "where masculine men would be in control with sexually submissive competent homemakers at their side" (May 99). Physically mature mentally retarded females tended to be interpreted as harder to confine in such ways: since the eugenics movement of the early 1900s, their sexuality was codified as excessively spontaneous. *The Light in the Piazza* reflects how, drawing on the models of the previous decades, the fifties thus considered mentally retarded women to be more terrifying than normate women.

In analyses of the fifties' discourse, the fears of out-of-control sexuality are often intertwined with the threats of the cold war for it was believed that sexually depraved men could be easily duped by immoral luscious women working for the communists (May 93–94, Dean 176–77). But such fears, in various forms, predate the 1950s by centuries and are also susceptible to a psychoanalytical explanation. Sexual spontaneity is viewed as dangerous because it violates the borders between human and animal identity. Julia Kristeva's theory of the abject illuminates how unrestricted sexuality violates those borders. In *Powers of Horror*,

Kristeva introduces the definition of abjection as a psychological mechanism through which an individual and group identity are produced by excluding anything that may potentially violate their boundaries. In her words, the abject is "what disturbs identity, system, order. What does not respect borders, positions, rules. The in-between, the ambiguous, the composite" (4). Accordingly, the abject confronts individual psyches not only in their attempts to separate themselves from the maternal body but also "with those fragile states where man strays on the territories of *animal*" (12; emphasis Kristeva). Therefore, the psychoanalyst adds, primitive societies have demarcated a precise territory of their culture to distance themselves from that which was understood as representative of the transgressive world of animals—murder and sex (12–13). The social construct of retarded females as sexually promiscuous and the corresponding efforts of normalcy to coerce their behavior involve such fears of animalistic sexuality.

Spencer's novella reflects these encodings of the abject. The sexual maturation of Clara signals to Margaret, and, by analogy, to those similarly socialized, an impending violation of the delicate boundary between the domain of culture and the state of animals in the territory of the sexual. Margaret is opposed to the couple's romance because it reminds her that sexuality—including her sexuality—exists also on the level of the irrational, the level of drives traditionally configured as the "not me," the inhuman, the animalistic. Immediately upon mentioning Clara's impulsive embrace in the grocery store and the sexual subtext of Clara's relationship with Fabrizio, Margaret looks at the scar on the right side of her daughter's head, recalling an episode in which Clara was hurt by her Shetland pony—the supposed cause of her daughter's impairment. In associating the horse that "had kicked in a temper at whatever was annoying him" (25) with the instances of Clara's interest in men, Margaret connects the retarded female's sexuality with unreasoning animal impulse, and, therefore, considers it uncontrollable and beastly. While Margaret admits that impulsive behavior cannot be judged because it "is innocent about what is good or bad" (25), she is sure that it represents a threat and will have negative consequences. She vividly remembers her daughter's "sidelong fall" and the "heart-numbing" silence that followed the pony's kick (26). She suspects that her daughter's sexuality will "scar" her, result in a wound that time can never completely heal. Margaret's mental associations thus suggest that animalistic sexuality as a form of the abject and stigmatizing punishment are inherently connected, which, according to fifties America's practices and beliefs, was a correct assumption. Such reasoning explains Margaret's efforts to prevent Clara from achieving sexual satisfaction. She, as the self-appointed guardian of patriarchal social rules, assumes that she must make her daughter forever subject to parental supervision that will limit the young female's sphere of action.

Given the fact that the readers of *The Light in the Piazza* are locked in Margaret's consciousness, the narrative initially seems to endorse the efforts of agents of normalcy to construct the retarded female Other as the abject and her sexuality as a threat, while attempting to coerce her behavior accordingly. Yet, at a closer look, Spencer does significantly challenge such stereotypes by refusing to portray Clara's sexuality as necessarily destructive on several levels. More specifically, the novella questions the interpretation of retardation as genetically transmittable. Clara's mental condition is a result of an accident she suffered as a child, not a sign of the Johnsons' genetic degeneration. Moreover, Margaret believes that, however dangerous the physical maturation of her daughter may be, it will not result in the conception of retarded children. As she mentions, "Even if marriage were ever possible to [Clara], the doctors say that her children would be perfectly all right" (63). Therefore, unlike some of Spencer's southern predecessors, such as Faulkner in *The Sound and the Fury*, Spencer disrupts the formerly dominant paradigm of retardation as a negative genetic change inherited through "bad blood."

Spencer further contests the eugenic notions of mental particularity by suggesting that women who are retarded do not have to be bad mothers. Margaret notices that her daughter adores children: she "had a large collection of dolls at home and had often expressed her wish for a real live little baby brother" (39). Similarly, in the Christmas pageant, Clara reaches to the manger for the little Lord Jesus, disappointed to find only a flashlight, placed there to represent the divine figure (49). Her fascination with the Holy Infant surfaces again at the Naccarelli household, where Clara admires the painting of a Madonna and Child (39). These religious images undermine interpretations of her sexuality as an obsessive, transgressive drive that would result in a procreation of defective children later abandoned by her. The Holy Family is often configured as the noblest of all, with the Madonna figure that Clara associates herself with signifying purity.

More importantly, the novella shows that the interest in the opposite sex figures the previously passive Clara's individuation (Seidel 20). The book introduces Margaret's daughter as an extremely obedient child, a "girl [that] had not a rebellious bone in her, and under her mother's eye . . . could be kept in tune" (29). Later, Margaret adds that she "had never known Clara to show a mean or stubborn side" (42). However, as Clara's romance with Fabrizio advances, Margaret begins to complain that the relations between her and her daughter have "deteriorated" (41). Since she equates the ideal state of their relationship with Clara's following her every order, the readers realize that what Margaret describes as deterioration stands for Clara's growing independence. Margaret proceeds to complain that Clara "calculated that she could afford to stick out her tongue at her mother" (42). The daughter also "refuse[s] to pick up her clothes or be on time for any occasion that [does] not include Fabrizio," argues with her mother, will not do what she does not feel like doing, pretends not to hear when called by Margaret (42), and one afternoon even goes off by herself (51). These instances of disobedience annoy Margaret. Her resistance to Clara's sexual maturation, as reflected in her interest in Fabrizio, triggers Margaret's emotion that "she had let things go too far . . . and whereas before she had been worried, now she was becoming afraid" (42). Margaret's angry comment suggests that Clara's sexuality aids her in establishing a separate existence from her controlling mother, signaling the possibility that her domination over her daughter will be replaced by a more balanced relationship between the two.

As might be expected, Clara's attempts at individuation cause her mother to come up with more complex maneuvers to regain her position of dominance. Following her previous strategy of an imposed change in location as a means of controlling her daughter, Margaret decides to take Clara for a trip to Rome, hoping that she will forget about Fabrizio. The most immediate trigger for Margaret's decision is a gift of a bouquet of flowers she and Clara receive from the Naccarellis. According to her, the lilies are almost obscene "with their enormous naked stamens, based in a back-curling, waxen petal" (54). Watching Clara arrange these "blatantly phallic" stalks "with their sensual bloom" one by one in a vase becomes unbearable for Margaret, for it once again highlights the explicit sexual dimension of her daughter's courtship (54). She falsely claims to be ill to make them leave for Rome immediately.

Ironically, Margaret's actions ultimately lead to the fulfillment of her retarded daughter's original wishes, causing her to modify her negative opinions of Clara's sexuality. Observing Clara sitting on a fallen marble block and weeping, Margaret notices that "something of a warm, classic dignity had come to this girl, and no matter whether she could do long division or not, she was a woman" (59). As the expression "dignity" suggests, Margaret no longer associates her daughter's interest in Fabrizio primarily with the unrestricted animalistic instincts that she dreads. What inspires her to change her opinion is the steadiness and intensity of Clara's affection. Margaret seems to rid herself of stereotypical thinking and to admit that even though Clara is retarded and sexually mature, she does not necessarily have to be promiscuous: with "proper" guidance, she can comply with the fifties' social norms of sexual behavior. She realizes that Clara's sexual feelings, since focused on one person, can be contained in a patriarchal marriage, and thus serve as an instrument for the fulfillment of her dream that Clara will be "normal" one day by becoming a mother and a wife. Correspondingly, from now on, Margaret supports Clara and Fabrizio's romance by returning to Florence, where she "single-handed and unadvised" plays what she calls "a tricky game in a foreign country" (107) in trying to make sure that Clara and Fabrizio's courtship will evolve into marriage without the Naccarellis becoming necessarily aware of her daughter's cognitive disability.

Margaret's willingness to revise her opinions of the sexual aspects of Clara's existence indirectly results in her rediscovery of her own sexuality. As Kathryn Lee Seidel poignantly observes, Margaret, nurtured by the fifties' capitalism, repeatedly uses flirtation in her premarital negotiations with Signor Naccarelli (19). For instance, during their little outing in Fabrizio's father's car and their subsequent meeting in the lobby of her hotel, she not only mentions the five thousand dollars her husband gave to their son when he got married, but also allows Signor Naccarelli to lean "flirtatiously at her over a small round marble-topped table" (69). With the whole scene reminding Margaret of "middle-aged adultery," she is relieved to know "that sin was not expected of them" (69). When problems arise in the form of Clara's physical age (Signor Naccarelli minds that she is slightly older than Fabrizio), Margaret sells even more of her sexual appeal in order to seal the marriage deal: she tolerates a kiss from Fabrizio's father (100). While some readers may frown at Margaret's decision to rely on flirtation to ensure that the marriage plans materialize—after all, such maneuvers reinforce historical views of female bodies as their main or only capital—recent feminist scholarship offers the possibility of viewing such behavior as liberating if it can be assumed that the woman involved is in control. According to Seidel, the close encounter between Clara's mother and Signor Naccarelli not only aids the marriage negotiations, but assures Margaret of her sexual appeal, helping her gain more freedom as a woman (19). Specifically, Seidel, referring to Irigaray, states that "women's rights include asserting sexual rights so that they are valued as women, not simply mothers" (19). Along these lines, in an interview Spencer noted that, by fighting for the marriage, Margaret "liberated herself. . . . This gesture shows that Margaret Johnson will not be dominated, not by her husband, her doctor, her culture—or even by honesty" (Broadwell and Hoag 123). This empowerment promises to rekindle Margaret's relationship with her husband (Prenshaw, *Elizabeth Spencer* 72). With Clara married and away from the family, Margaret wonders "what degree of delight . . . they [she and Noel] might not be able to discover (rediscover?) together" (109). Therefore, by allowing her daughter to experience a sexual awakening and to get married, Margaret herself learns to become more confident as a woman and a wife.

Nevertheless, Clara's matrimony deserves a closer analysis because of the ambivalence as to its meaning in a narrative offering a revision of misogynistic paradigms of female retardation. While it has been established that both women do benefit from Clara's future marriage—it is linked to their reclaiming of their sexuality—speculations on what happens after the wedding problematize the readings of Spencer's portrayal of female mental particularity as fully liberatory. In fact, some critics go as far as to describe *The Light in the Piazza* as generally unfavorable in its presentations of both femininity and retardation. Very recently, at the 2006 MLA Convention in Philadelphia, Samuel Delany labeled the novella a "rather appalling story," illustrative of the 1950s as a period that does not "have a particularly good reputation either for women's right or for disability rights." Indeed, the Johnson-Naccarelli matrimony suggests conformism to patriarchal social norms. Rachel Blau DuPlessis observes in *Writing Beyond the Ending* that marriage was an expected plot resolution for nineteenth-century fiction featuring both female Bildung and romance (3).[5] As DuPlessis explains, the romance plot stifles the female character, repressing her quest and endorsing traditional roles of the heterosexual couple (5). The fifties culture in which DuPlessis came of age indeed used marriage as a tool to impede the growing threat of female independence, presenting marriage as "the only sanctioned goal for girls" (Breines 107). Correspondingly, the average marriage age dropped dramatically compared to the previous decades: most Americans agreed that twenty-one was a healthy age for one's choosing a spouse and starting a family (May 102). Women passing this age mark without getting a wedding ring were stigmatized. According to Stephanie Coontz, "In 1957, 80 percent of Americans polled said that people who chose not to marry were 'sick,' 'neurotic,' and 'immoral'" (186). Thus, the fifties forced women to trade what was perceived as their increasingly dangerous sexual and economic emancipation for a traditional family life of homemaking and childrearing. Given this cultural framework, readers have the right to suspect that Clara will ultimately become anything but empowered through the legalization of her liaisons with her Italian beau.

Such suspicions of Clara's impending loss of her newly gained agency after the wedding are further supported by the narrative's description of her behavior in Fabrizio's presence. Margaret notices that while Clara is rebellious towards her, she becomes obedient when her lover is around. In the narrator's words, "the minute the girl fell beneath the eye of Fabrizio, her rapt, transported, Madonna look came over her, and she sat still and gentle, docile as a saint, beautiful as an angel" (42). As this quotation suggests, two authorities—matriarchal and patriarchal—will exchange a position of power through Clara's marriage to Fabrizio, with Clara remaining in subjection. As Fabrizio's wife, she will be anything but free. She will adopt the role of Signora Naccarelli, confined in her home, surrounded by her religious artifacts and her family (Seidel 21). Therefore, becoming Fabrizio's wife threatens to end the individuation Clara achieved by partially separating herself from her mother.

However, if Clara's marriage is a traditionally unfeminist element because it can suppress the young woman's agency, it can also be read as partially progressive in the light of disability studies theory. Given the eugenic stereotypes of female retardation, love plots involving cognitively disabled women do not necessarily represent instances of the authors' acceptance of social norms since, historically, these individuals have been treated as unfit for marriage and parenthood. Even in the fifties, notwithstanding the hegemony of marriage, people with disabilities were not supposed to marry. As Coontz documents, "the mentally defective," together with "the sick, the badly crippled, the deformed, [and] the emotionally warped" were excluded from the marriage scene (33). Viewed from this angle, Spencer's decision to have Clara married, though her narrative indicates that such a marriage may be short-lived[6] and repress Clara's budding individuation, is also a sign of the novella's dissenting potential. Along these lines, Spencer told an interviewer that she was pleasantly surprised to have received numerous letters from people with retarded children, because they wrote to her that, "What we have to have as we live day to day is a sort of hope which you have represented, even though we know it'll never be realized" (Bunting 448–49). It is the novella's pointing towards a positive reinterpretation of retarded women's sexuality and of spontaneous sexuality of women in general that helps nurture such hopes.

The readings of *The Light in the Piazza* as an unfeminist "appalling story" that does not take into account disability rights (Delany) can be further contested as too exaggerated also because they overlook the satirical tone of the narrative. Through a series of ironies, the author offers a harsh critique of the domestic containment of women in the 1950s while highlighting the constructed character of culturally sanctioned women's roles. Spencer shows that the fifties' definitions of femininity, like those of mental particularity, are conditioned geographically as well as temporally. As for retardation, Margaret makes it clear that while in America, Clara is marginalized because she cannot "do long division" (59), but in Italy she "seems no different from the rest" (72). All dressed up like her friends, she spends her time with them in outdoor cafes, talking about celebrities, pets, cars, and men (72–73). Clearly, even though she has a mentality of a ten-year-old, Clara easily passes for an average middle-class Italian in her twenties because the activities they usually engage in do not put much demand on intellectual abilities. Consequently, Margaret comes to think that, unlike Americans, Italians do not judge people "in terms of IQ, 'retarded mentality' and 'adult capabilities'" (79), and presents these differences in the context of what her husband would be likely to describe as the "inefficient way of life" in Italy in general (78) and the lack of American "ordinary sense" in this sunny culture (81).

The novella emphasizes that the Italian acceptance of Clara is closely linked to her gender. Spencer commented that "there's kind of an Italian mentality that really doesn't want women to be very, very bright"; she was writing a comedy about it, while aware that Italians resist such notions (Girard 327). Based on statements like these, several scholars have concluded that the novella is a critique of the Italian scripts for women. For instance, Prenshaw in "Elizabeth Spencer" observes that *The Light in the Piazza* includes "interesting feminist ironies" since it indicates that the mentality of a child poses hardly any problems for an Italian marriage (510). The text supports such arguments. According to Margaret, Clara does not have much value on the American marriage market because her limited intellectual abilities do not allow her to become a woman like her mother: "the busy American housewife, mother, hostess, cook, and civic leader, who paid attention to her looks" (24). Nevertheless, as Margaret gradually comes to realize, Clara's medical condition is not necessarily an issue on the Italian marriage scene. In a letter to her husband, she writes, "The thing that impresses me most, Noel . . . is that nothing beyond Clara ever seems to be required of her here. I do wonder if anything beyond her would ever be required of her. Young married girls her age, with one or two children, always seem to have a nurse for them; a maid does all the cooking. There are mothers and mothers-in-law competing to keep the little ones at odd hours. I doubt if these young wives ever plan a single meal" (72). Margaret is never sure whether or not the Naccarellis have realized that "Clara was a child" (79), but she gradually comes to assume that even if they had, Clara's good physical and genetic health would satisfy the Florentine family. Signora Naccarelli confirms such notions. In her eyes, Clara is the ideal bride for Fabrizio because she is "so sweet and gentle, [and] would bear children for him" (89). Likewise, Fabrizio, while often painfully aware of Clara's physicality, values Clara for "her gentleness, her sweetness and goodness" (73). He thinks of her as a religious icon, "a lost work" of art, "on the wall a fresco" (102). Therefore, to him, Clara is an exemplar of female purity. Supporting his wife's and son's assumptions, Signor Naccarelli implies that, according to the Italian norms, Clara's condition may actually turn out to be to her advantage. As he points out, "American women [are] too confident and brisk" (65), but Clara is "Not like other American girls" because of her "innocence" (67). Such statements, associating Clara's intellectual level with chastity, further deessentialize Margaret's culturally conditioned stereotypical suspicion that Clara's mental particularity may imply irresponsible sexuality. The radical twists in interpreting difference in Spencer's narrative are highly ironic. How can the same set of characteristics pass for an ideal, pure femininity in one geographic space and for dangerous deviation in another? The implication is that the roles of women in both regions are scripted.

At the same time, the narrative shows that the American version of femininity is conceptually much closer to its Italian counterpart than Margaret would make the readers initially think. As Seidel insightfully observes, the novella is equally "a searing critique of expectations in the 1950s for American women" (22). Seidel, in agreement with May's, Coontz's, and Breines's discussion of women's roles in fifties culture, points out that the healthy, well-adjusted American female of the decade was encouraged to be more like Clara than Margaret: she was supposed to be nonintellectual, adoring of children, and dependent first on her parents and later on her husband; her calculating abilities were valued only when applied towards saving money for the home (16). In this way, Clara is "the perfect product of her culture, the southern belle, the most important work of art of her culture" (Seidel 20). Indeed, as Margaret recalls, Clara's aunt Isabel always promoted "the theory that Clara had as much sense as most of the women she sold hats to" (83). The only difference between the ideal American woman of the fifties and Clara is perhaps that Clara became that way not by nurture but by accident, and ended up married partially because of freely accepting her sexuality. Ironically, she will also probably be one of the few women who will take on the limited and limiting roles prescribed to them by their respective society and be satisfied.[7] Through such intimations, Spencer's narrative clearly voices dissatisfaction with the objectifying patriarchal paradigms prepared in the fifties for women both in the American South and in Italy. It prompts the readers to notice the ironically close affinity of scripts of ideal femininity and mental retardation.

The social framing of femininity as somehow disabling has a long tradition. Conventionally, all women, irrespective of their cultural, ethnic, or economic backgrounds, have been viewed as the inferior gendered Other, as reflected in Aristotle's equation of them with deviant males in *Generation of Animals* (401). Garland Thomson explains that many parallels exist between the social categories of gender and disability.[8] Focusing on the social meanings ascribed to female and disabled bodies, Garland Thomson observes that both "are cast as deviant and inferior; both are excluded from full participation in public as well as economic life; both are defined in opposition to a norm that is assumed to possess natural physical [and, we could add, mental] superiority" (19). As she also mentions, based on these parallels, theorists have often tended to conflate disability and femaleness: even contemporary feminist theory invokes negative images of disability to portray the oppression of women (19).

Jessica Benjamin's *The Bonds of Love* further explains this constant intertwining of femininity and disability and society's marginalization of both by pointing out that in Western culture dependence is constructed as female and repudiated. Specifically, we tend to consider the Oedipus complex as central to the development of a human being, rather than as just one step in psychological growth, which results in our worship of independence and autonomy conceived of as male, with femininity perceived as submissive and devalued (Benjamin *passim*). Therefore, Benjamin adds, our society tends to feel contempt for all those in need, worship individual self-reliance, and reject social forms of providing nurturance (171–72). When applied to mental or physical particularity, Benjamin's comments suggest that femininity and disability are often treated as interchangeable because of society's perception of disabling features as signaling dependence, and, as such, being opposed to the one-sided masculine ideal. Benjamin's theory also explains that, to free both people with disabilities and women from the position of ultimate social Other deprived of subjectivity, society needs to overcome gender polarity, to sustain "the essential tension of . . . asserting the self and recognizing the other" (53) rather than attempting to strive for dominance configured as masculine.

As we have seen, Spencer's *The Light in the Piazza* uses such traditional conflations of femaleness and disability subversively by satirizing the fact that fifties mainstream society still tended to present helplessness, dependence on others, and deficient cognitive abilities as a female ideal that all women should aspire to. In this way, the narrative attacks the period's patriarchy as well as that of the regional culture, unrelenting in its efforts to maintain control over gender identity scripts. Theorists have repeatedly indicated that in the South, gender polarity, and, by implication, the configuration of women and people with disabilities as the ultimate social Other, is harder to overcome than in other regions. In Anne Goodwyn Jones and Susan V. Donaldson's opinion, gender dichotomy has traditionally been seen as more clearly defined and observed in the South than anywhere else in American culture (6). As Jones claims in *Tomorrow Is Another Day*, while the definitions of southern womanhood resemble those of the British construct of a Victorian lady and the American construct of true womanhood, only in the South has the lady been "at the core of a region's self-definition" (4); the South shows more dependence on the preservation of its traditional image of a lady than any other region (4). In accordance with this argument, but working towards a goal diametrically opposed to that of Jones and Donaldson, Richard M. Weaver, a conservative ideologue nostalgically looking for ways to resurrect the Old South with the gradual decline of its patriarchal structures, suggests that the region must re-accentuate gender polarity, "the fruitful distinction between the sexes, with the recognition of respective spheres of influence" (378). Correspondingly, Weaver believes that the "re-establishment of woman as the cohesive force of the family, the end of the era of 'long-haired men and short-haired women,' should bring a renewal of well-being to the whole of society" (378). Such comments demonstrate that the southern patriarchy has been even more adamant in their fight for preserving conventional gender scripts in the time of the emergence of the New Woman than other parts of America. Spencer, from her own position of a female Other traditionally configured as dependent and inferior, counters such efforts in *The Light in the Piazza* by pointing out the problematic aspects of these scripts, and fighting for the individuation of all women as the social Other. In the process, she revises the eugenic degeneration paradigm of retardation, another site on which society projects its fear of dependence gendered as feminine, to support the movement of the southern culture and the American culture of the fifties in general closer towards gender parity.

Recent disability studies theory asks critics to analyze carefully any such claims of the revisionary character of representations of disabilities, whether for feminist or other purposes. For example, Robert McRuer, in his discussion of the popular show *Queer Eye for the Straight Guy*, warns scholars against falling into the trap of what he identifies as the progressive narrative currently popular in disability studies (588, 590). Accordingly, he emphasizes the importance of employing the counterhegemonic in portrayals of disability to achieve social change (589–90). Similar caution has to be applied to the analysis of *The Light in the Piazza*. After all, as explained above, the novella does contain such pro-normalizing moments as making Clara marry into a traditional patriarchal family. At the same time, the perfect housewife stereotype of the fifties is criticized by showing that only a woman who is retarded can take on this confining role and be content. In this way, it could be argued that the text does not grant Clara a status of full equality to normate women, and still points to the encoding of cognitive disability as a sign of inferiority rather than an unmarked difference. However, Clara's difference also has a clear subversive potential, particularly in its fifties' context: Spencer's revision of core tenets of the prevailing eugenic paradigms of mental particularity through the character of Clara aids the novella's anti-establishment agenda by granting all women, irrespective of their cognitive abilities, the right to their sexuality and independence.

More specifically, Spencer challenges previous literary assumptions about two groups oppressed in the fifties: people who are retarded and American women. She deconstructs the eugenicists' notions of mentally retarded females as promiscuous and genetically dangerous by showing that Clara's acceptance of her sexuality can lead to her female empowerment and individuation—even if temporary and limited—rather than destruction. Correspondingly, her narrative moves closer to the broken down tension between the self and the Other advocated by Benjamin. Clara's individuation figures a kind of assimilation into human community that was formerly foreclosed by repudiation—she can get married and enjoy the prospect of having children. While these simple pleasures could be interpreted as pro-normalizing, especially in the context of the fifties' use of marriage as a tool to contain growing female independence, they are employed to serve the purposes of a subversive narrative scheme revealing the constructed character of the decade's roles for all women. Through the differing geographical responses to the retarded female's sexual appeal, the novella reveals the performative aspect of all female identities, especially those of Euro-American white ladyhood. In this way, the slim book that has fallen out of canon aims at a quite ambitious task of serving as an antidote to the fifties' anxieties about social decline, most profoundly manifested in the South. It implies that traditional patriarchal hierarchies are not essential for the culture's survival and can be replaced by intersubjectivity of all individuals, regardless of their mental abilities or gender, as a more viable basis of the American community. *The Light in the Piazza* demonstrates that a work sometimes seen as exemplary of the quiet, conformist 1950s in fact anticipated powerful voices which helped ignite the women's liberation and disability rights movements of the late 1960s and 1970s.

Notes

1. For details on these reviews, see, for example, Anderson 19; Roberts, "Italy: Dream and Nightmare" 50; and Prenshaw, *Elizabeth Spencer* 76.

2. The work continues to be known as a Broadway musical, the winner of six 2005 Tony Awards.

3. Thus far, most criticism has focused on the central consciousness of the novel, Margaret Johnson, and her response to the dilemma of whether she should let her retarded daughter Clara marry her Italian suitor Fabrizio (see, for example, Prenshaw's "Mermaids,

Angels and Free Women"). Given the European setting of the novel, critics have also repeatedly compared Spencer to Henry James. For instance, Nettels analyzes Spencer's stylistic as well as thematic affinities with Henry James (84–85); similarly, Anderson highlights the revisions of Jamesian concerns in the novella (19–26, 33). The exception to these interpretative trends is Seidel, who pays close attention to the text's portrayal of mental retardation. Seidel argues that Margaret sees Clara as a "flawed product" that can be successfully marketed abroad (*passim*). However, only briefly does Seidel consider the intersection between gender and retardation, as reflected in Margaret's fears of Clara's budding sexuality, a key issue in the variations of paradigms of mental particularity.

4. For a more detailed analysis, see Khailova 79–82.

5. According to DuPlessis, the other possible resolution of the tension between quest and love in nineteenth-century fiction featuring women was death (3–4).

6. Prenshaw in *Elizabeth Spencer* observes that the narrative contains clear indications "by which the reader is given to understand that malevolence can threaten the romantic interlude at any moment" (73). The cannon misfire killing an onlooker, the rude carriage driver, and a pushy Signor Naccarelli are all signs of the more sinister realities of life in the sunny Italy (73). Spencer herself, when asked, repeatedly mentioned that she was not sure at all if Clara's marriage would have any duration to it; she described the whole arrangement as "a fantasy that could explode five minutes after the book is over" (Broadwell and Hoag 123, 129).

7. Coontz documents an awareness that, under the façade of happiness, women in the fifties were frequently suffering from deep discontentment. A 1950 issue of *Life* magazine reported that " 'suddenly and for no plain reason' American women were 'seized with an eerie restlessness' " (Coontz 37). Similarly, Coontz quotes a former editor of the *Ladies' Home Journal* in 1956 stating that "We suddenly realized that all those women at home with their three and a half children were miserably unhappy" (37).

8. Of course, the categories of race, sexuality, and class also belong to this nexus.

The Mid-century Pulp Novel and the Imagining of Lesbian Community

Jennifer Worley

IN 1952, THE House of Representatives Select Committee on Current Pornographic Materials targeted a little-known novel as an example of the obscenity being fostered by the rise of cheaply produced, pocket-sized paperback or "pulp" novels. The book was Tereska Torres's *Women's Barracks* (1950), the first paperback to feature lesbian characters and situations. After the House of Representatives called the nation's attention to the title, *Women's Barracks* became a best-seller and set off an avalanche of sorts in the publishing industry: over the next twenty years, thousands of paperback originals, or PBOs, featuring lesbian characters and situations were published and distributed across the United States. The popularity of *Women's Barracks* and the flood of lesbian-themed pulps that quickly followed in the wake of its success allowed for the first truly mass circulation of lesbian narrative.[1] This essay examines the interplay between this mass-circulation and the lesbian communities that both read and were depicted in the lesbian pulp fiction of the 1950s and 1960s.

Although this decade saw the publication of the largest number of lesbian-themed novels in history to that point, the 1950s also stand out as a particularly oppressive decade for gays and lesbians. Political, legal, medical, and social forces all took aim at homosexuals in this period, creating a climate of fear and secrecy. For example, during the fifties, homosexuals were considered a grave threat to national security, and gays were key targets of the relentless search by the House Committee on Un-American Activities for communists, traitors, and other enemies of the American way of life. In spite of the fact that the Communist Party actually forbade membership by gays, official policy and stereotyping alike linked sexual "deviance" with national weakness: Republican National Chairman Guy George Gabrielson railed against the "sexual perverts who have infiltrated our government in recent years, perhaps as dangerous as the actual Communists." In 1950, the Republican party charged the Truman Administration with "harboring sexual perverts," and the exposé *Washington Confidential* used the phrase "lavender menace" to describe the supposed cabal of gays in the State Department and elsewhere in the federal government. Senator Kenneth Wherry of Nebraska claimed that "There should be no people of that type working in any position in the government," and that "You can't separate homosexuals from subversives." (Mann 295). The results of all this mudslinging between warring parties were very real for gay government employees: in the early 1950s, the State Department purged 425 suspected homosexuals from its ranks.

While the State Department purge and similar efforts in the armed services certainly created a climate of fear among gays and lesbians, the most direct, visible manifestation of this era's oppression of those outside the sexual norm were the increased police raids on gay bars. One historian of American lesbian life relays stories of a raid in San Francisco in which dozens of women were arrested simply for being in a "house of ill repute," one in which NYPD officers lined up female patrons and put their hands in the women's pants, and one in Greenwich Village in which a woman ate her drivers license in the police paddy wagon in a panicked effort to avoid having her name printed in the paper (Faderman, *Odd Girls* 166). The repressive force of these raids is difficult to overestimate; because homosexuality was taboo and had to be hidden from families, co-workers, friends, and employers, the gay bars offered the only physical space where gay people could openly associate, find romantic or sexual partners, and express their gender and sexual orientation in a relatively open manner. The bars were particularly important to lesbians, since social conventions and economic inequality often demanded that unmarried women live at home with their families and thus could not even use their own homes for socializing openly with other gays. One historian of lesbian culture describes the role of the gay bar thus:

> . . . the most important aspect of the bars to young and working-class women was that they provided a relatively secure place where lesbians could connect with other lesbians, whether for friendship, romance or (more rarely) casual sex. How else might a young or working-class woman meet lesbians? It was certainly not safe simply to approach a woman at work or in the neighborhood. If you suspected that another woman was gay you went through lengthy verbal games, dropping subtle hints, using jargon of the subculture (not many straights even knew that the word "gay" meant anything other than "merry" in those days), waiting for her to pick up your clues before you dared to reveal yourself.[2] It required great effort and some risk. In the bars there were no such difficulties. (Faderman 163)

Because the bars were so central to gay life, the police raids of the 1950s forced gays and lesbians to choose between risking arrest, violence, exposure, and financial ruin on the one hand, and living in complete isolation and secrecy, on the other.

For many, particularly drag queens, men who presented as effeminate and butch lesbians, police harassment and brutality spilled over into life outside the bars. One butch lesbian recalls the routine harassment gender-deviant gays experienced on the streets: "I've had the police walk up to me and say, 'Get out of the car.' I'm drivin'. They say 'Get out of the car' and I get out. And they say, 'What kind of shoes you got on. . . . You got on men's shoes?' . . . At that time when they pick you up, if you didn't have two garments that belong to a woman you could go to jail. . . . It would give them the opportunity to whack the shit out of you" (Kennedy and Davis, 180). With no hope of legal protection, street harassment and violence from male civilians also created a constant, steady stream of degradation as well as grave physical danger in the daily lives of gays. One butch woman recalls that in the 1950s "When I walked down the street, cars used to pull over and say, 'Hey faggot, hey lezzie.' They called you names with such maliciousness" (180). Another recalls "you walk down the street and they knew you were gay and you'd be minding your business and there'd be two or three guys standing on a street corner, and they'd come up to you and say, 'You want to be a man, let's see if you can fight like a man.' . . . I actually had walked down the street with some friends not doing anything and had people spit at me, or spit at us, it was really bad" (181).

When we consider such examples of the oppression of homosexuals in the 1950s, it may seem surprising that this decade yielded the first true boom in lesbian publishing, but in another sense, this is quite logical. We might explain this apparent irony using Michel Foucault's concept of discourse and reverse-discourse, which he illustrates, conveniently, with the example of homosexuality: "There is no question that the appearance in . . . psychiatry, jurisprudence and literature of a whole series of discourses on . . . homosexuality . . . made possible a strong advance of social controls into this area . . . but it also made possible the formation of a 'reverse' discourse: homosexuality began to . . . demand its legitimacy or 'naturality' be acknowledged" (101). In other words, the emergence of a given concept "in discourse," (above, the emergence of the idea of "the homosexual" as a type of person) simultaneously enables repression and social control, on the one hand, and identification, defense and even celebration, on the other. And so it was with the proliferation of lesbian pulp novels. The pulps were part of a broader trend in the popular media of voyeuristically and judgmentally revealing the supposedly sleazy "twilight world" of gay culture to a presumably straight audience. By making queer life more visible to those who policed, punished and controlled it, such "exposés" helped deprive homosexuals of the survival strategies of secrecy and discretion; at the same time, the public discourse on homosexuality gave gays a point of identification and commonality, made it possible for them to speak out on their own behalf, and enlisted the support of sympathetic heterosexuals.

Thus, while *Women's Barracks* and the novels that followed both set off a new backlash against homosexual "deviance," at the same time they allowed lesbians an important public point of identification, pleasure, and representation. For example, if the prosecution of *Women's Barracks* for obscenity illustrates a homophobic backlash, as a novel set in a French women's army unit during World War II, *Women's Barracks* also reflected and reified the wartime experiences of many lesbians, to whom military service offered their first experience of paid work, independence from family, and belonging to a community of women, experiences that allowed some to imagine a life outside the confines of the nuclear family and the possibility of a lesbian life.[3] Similarly, the barrage of novels that followed *Women's Barracks* honed in on the book's depiction of lesbian sexuality as an outgrowth of the all-female institution, revealing an increasing cultural uneasiness with women's changing roles on the home front, but also reflecting the possibilities that these homosocial institutions presented for lesbian life. For instance, the postwar period saw greater access for middle-class women to higher education. Not coincidentally, many lesbian pulps of the late fifties, such as *Dormitory Women* (1955), *Sorority House* (1956), *Whisper Their Love* (1957), *Spring Fire*, and *Odd Girl Out* (1957), were set in girls' college dormitories and featured these homosocial settings as both covers and breeding grounds for rampant lesbianism.[4] Similarly, the pulps of the early 1960s appropriated all kinds of settings associated with women's paid labor, particularly those which involved homosocial "worlds" represented by such titles as *Nurses Quarters, All Girl Office, Two Reel Gay Girls* (about the porn industry), and *Lady Boss*. This obsession with figuring lesbian sexuality as an infectious outgrowth of all-female social worlds makes them a particularly rich archive for exploring the relationship between lesbian community and lesbian narrative.

Of course, the pulps' depiction of the homosocial is basically homophobic—that is, they use the specter of lesbianism as a dangerous contagion to express anxieties about women's increased visibility in public life, outside the domestic sphere and under the aegis of neither parental nor matrimonial protection/control. Nevertheless, lesbian pulp fiction's preoccupation with women's worlds also allowed these novels to reimagine the figure of the lesbian as a social creature embedded in a community of like others, a radical departure from earlier depictions, such as the long suffering heroine of Radclyffe Hall's 1928 classic, *The Well of Loneliness* which depicts lesbianism as an isolated, loveless existence. In contrast, many pulps depict lesbian desire not so much as a harbinger of isolation and alienation, but as a marker of belonging in an alternate "world." As a result, the heroines of many lesbian pulp novels seem to have abandoned Hall's lonely well in favor of the more densely populated and enticing imaginary terrains indicated by titles such as *City of Women, Lesbian Jungle, Lesbo Lodge, Queer Beach, Strumpet's Jungle, The Gay Scene, Sex Salon,* and *A Gay, Gay, Gay World.*

While the pulps are certainly notable for their *depiction* of lesbian communities, I am particularly interested in how the pulps served also to *constitute* what Benedict Anderson might call an "imagined community" through reading.[5] Anderson's well-known trope of the imagined community helps us to understand lesbian pulp novels as not simply a realist mode of *representing* mid-century lesbian culture, but as a technology by which this culture was constituted, and by which membership in queer communities—previously available only to those who lived in large urban centers—was extended to a "nation" of lesbian readers. The testimony of one interview subject in the 1993 documentary *Forbidden Love: The Unashamed Stories of Lesbian Lives* reveals some very specific ways in which the pulps served this function: "Well, a friend of mine, she got in the habit of reading these paperbacks, and she started lending them to me, and I got addicted." The two devoured the pulps addictively, passing them on to one another when they finished. One day the friend confessed that she thought she was "like that" and, despite the subject's initial reaction ("Oh no! Not like *that*!"), the subject herself eventually decided that she, too, was "like that." The pair became lovers and decided to take a trip to Greenwich Village to "look for the lesbians." The subject recalls that the couple deliberately dressed in butch and femme clothing so that they would be recognized by the Greenwich Village lesbians about whom they had been reading in the pulp novels. They asked a taxi driver to take them to where the lesbians were, and he did his best. Alas, they did not manage to locate the lesbian world of their pulp-fiction-fueled imaginations and so returned home disappointed.

This anecdote illustrates the role that lesbian pulp novels played in the shaping and regulation of lesbian sexual identities. Passing the books back and forth, feeding one another's addictions, the two at first use the books as a means of exchanging pleasure by sharing an eroticized experience of reading. Indeed, the women's very coming out process is mediated through the pulps as physical objects of exchange, as conduits to a shared pleasure, and eventually as a way of rendering meaning from these bodily experiences. But these women's experience also illustrates a more complex relationship between queer reading practices, the lesbian public sphere, and the performance of sexual identity. In addition to offering readers, through the act reading itself, a form of queer erotic pleasure, the pulps, in this example, function as tools for articulating a legible queer identity; that is, the pulps offered their readers a vocabulary of dress, language, gesture, sexual practice, and public behavior from which they could both forge their own performance of sexual identity and "read" the performances of others. For example, the women in *Forbidden Love* learn from the pulps how to dress (in butch/femme clothing), where to go (to Greenwich Village), and how to speak (asking the cab driver where to find "the Lesbians"—a term not, at that time, as commonly used as it is now). For these interview subjects, then, lesbian identity does not preexist its representation in literature and find reflection there; instead, they find in pulp novels an aesthetic vocabulary from which to forge and perform queer identities legible in the context of real-world queer communities. This anecdote illustrates how the private act of reading pulp novels may have allowed lesbians to rehearse and become proficient in the public reading of bodies and practices in the real world.

In this sense, we might understand the lesbian pulp novel to have played a role similar to the one that real lesbian bar communities played in this period.

For lesbians, according to various histories of twentieth-century gay urban culture, the city provided a public sphere for social interaction, a place apart from the domestic sphere and the family, key institutions in the production of women's sexuality as heterosexuality. In these historical narratives, the urban lesbian community is accorded the authority to produce, interpret, and police sexual identities and practices. Kennedy and Davis discuss the role of the urban lesbian community in policing such supposedly private domains as sexual object choice and sexual practice: "For butches [in the 1950s], the actual coming to sexual subjectivity was a slow process, which they describe as moving from 'bumbling' to excellence. The community was central in this process. In contrast to those of the 1940s, few butch narrators of the 1950s had their first full sexual experience before they had some contact with the public lesbian community, suggesting that women needed explicit social support to become competent leaders in lovemaking" (215).

The interplay between community and sexual practice is particularly striking as Kennedy and Davis trace the emergence and eventual hegemony of the idea of the butch as stone, or sexually non-receptive: "In the 1950s, the stone butch became a publicly discussed ideal for appropriate sexual behavior, and by the late 1950s it was the standard that young butches felt they had to achieve to be a 'real' or 'true' butch. In contrast to the 1940s, a 1950s fem who was out in the community would not have to ask her butch why she was untouchable and if there were others like her. She would have known it was the expected behavior for butches" (204).[6] The fact that an increase in communication about sex in the 1950s lesbian bar communities led to a codification of sexual practice demonstrates the extent to which communities shaped and policed the performance of queer identity, even the supposedly "private" performances of sexual practice.[7] To this extent, lesbian communities were in a very real way the sites where the practices, codes, and markers of lesbian identity were regulated through recognition and the refusal of recognition.[8]

While such histories of lesbian culture have demonstrated that urban bar communities served to shape, regulate, and disseminate a fairly codified lesbian culture, these studies have located such dynamics firmly in real-time, real-space lesbian communities. But just as the communities of urban bar culture shaped lesbian gender performance, sexual practice, and even desire, so did the pulps dictate and shape the imagination of a nation of readers in relation to the spectacle of the sapphic city they upheld. As the mass-production, low cost, and wide-scale distribution of pulps in drugstores, magazine stands, and train stations allowed women across the continent the affective experience of belonging in a community of like others, this regulatory function that Kennedy and Davis locate in the urban gay bar began to transcend the spatial and temporal confines of that space. In this sense, the lesbian pulp novel not only gave women in small towns and suburbs a discursive sense of belonging to this lesbian world, as I suggest above, but also served to extend the regulatory function of the urban lesbian community across time and space. Certainly, literary scholars have drawn a connection between the proliferation of gay and lesbian publications—including lesbian pulps—and the emergence of queer communities strong enough to generate and sustain the gay liberation movement of the 1970s. For example, Alexandra Chasin has explored in detail the role that the proliferation of gay and lesbian periodicals played in the creation of the early homophile movement in the United States. Similarly, Yvonne Keller has argued that lesbian pulps "helped create the largest generation of self-defined lesbians up to that point" (387). Keller's essay bases this argument upon an astute analysis of the visual address of pulp covers, a detailed and careful study of the genre's publication and distribution history, and a useful taxonomy of some basic distinctions between types of lesbian pulps.

But while Keller and others have argued for the inclusion of lesbian pulps in serious considerations of lesbian literary history, few, even of those who have championed the pulp's worthiness as objects of study, have looked closely at the content of these neglected redheaded stepchildren of our lesbian literary heritage to examine the specific strategies these texts used to imagine, address, and encourage the formation of what was to become a "lesbian nation" of readers.[9] That is, if local communities functioned to shape and regulate the public performance of lesbian sexual identity as well as the private practices of lesbian sexuality, we might understand the mass- distribution of lesbian pulp novels as a means by which this function was extended to a lesbian "nation" of readers who learned from the pulps how to "read"—and eventually, to "write" in the language of their own dress, speech, and behavior—the conventions of queer female culture and identity. Indeed, some pulps were even advertised as discursive substitutes for the lesbian bar experience. For example, an ad appearing in the journal of the lesbian homophile organization, *The Ladder* (1956–1972), trumpeted a book entitled *Gay Bar* by promising readers an experience of community and belonging: "You, too, can go to Helen's. . . . For now Helen has put her bar between covers. Her readers can become happy habitués of the place—at least for a time. So pour out a beer for yourself. Cold glass, of course. And settle down to the pleasure of a night in Helen's *Gay Bar*" (*Ladder*, 1, 11).[10] Here we see the urban gay bar offered as a commodity, purchasable and consumable in the form of a novel entitled *Gay Bar*. The ad's visible slight of hand—its promise that the affective experience of reading *Gay Bar*, the novel, will prove to be more or less indistinguishable from the affective experience of going to a gay bar, the place—produced a simulacra of sorts. That is, even as it positions the lesbian pulp as an attractive substitute for a real experience of space and time, it does so by imagining the real gay bar as "original," and the novel as a "copy" of this original experience. In this sense, the ad not only depicts, but effectively *produces* the city as the center of queer culture in relation to a provincial or suburban reading public, in turn *producing* the suburbs and small towns as sites of heteronormativity which must be escaped, if only through the act of reading.[11]

In this way, the lesbian pulp novel both affirms and undermines the role of the urban milieu as the center of lesbian life. That is, the pulps reify the centrality of the city by depicting it *as* center, but at the same time make this center habitable from the farthest reaches of the provinces, where magazine-rack pulp novels suddenly proffered visions of an enticing lesbian city to an imagined lesbian nation. In doing so, the pulps enabled the momentary formation, in the far corners of the heterosexual empire of 1950s America, of "queer space"—"the place-making practices within postmodernism in which queer people engage" (Halberstam 6). The role played by the pulps in the dissemination of queer culture might be seen, then, as a technology of queer "reproduction," for they "reproduce," across time and space, the queer practices and conventions through which identities are performed, recognized, and reified, through which queer subjects learn to perform their own queerness and witness that of others. As such, the pulps offer an alternative to heteronormative modes of "reproducing" the subject—biological reproduction, the family—and allow a way out of the "temporal logic" of what Lee Edelman has called "reproductive time," and into what Halberstam has called "'queer time,' a term for those specific models of temporality that emerge within postmodernism once one leaves the temporal frames of bourgeois reproduction and family, longevity, risk/safety, and inheritance" (6).

Indeed, many of the pulps self-consciously, almost prescriptively, portray their own role as arbiters, disseminators, and monitors of queer identity and its practices. To this end, they frequently depict lesbianism as a species of diaspora and lesbian pulps as a force that unites the dispersed tribe, often drawing them to their rightful homeland, frequently located in Greenwich Village. In this model, urban lesbian culture is constructed as an ontologically separate space. For example, the heroine of Ann Bannon's *Journey to a Woman*, sees New York City as a kind of lesbian homeland, not just geographically distant from the California suburb where she lives, but ontologically separate, "another world where she longed hopelessly to be" (73). Similarly, the narrator of Paula Christian's *Amanda* (1965), herself a writer of lesbian pulps living in New York City, tells us of the "far out" letters she receives from her readers, "letters airmailed from New Jersey to New York" (8). This image suggests that the city is not just a real site of queer community, but a powerful imaginary force, a place figuratively far from small town readers' own lives, "another world" to which even letters that need only cross the Hudson must be airmailed, but nevertheless, a world whose experiences and pleasure can be accessed through pulp reading.[12]

Bannon's *Journey to a Woman* traces the entire trajectory of one lesbian's diasporic journey from exile to belonging, the journey of a heroine spurred on by reading lesbian novels to leave her husband and children in search of her lost lesbian love. In this novel, reading and writing figure as practices of sexuality as well as technologies for the reproduction of lesbian identity. *Journey to a Woman* reintroduces Beth, a character from Bannon's first, girls'-dormitory novel, *Odd Girl Out*, picking up Beth's story nine years after the close of the earlier novel. Now married and trapped in the suburbs of Southern California with a husband and a pair of children, Beth longs for Laura, her lost love from *Odd Girl*, and flees to New York to find her. One of the factors leading Beth to embark on her journey to a woman (or as it turns out, quite a few women) is her practice of reading, which is portrayed as a mode by which she begins to imagine herself as member of a lesbian world and a subject of lesbian desire, even as she enacts her daily duties as a suburban wife and mother: "To while away the hours, she read. On her shopping trips she picked up books—every book she could find on the subject of homosexuality and Lesbianism. She read them with passionate interest, and found a release in them she had not expected" (74).[13] In this passage, Beth's lesbian desire is manifested through the practice of reading, an act through which she eventually begins to imagine herself as a member of a lesbian world from which she has been wrongfully separated. This new vision of herself in relation to a lost lesbian world leads Beth to attempt contact with this world by entering into correspondence with her favorite pulp writers: "She gained a feeling of companionship with some of the writers which alleviated her solitude a little. She wrote letters to a few, the ones who impressed her most, who seemed to understand best what it was like to be gay and to be alone and starved for love; for less than love, even—for sympathetic companionship. . . . She looked forward to their letters eagerly and poured out her desperate lonesomeness and bewilderment to them" (74–75). Beth images her communion with a lesbian public sphere through the pulps, and specifically through the figure of the pulp fiction author, who functions as the discursive point of genesis for this feeling of communion across time and space. Ironically, it is the very experience of aloneness and isolation among the straights that defines the members of the lesbian community insofar as Beth imagines it; the common experience of *lack*—lack of community, lack of love, lack of sympathetic companionship—is the basis for membership in Beth's imagined lesbian public. Distance and separation themselves are the stuff of commonality.

Beth's contact with these authors of the imagined lesbian community leads quickly to the re-ignition of her passion for Laura, and she leaves her husband and children to find her lost love in New York City. When Beth arrives in New York, she contacts Nina Spicer, the pulp writer with whom she has corresponded from California, and through whose books Beth has forged her newfound sense of connection to an "imagined community" through reading. And while Beth enters that lesbian world seeking Laura, the object of her emotional and physical desires and her bodily experience, it is the pulp writer Nina who serves as Beth's guide to the real world of the Greenwich Village bar community. Under Nina's guidance, Beth witnesses a world that seems brazenly to reference Beth's own imagination, an imagination that has itself been constructed by the practice of reading pulps: "After dinner Nina took Beth around to some Lesbian bars. It was the first time in her life that Beth had ever been in such places. They recalled scenes from Nina's novels to her" (106). Here, Beth inverts the relationship between real and representation, recalling scenes from Nina's books and perceiving the real bars as imitations of pulp. It is through this experience of recognition—of recognizing in the outside world a world of her own imagination—that Beth begins to insert herself into this world, first by adopting the vocabulary she has learned in the pulps to perform her own belonging: "Beth was surprised to see so many men sitting at the bar. 'Who are they?' she asked. 'Johns?' She remembered the word from one of Nina's novels and she asked her question in a firm clear voice that made Nina duck and laugh" (106). In effect, once inside this queer public world, Beth begins to articulate her own queerness, though clumsily at first, by culling from the representational repertoire of the pulps to render herself legible in a real-world lesbian community. She needs the pulps to be true in order that she might correctly read other queer bodies and be correctly read herself.

While the novel trades in various theories of homosexuality and its origins—sexological, psychoanalytic, libertine, and liberal—the fact that Beth's voracious readership is the conduit to her coming out suggests that while her lesbianism might have been contained to adolescence and the homosocial environment of the sorority house, she is reinfected by reading lesbian pulp fiction. The discursive mode of pulp fiction and the addictive narrative desires that feed and are fed by it are portrayed as the sources of Beth's queer desires, as if the representation preexists its referent and produces it. Indeed, it is the author Nina who pronounces, "You're gay, Beth," after they finally sleep together, giving Beth the answer she has sought in her search for the elusive Laura. As in the example from *Forbidden Love*, in which the interview subject recounts first reading lesbian pulps at her friend's insistence, then actually enacting the desires and the sexual identity that the books portray, Beth encounters a discursive lesbian identity and desire before she actually experiences this desire or assumes this identity.

The relationship between Beth and the writer Nina mirrors Bannon's own "communion" with the world of New York lesbian life through Marijane Meaker, author of the first American lesbian pulp, *Spring Fire*. After reading *Spring Fire*, Ann Weldy, a married mother of young children living in the suburbs of Philadelphia, wrote to Meaker (a.k.a. Vin Packer and Ann Aldrich), who encouraged her to send in her own manuscript, which was published by Gold Medal in 1957 as *Odd Girl Out* by Ann Bannon (Zimet, 20). Bannon's own "communion" with a lesbian world, like Beth's, was routed through the reading, writing, and mentorship of an established lesbian writer. Beth's journey to a woman, like Bannon's connection to lesbian life, begins and ends with acts of reading: first as a practice of imagining community and imagining the self in community, and later as the means by which she is integrated as a legible subject within a queer world.

While *Journey to a Woman* is focalized through the figure of the pulp reader, the production of queer desire in the writing of lesbian pulp is explored from the point of view of the pulp author in *Amanda* by Paula Christian, another of a handful of lesbian authors who contributed to the lesbian pulp boom in the 1950s and '60s, along with Bannon, Meaker, Patricia Highsmith (as Claire Morgan), Valerie Taylor, and Marion Zimmer Bradley (as Miriam Gardner). Like *Journey to a Woman, Amanda* is compellingly self-conscious with regard to its own cultural function as a lesbian pulp, taking as its protagonist a heterosexual writer of lesbian pulps and as its subject her struggles to simultaneously break away from pulp-writing and produce a "real" novel, to mentor another aspiring lesbian pulp writer, and to make sense of her own first queer affair (with the aspiring writer). Ev, the protagonist and narrator, is almost a parody of the "career girl" that so many pulps portray as vulnerable to the wiles of the predatory lesbians who hunt the city streets, nurses quarters, prisons, and dormitories in the pages of the pulps. Like a female version of *Playboy* magazine's urbane bachelor, Ev lives in her own New York apartment where she pursues a successful freelance writing career, smokes, drinks martinis, and has casual sex with male friends. She characterizes herself in the first pages of the novel: "My life had always been a flexibly regulated one. I've a garden apartment in the Murray Hill section of New York. I do my writing and whatever freelance editing and copywriting I can get my hands on in my home. . . . No steady boyfriend, but I date frequently, go to parties, and enjoy a healthy sex life unencumbered by matrimonial demands" (7–8). Ev's comfortable playgirl lifestyle is disrupted by near simultaneous and near contradictory messages from the opposite ends of the chain of literary production: her editor begins pressuring her to produce a "real" (meaning heterosexual-themed) novel instead of more junky lesbian pulp, and a fan, Amanda, writes her a letter asking for feedback on a draft of her own lesbian novel. She struggles (though not very hard) to write a "real" novel, and this struggle becomes synonymous with her struggle to resist the pull toward pulp, a pull that begins to resemble lesbian sexual desire as it is portrayed in the pulps—as an undeniable force, a subconscious drive, the repression of which only leads to its more ferocious return. Ev agrees to collaborate with Amanda on the novel, and the two fall madly into bed. But once they have finished the project, Amanda moves back to California and becomes mentor to another ingénue trying to write yet another lesbian novel.

While the received pulp narrative tells of the closeted small-town outcast who comes to taste the pleasures and freedoms of the big city, *Amanda* gives us a hyper-hetero urban sophisticate who is comfortable if not blasé in the gay clubs and restaurants in the Village. And instead of this jaded urbanite preying upon the naiveté of the new arrival, it is Amanda, the out-of-town ingénue, seemingly fleeing the chains of heterosexual domesticity in the California suburbs, who seduces Ev and takes advantage of her. This novel's reversal of the standard narrative suggests that the city, presumably the center of the lesbian nation, depends as much upon the provinces for its status as the lesbian "homeland" as the suburbs and small towns depend upon the city as the imaginary center of queer life. Similarly, it suggests that the queer author and her narratives are as vulnerable to transformation in the process of reception by the desires of the reader as the reader is to the seductions of the text. In this self-conscious novel of reading, writing, and seduction, text, reader, and author all become pulp in each other's hands.

Foregrounding this complex play of desire among reader, writer, and written word, *Amanda* uses direct address to confront and implicate its reader in the issues of identity, experience, and realness that permeate the novel: "You've never heard of me but you've probably read some of my books. Naturally I use a pen name as do most authors of frowned upon books. You see, I write lesbian novels. And to answer the question you've already formed in your mind, I'll give you my standard reply: A mystery writer doesn't have to commit murder to write about it" (7). This opening carefully collapses character, narrator, and author by focalizing the narrative through a figure who is all three at once. But in doing so it collapses the reader of *Amanda* with the readers of pulps depicted in the novel, and with Amanda herself, casting the reader as herself a partner in the dance of reader-author desire and seduction that Amanda herself performs with Ev. By thus aligning its readership with the character of the pulp reader-as-lesbian-lover, *Amanda* performs the cultural function it imagines for itself and for other pulps: the positioning of the reader as subject to lesbian desire through the very act of reading.

This interpellation of the reader as a desiring subject is accomplished in part by *Amanda*'s construction of reading and writing as technologies of both sexuality and reproduction, practices through which lesbian identities and desires are transmitted, enacted, and inhabited. We see this as Ev reads Amanda's letter and is seduced, attracted to Amanda's discursive contact as to a body: "I opened it and was immediately struck by the neat typing and broad margins. . . . [T]here was something warm and captivating about the letter which compelled me to read the paragraph twice. . . . Her grammar and vocabulary, even her metaphors, were quite above average and in an instance or two superior to mine" (9). This sexy letter seduces Ev and leads her to invite its author to forward her manuscript. Like Bannon's Beth, Ev reaches through the imagined communion of reading toward a more personal connection.

This communion is achieved less in the eventual sexual contact between Ev and Amanda than through the pleasurable acts of writing and reading, which are figured as in themselves acts of lesbian seduction, as in Ev's sensual description of the process of reading Amanda's manuscript:

> I laid the M.S. on my desk and went into the kitchen to make myself a cup of coffee. I opened a fresh pack of cigarettes and put them next to the manuscript. I had to smile at myself; anyone watching would have thought I was lining my tent for the winter siege. . . . It wasn't until the sunlight had passed behind the tall buildings beyond my garden leaving me in dull daylight that I realized that I'd been reading nearly the whole day. And that I was famished. While fixing myself a sandwich, I couldn't keep my mind off Amanda's story. Thus far, about halfway through the novel, she had not introduced any overt sex into the book and I wondered if the two heroines would ever get it on and how Amanda would handle the scene. I opened the beer and took my sandwich back to the desk and resumed reading. . . . By my appointed Martini time, six o'clock, I'd finished Amanda's book and sat back in my chair, totally exhausted emotionally and cramped. (17)

This leisurely, detailed account of what could be said in four words ("I read the manuscript"), and the weaving together in this passage of reading with other bodily pleasures—smoking, coffee, beer, martinis, food—suggests that reading itself has become an act of sensual pleasure. Here, reading becomes not a mere technology for the representation of pleasure, but the *referent* of this near-pornographic representation. Indeed, when she finishes reading the manuscript, Ev finds herself "famished" and "emotionally exhausted" and "cramped." In contrast with the sensuality of this passage on the act of reading, lesbian sex itself is never represented: the chapter closes as the pair go to bed, and the next one opens the following morning.

Like *Journey to a Woman*, *Amanda* frames the issue of the origin of the lesbian subject in terms of narrative, setting up the queer pulp novel, with its capacity to attract, seduce and even addict the reader as a technology for reproducing the lesbian subject. In this sense, *Amanda* imagines lesbian identity as originating in a discursive communion between the pulp-fiction reader and writer, a communion which is mirrored in but never matched by the eventual sexual communion between these two figures. By eliding sexual and textual reproduction of the lesbian subject, the novel illustrates metatextually the ways in which reading functions as a queer mode of reproduction. In Bannon's and Christian's intratextual portrayals of the urban writer and the provincial reader, and of pulp reading as itself a mode of mastering lesbian sexual identity, we see the lesbian pulp novel holding itself up as a mode by which lesbian readers might imagine themselves and their desires in relation to a community, albeit a community of people they had never met, and might never meet.

The discursive function of reading in mid-century lesbian pulps is perhaps best illustrated in the complex address of the reader in Ann Bannon's final and most beloved lesbian pulp novel, *Beebo Brinker*, the story of a seventeen-year old gender outlaw who flees the ostracism she faces in her rural Wisconsin hometown after she is discovered passing for a boy at the rodeo. Arriving in New York City, Beebo is adopted by Jack, a gay man who introduces her to queer life in Greenwich Village. As luck would have it, she delivers a pizza to a bombshell movie star, a closeted femme-dyke, who seduces her, moves her to L.A. and finally sends her home when the Hollywood tabloids start to catch on.

The novel's narrative voice is third person, but *Beebo Brinker*'s narrative is focalized quite distinctly through particular characters, and it is through this shifting of focalizing figures that the novel produces and orders knowledge, strategically positioning the reader in relation to that knowledge.[14] The first third of the novel is focalized through Jack, the gay man who "adopts" Beebo, so that the reader's view of Beebo is Jack's view, and it is through his privileged, queer gaze that the reader, too, is afforded sight. *Beebo Brinker* uses this kind of focalization carefully to position the reader on the side of the insider, the knowing "reader" of queer bodies. The passage in which Jack comes out to Beebo is an excellent example: because the reader has been introduced to Jack first, has, in fact, been privy only to that which Jack knows and sees, she knows that Jack is gay long before Beebo does. As a result, when Beebo fails to see Jack's queerness until he declares, "I swear to God, Beebo, you can be thicker than bean soup. I've done everything but sing it for you in C sharp" (640), the reader gets to feel comparatively cosmopolitan, for she is already on the "inside" of the queer world to which Jack is introducing Beebo. This strategic alignment of the reader with Jack's epistemological position offers membership in an imagined queer community and access to its domain of knowledge as an effect of reading and as a position of privilege and power. This use of narrative focalization to interpellate the novel's reader as a member of a queer community and subject of a queer epistemology comes to the fore as Jack begins to take Beebo out to lesbian bars, to "teach her gently what she was, and teach her not to hate the word for it: Lesbian" (610). This process presents an alternative to the coming out narrative in which sexuality emerges as a truth from within the subject, instead offering a model in which sexual identity does not arise spontaneously from an essential self, but is rather given to the subject through a complex process that is both linguistic and visual. Jack must "teach [Beebo] the word," but this is not enough, he notes: "Jack wanted to comfort her, to explain that she wasn't alone in the world, that other people were different in the same way she was. But he couldn't speak of it to her until she admitted it first to him" (607). Because the reader is privileged with Jack's "queer eye" and enfolded within the novel's queer epistemology, she sees Beebo's own queerness before Beebo herself does. Again, the pleasures of the text are made contingent upon the reader's alignment with a queer community and its knowledge.

As Jack takes her out to view the spectacle of urban lesbian culture, the narrative begins to align itself with Beebo's gaze, and Beebo herself is seduced by the lure of "knowing" this world. And yet it is also this relationship of spectatorship that keeps her outside the community, at a gazing distance, an ethnographic observer: "She wanted to talk to them, see what they were like. She was often drawn to one enough to daydream about her . . . she was eagerly curious about the Lesbian mores and social codes. The gay girls seemed so smooth and easy with each other; talking about shared experiences in a special slang, like members of an exclusive sorority" (631). While the overt metaphor of the previous passage is that of "an exclusive sorority," its language echoes the language of the anthropologist, with its talk of "social codes" and "mores," and its reference to "shared experiences," "special slang" and membership. The categories by which Beebo defines and delimits the community she observes—recognition of membership and shared language, experiences, and social codes—resemble the categories of anthropological taxonomies of races, tribes, and other "primitive" cultural configurations.[15]

Indeed, the pulps draw heavily on the discursive strategies of ethnography, "urban-spectator" writing and early twentieth-century anthropological writing, particularly in their production of the "other" as visual spectacle, and of "seeing" as the primary metaphor for "knowing." We see this dynamic of seeing and knowing at work as Beebo confronts and is confronted by the visual spectacle of a lesbian world, for in subjecting this urban spectacle to her own gaze, she is herself transformed into a desiring subject: "Beebo watched them [the women in the lesbian bar dancing and kissing] for less than a minute, all told; but a minute that was transfixed like a living picture in her mind for the rest of her life . . . and she was obsessed momentarily by the desire to grab the girl nearest her and kiss her" (626). Here what Anderson would call the "image of . . . communion" is presented *as* image, as spectacle of sight, as "living picture." And it is from the position of spectator—"Beebo watched them"—that the protagonist's desire is evoked, a desire that does not preexist sexual community, but is in fact called forth by its visualization. In this sense, it is the "living picture"—the image—of a lesbian community that renders Beebo "obsessed . . . by the desire" not for the female body, but for the body of this imaged/imagined community itself. That is, Beebo doesn't desire one girl in particular, just the nearest one as a conduit to communion with this spectacle of queer life. It is through the visual register that Beebo imagines herself in relation to a lesbian public by accessing her desire through the exercise of the gaze. The importance of Beebo's visual image of community as that which produces Beebo's own queer desire is emphasized by her vitriolic and excessive repudiation of this image: "She covered her face with her hands and rubbed her eyes roughly. Through her fingers she said, 'I don't want to watch them. I just don't want to stand there and watch them'" (627). Beebo refuses this vision precisely because of the way in which it interpellates her as a member of this community of desiring subjects.

Unlike the proper ethnographer and urban spectator, Beebo cannot maintain her separation, for she cannot maintain the illusion of her own invisibility to the gaze she trains so powerfully on others. Eventually, it is through her very positioning as *flâneur*, and through the visual register which she at first finds so jarring, that Beebo negotiates a peripheral relationship to the lesbian community and is seduced by its visual pleasures. As a result she begins to adopt their gaze in order to envision her queer self. In the above passage, it is not through identification with like, but through the separation of viewer from spectacle that Beebo is able to experience self-recognition. And it is her witnessing of this lesbian "world," and her eventual recognition of herself as, too, an object of that world's own gaze, that allows her to re-see, to re-envision herself. She tells Jack, "'Back in Juniper Hill, I could only see what other people saw, and I was afraid and ashamed. But here, I look all different. I even feel different.' She looked at her hands" (628). Assuming queer identity, here, is constructed less as a process of revealing the secret self to the public, than of having that self "read" and revealed to oneself by the public. Looking at her hands, Beebo re-envisions her own body at this moment, for having submitted to the gaze of the lesbian world which she had gazed upon so longingly, feeling herself "read" by this world to whom she is legible, Beebo is suddenly able to "read" herself, to take the correct spectatorial position with regard to her own performance of sexual identity.

While lesbian pulp novelists of the cold-war era were forced to conform to publisher's demands for punitive endings or negative stereotyping, their narratives recast the structural relationship between reader, narrative, and writer in a way that offered readers the experiences of membership, belonging, and pleasurable communion with a body of like others as effects of reading. By allowing women to experience the pleasures of queer desire through the act of reading, the pulps positioned readers as subjects of queer desire, simultaneously offering them the pleasures of membership in an exotic lesbian world with which their readers might never have real contact, but whose pleasures and power they could nevertheless experience through the act of reading, of knowing, and of re-seeing themselves as legible within such a lesbian world.

By simultaneously evoking and engaging their female readers' desires for escape from the stifling prison of postwar gender ideology, lesbian pulp novels emplotted queer desire in ways that lent it cultural and eventually political meaning. Utilizing the powerful and seductive tools of the realist novel to focalize narratives through the figure of the lesbian subject and align the reader with an imagined lesbian public, the pulps began to articulate lesbianism as a privileged position from which to gaze back critically upon the social fabric of cold-war American culture. By providing a place of common identification, an alternative position from which to view 1950s America, lesbian pulps fostered the collective resistance to this oppression.

The pulps' re-signification of the figure of the lesbian as privileged social "eye," on the one hand, and their affective constitution of their own readership as an "imagined community" of national scope, on the other hand, entwined a feminist social critique, a lesbian desiring subject and an imagined reading community. Embedding a desire for escape from normative mid-century gender roles in sensational stories of queer passion and urban adventure, these narratives produced the position of the lesbian as not simply one of sexual preference, but as one of profound dissatisfaction with the culturally proscribed apparatus of heterosexuality: marriage, motherhood, domesticity, and family. Such a constitution of the figure of the lesbian set the stage for the development in the 1970s of a lesbian-feminist politics that saw lesbianism as a strategic feminist position of solidarity and resistance. In this sense, mid-century lesbian themed pulp novels articulated a vision of lesbian identity that can be traced into feminist and lesbian political discourse over the subsequent twenty years.

Notes

1. For an excellent history of the "golden age" of the lesbian pulp novel, see Yvonne Keller's "'Was It Right to Love Her Brother's Wife So Passionately?' Lesbian Pulp Novels and U.S. Lesbian Identity, 1950," *American Quarterly* 57.2 (2005) 385–410. See also Susan Stryker's *Queer Pulp*. San Francisco: Chronicle Books, 2001.

2. Gay jargon even had a term for this very strategy: gays referred to the practice as "dropping a hairpin." Thanks to Dennis H. Conkin for reminding me of this phrase in a discussion of the novel *Stone Butch Blues*, Feb. 22, 2007.

3. Scholarship in LGBT studies has attributed the rise of queer identities, communities, and cultures since the mid-twentieth century to a variety of economic, demographic, and other factors, including the proliferation of wage labor and commodity culture that made traditional family structures and marriage at least economically non-compulsory. But nearly all historians of gay and lesbian culture in this period, including John D'Emillio, Kennedy and Davis, and Lillian Faderman, agree that the expansion of the military during World War II had a tremendous impact upon the formation of gay communities during and immediately following the war. One of the subjects of journalist Brett Harvey's oral history of American women's experience in the 1950s illustrates the particularly important role played by the military in the creation of lesbian communities in the 1940s: "I went through basic at Fort Lee, Virginia. Now when I walked in there, it turned out *everyone* was gay! My captain, my first sergeant, right on down. Man, I was like a kid in a candy store. I went berserk. And I was the supply sergeant: I met them first! They had to come to me to get their supplies" (Harvey, 181). While this testimony may seem like an exaggeration, it is important to consider the appeal of the WAC (Women's Army Corps) to lesbians in the 1940s. Certainly, the service was attractive because it provided an all-female context which offered both an opportunity to meet and interact with women, and because it provided the means by which women could support themselves financially and thus to avoid marriage. Moreover, the military provided a legitimate (indeed, patriotic) opportunity for women to transgress gender norms, performing traditionally male jobs, assuming titles previously reserved for men (lieutenant, captain, and sergeant) and wearing masculine uniforms (albeit feminized versions thereof) rather than the era's floral rayon dresses and high heels. Thus military service would have appealed strongly to butch lesbians as a space where deviations from feminine gender presentation were not only tolerated, but even rewarded. When we consider these factors, the subject's estimation that "everyone" in her unit was gay may not have been much of an exaggeration.

4. Indeed, Marijane Meaker (Vin Packer) claims to have based her sorority house novel, *Spring Fire*, on her own and her sorority sisters' experience college (Zimet, 19).

5. Theorizing the role of print culture in the creation of the European nation-state, Anderson ponders the seemingly impossible coherence of communities as large as nations, even empires, in spite of the fact that the members of such communities as, for example, the nation, consist of individuals who "will never know most of their fellow-members, meet them or even hear of them, yet in the mind of each lives the image of their communion" (15). Anderson concludes that it is the *image* of a communion of disparate subjects (who are in fact unrelated by shared experience or actual daily contact—emotional, economic, social, etc.) that allows the nation-state to cohere, to function as a discrete political and economic unit: "communities are distinguishable not by their falsity/genuineness, but by the style in which they are imagined" (15). Thus, it is at the discursive level, in what Anderson calls the "imaginary" register, that nations and empires cohere. For Anderson, print capitalism was the lynchpin of the European bourgeoisie's ability to "achieve solidarity on an essentially imagined basis," for it was the commercial circulation of newspapers and books that allowed members of this emergent bourgeoisie to constitute themselves as a distinct class a "literate elite"—connected to one another through the mediation of the printed word.

6. The reference here is to Joanna, a 1940s fem who recalls asking her butch lover about her nonreceptive sexuality: "Because I asked her one time, I said, 'do you think that you might be just the only one?' 'Oh no,' she said. 'I know I'm not, I've discussed it with . . . different people.'" (196) The channels through which this community construction of sexual behavior operated changed with time, and even from bar to bar: For instance, a butch narrator from one group recalls a fem who instructed her quite explicitly: "she took a piece of paper and drew me a picture. She says, 'Now you get this spot right here.'" (217). In contrast, "By the late 1950s many butches received their instruction from other butches, particularly if they were young and just entering the community. . . . It was not uncommon for someone to have her first affair with a butch and learn from the experience that she wanted to be butch herself" (217). The '50s also saw another shift in the channels through which sexual practices were policed and reproduced: "the 1950s also was the advent of another completely new practice—experienced butches teaching novice butches about sex through discussion and support" (219). Indeed, for many butches, sexual practices eluded their imaginations until they were able to access them discursively. For instance, one narrator recalls telling an older butch, "I feel sexually aroused by this woman, but if I take her to bed, what am I gonna do?" The experienced butch replies, "Well, what do you want to do?" But this question, which posits sexual practice as already inscribed upon desire itself—as if desire is always a "desire to"—gets the young butch nowhere, and the more experienced one ends up giving her explicit instructions. Another recalls, "I wanted it but you didn't know what the hell to do. You were filled with passion but you just didn't know how to go about this thing" (216).

7. This is an excellent illustration of the fallacy of what Foucault calls the "repressive hypothesis," or the notion that power, particularly with regard to sexuality, operates primarily through censorship and repression, for here is an example of an increased willingness to talk about sex, a lifting of repression, which results in a much more rigid social systems for policing sexual behavior in a community.

8. For example, the hegemony of butch-femme in 1950s lesbian communities was marked by the refusal to recognize those whose gender presentation was neither clearly butch nor clearly femme.

9. Keller's taxonomy of the lesbian pulp genre includes a primary division of pulps into "virile adventures"—semi-pornographic books written primarily by male authors and for heterosexual male readers—and "pro-lesbian" pulps—books written almost exclusively by female (generally lesbian) authors in deliberate and calculated response to the

voyeurism and homophobia of the more common "virile adventure" sub-genre. Indeed, as Keller points out, many of these lesbian authors have commented in retrospect about their very conscious attempts to address other lesbians through their work in the genre, suggesting that the impact Keller claims these books had upon the identification of a great number of women as lesbians in the post-pulp period was in fact quite deliberate.

10. Indeed, *The Ladder* also positioned *itself* as a substitute for the lesbian bar as a source of community. For example, in one issue, a reader writes to ask that her name be removed from *The Ladder*'s mailing list because she fears the repercussions of appearing on such a list. The editor responds: "I personally know the lass who wrote those words. In a later paragraph of her letter she gave me the details of all the gay bars in a certain city. She frequents these bars and apparently is not afraid to be seen in them. Yet, she doesn't want her name on our mailing list" (*Ladder*, v. 1, #2, 10). Here, being present on a list, being written, is compared favorably to being present in the bars—a site of sexuality, of physicality, of embodiment. Martin Meeker explores a similar struggle over the role of lesbian representation in relation to the public articulation of lesbian identity and the modes through which lesbian communities would be produced and extended. Between 1957 and 1960, *The Ladder* printed a series of book reviews and editorials on the nonfiction paperbacks of lesbian author Ann Aldrich (who also wrote lesbian pulp fiction under the pen name Vin Packer). Meeker points out that *The Ladder* took Aldrich to task for her highly pathologizing portrayals of lesbians because the Daughters of Billitis saw pulp fiction as a potential medium not only by which the lesbian community was represented to the straight public, but also by which the homophile movement could communicate and connect with lesbians around the country. Thus, Meeker argues, the question of who would represent the lesbian in pulp and how she should be represented became central to homophile strategies for reaching potential members and achieving its goal of integrating the lesbian into society. This argument eventually came to a head in the lesbian feminist movement of the '70s, which witnessed the expurgation of butch-femme, the movement from urban community to rural commune, and the deliberate articulation of lesbianism as ideology. And the repressed of that period returned in the sex wars of the 1980s with the revival of butch-femme sexuality, of urban dyke cultures and other changes.

11. Recently, rural queers as well as queer theorists have begun to question the received notion that the city is uniquely situated to foster queer life, community, and culture. For example, Judith Halberstam discussed the problems with this construction of the rural/urban divide in relation to discussions of the murder of Nebraska transgender youth Brandon Teena in her recent book *In a Queer Time and Place*. Halberstam suggests, for example, that urban queers tend to blame a specifically rural homophobia for the murder of Brandon (as well as Matthew Shepherd in Wyoming five years later), and to imagine that such youths might meet a happier fate if only they migrated to the cities. However, Halberstam points out, Brandon himself seems to have found a greater sense of belonging in a rural setting than in an urban one, for he deliberately moved from urban Lincoln to rural Falls City, Nebraska. Halberstam suggests that the move actually allowed Brandon to live more seamlessly as a young man, by performing a middle-class masculine identity that appealed quite neatly to the romantic fantasies of the working class, rural girls and women he dated in Falls City.

12. Victoria Hesford explores the connection between the imaginary terrain of the city and the possibilities evoked by lesbian desire in Patricia Highsmith's 1952 lesbian novel (written under the pseudonym Claire Morgan) *The Price of Salt* (Hesford). Hesford argues that Highsmith (like Paula Christian in the above example) maps New York and New Jersey as sites, respectively, of lesbian possibility and of heterosexual limitation. Hesford's analysis of Highsmith's construction of the relationship between urban space and the possibility of lesbian futurity also throws into high relief similarity between the work of various lesbian authors who wrote pulp fiction in the 1950s and '60s. Highsmith's influ-

ence upon Ann Bannon in this regard is striking, as I note below in my discussion of Beebo Brinker. And, while lesbian pulp fiction has generally been treated as popular culture quite outside the cannon of lesbian literature, this repeated trope of the city, of the female *flâneur* (discussed by Sally Munt) suggest a fascinating genealogy of influence—which is visible at both the textual and the biographical levels—from Janet Flanner to Highsmith (who was mentored by Flanner) to Marijane Meaker aka Ann Aldrich/Vin Packer (who was Highsmith's lover in the late 1950s), to Bannon (who was mentored by Meaker). This trajectory of lesbian sexual/literary heritage legible in the repeated trope of the city as the center of queer life reflects the intertwining of the sexual and the textual in as modes of queer reproduction which I discuss below.

13. Beth's illicit reading practice is strangely assimilable into her daily life as a suburban housewife: she pursues this discursive lesbian experience not by leading the double life that figures so prominently in narratives of male homosexuality, but simply by following the quotidian course of activities of the typical American middle-class wife and mother, picking up the books on her regular trips to the suburban shopping center and reading them in the leisure time of her husband's work day and her children's naps or school days. Beth's participation in an imagined lesbian community is possible, and was in fact historically possible for thousands of real women, because of the book distribution networks created around the pulps, which made them easily available in drugstores and magazine stands across the United States and Canada.

14. The term focalization is Shlomith Rimmon-Kenan's. She uses it to distinguish between narrative voice and perspective. While a narrative may be spoken from an outside voice, the events relayed may be accessed through a specific character's experience. She uses the metaphor of a movie camera to characterize the function of focalization in a narrative: we may see through that person's lens even if we are not addressed by her voice.

15. Susanna noted that the pulps offered themselves to readers almost as "travel guides to the seamy side of Village life, inviting the reader to venture into the bars and coffee shops and test her skills with the ladies. From these books, one could learn the terminology, dress codes, and etiquette necessary to negotiate the lesbian subculture" (Walters, 90).

Afterword: The Conditions of Reception

Josh Lukin

ONE MIGHT EXPECT that, with the decline of containment culture and the rise of the New Left, the U.S. would see a resurgence of the old values kept alive in the fifties by the likes of Nelson Algren and Martha Dodd, and a burgeoning of the newer movements anticipated by Elizabeth Spencer and the readers of lesbian pulps. That such a revival was delayed in coming demands some explanation. The domestic containment era, sometimes defined as contiguous with the "long 1950s," was over by 1962. In that year, John Henry Faulk successfully sued the Red hunters who had blacklisted him; Michael Harrington revealed the existence of poverty (*The Other America*); Stan Lee and Steve Ditko redefined the superhero as an impoverished young wisecracking rebel (*The Amazing Spider-Man*); Old Left icon John Hammond signed Bob Dylan to Columbia Records; and the Cuban Missile Crisis redefined public sentiments on U.S.-Soviet relations. Gay postmodern novelists Samuel Delany and Tom Disch made their debuts. *Rapprochement* was the order of the day: liberal *New York Times* reviewer Anthony Boucher decided that Mickey Spillane's novels of reactionary thuggery were no longer so bad; Harold Prince and Stephen Sondheim persuaded Red Scare survivors Jack Gilford and Zero Mostel to work with friendly witness Jerome Robbins on *A Funny Thing Happened on the Way to the Forum*. In an age when "folk group" meant a trio or quartet of identically dressed, crew-cut simulacra delivering condescending renditions of songs swiped from blacklisted artists, Albert Grossman created Peter, Paul and Mary, a diverse, energetic, and politically committed deformation of the Weavers. And 1962 was the year in which the Student League for Industrial Democracy renamed itself Students for a Democratic Society, issuing the Port Huron Statement as the New Left's founding document.

The era saw a great resurgence of cultural forms and figures with Old Left ties, as blacklisted musicians and filmmakers returned to visibility and marginalized poets and dramatists gained new influence. But a parallel outbreak in novels did not occur, as narrative fiction followed a path very different from that of music and movies. 1962's major novels of rebellion included *One Flew Over the Cuckoo's Nest*, *Stranger in a Strange Land*, and in some quarters *Mother Night* and *The Man in the High Castle*: the first two by Cold War Libertarians, the latter two by New Deal liberals writing of personal ethical dilemmas. The central modes of most classic 1960s fiction include existentialism, Black Humor, rejection of mainstream society, and the recovery of certain High Modernist styles; but by and large, the values we have come to associate with progressive movements do not appear in fiction until late in the decade, and some reasons for that delay can be traced to the fifties.

Among all artistic media, the containment era evidently was most successful in changing the landscape of American fiction: not only did few blacklisted publishers make comebacks after that era's end, the ideological standards by which many critics and editors judged fiction tended to retain Cold War strictures. In the broader context of suppressing political protest, such a success was a rather small victory. Fiction has rarely been the preferred medium of artists seeking to mobilize social movements, in part because it is usually consumed in solitude: poetry, music, and drama naturally seem more efficacious, with their capacity to attract public audiences. U.S. history shows few instances of an *Uncle Tom's Cabin* or *Jungle* that have directly influenced public policy: political fiction is more likely to validate experiences that a reader already possesses or to document lives that a reader can learn to empathize with than to motivate social action on a large scale.[1] But, as the scholars in *Invisible Suburbs* have shown, the field of fiction is not isolated from other social and artistic realms. Not only can the successful production and promulgation of a novel be liberating for the artist who creates it and for his or her community, it can have a direct influence on more "public" media, as for example in the case of the Popular Front literature that influenced Bob Dylan. Hence the question of why mid-sixties fiction retained strictures that other arts were throwing off deserves further study.

In view of the geographical concentration of the publishing and reviewing world, it makes sense that the New York Intellectuals' influence was most intensely felt in those media. And those critics had worked hard to exorcise Popular Front values in the name of good taste. Robert Warshow had famously condemned thirties Left culture as "a disastrous vulgarization of intellectual life" so appallingly un-American that the Rosenbergs' fondness for it exemplified their "absolute alienation from truth and experience" (34, 81). The postwar essays of Mary McCarthy, Lionel Trilling, and even the young James Baldwin had come close to stating that to engage in the Naturalist tactic of presenting lives in terms of determining social forces is not so much mistaken as *unbecoming*—to maintain one's credibility as a world power, one doesn't say these things in front of the French. While the CIA-sponsored Congress for Cultural Freedom worked to impress the intelligentsia of Europe with American values, our *litterateurs* and journalists tried to keep our own people in line, lest we succumb to philistinism or that other *bête noire* of fifties discourse, Ideology. David Riesman in 1953, at the height of the McCarthy years, had ridiculed "Intellectuals [who] try to cope with their anxiety by telling each other atrocity stories about America" (*IR* 239). The idea that social injustice was an issue worth addressing in fiction, or even a lived reality, seemed passé: Marcus Klein in 1962 praised the ability of the major fifties novelists to address conditions under which "there was no politics to speak of and there were no orthodoxies to speak of to restrict one's freedom, and when all theories of society had been shattered" (29). As late as 1963, Thomas Pynchon's editor at Viking exemplified the effects of this exclusionary mentality, urging Pynchon not to make *V.* a "protest novel" by including "Negroes" among its characters (Gerald Howard).

A related aspect of containment that demands our understanding is the extent to which it virtually eliminated, or rendered unintelligible, certain discourses that were extant in earlier and later eras. I have noted Coontz's, Douglas's, and Duchamp's work on this foreclosure as it applied to gender roles, but its effect was far broader. I. L. Peretz's classic socialist parable, "Bontsche Schweig" had originally been the ironic story of a man whose persecutions have left him so vitiated that, when offered all the rewards in Heaven for his mute sufferings, he can only think to ask for a hot roll with some butter; in the fifties, it was cherished as a charming fable in praise of humility, with Alfred Kazin styling it "old ritualistic praise of Jewish goodness" (286). Mailer's ironic elegy for the Old Left, *Barbary Shore,* and the reissue of Gide's homophilic *Corydon* met with incomprehension. As late as 1961, Daniel Hoffman, building on Richard Chase's reinvention of Melville as a Cold Warrior *avant-la-lettre,* was impervious to the antiracist irony in *The Confidence Man,* praising the novel's genocidal "Indian-Hater" as its moral center, a "hero dedicated to extirpating evil" (303).

With older literature of resistance retaining the stigmas that had been attached to it in the fifties, when it had been condemned as kitsch or gobbledygook or refunctioned to serve the status quo, an advantage accrued to protest fiction that did not claim the direct influence of the thirties and forties: Robert Stone, Thomas Pynchon, and Hubert Selby Jr. in different ways avoided the taint of Cultural Front associations. Other authors were able to reinvent the thirties for their own purposes: Leslie Fiedler, gradually mutating from a Cold War Liberal to a counterculture hero, reprinted his 1955 characterization of *Call It Sleep* and *A Cool Million* as typical novels of the thirties, notwithstanding the fact that no one had bought them in their time of publication. As ever, Fiedler knew the temper of his time: claiming Henry Roth and Nathanael West as forebears rather than Algren and Farrell, sixties novelists were able to play with Jewish identity and Black Humor in ways congenial to their temperaments and world views.[2]

A chief ideological obstacle to narratives reviving the values of Dodd, Algren, or indeed Elizabeth Spencer's correspondents was the New Left itself. The Port Huron Statement and the early SDS, and indeed much sixties activism, operated in the shadow of late-fifties ideologies that had exorcised some key values of earlier progressives. Tom Hayden still says with some pride, "We studied the lyrics of Bob Dylan more than we did the texts of Marx and Lenin . . . the early movement was able to guarantee its roots in American culture and traditions while avoiding the imported ideologies that infected many elements of the earlier left" (7, 9).[3] Hayden characterizes what the 1962 student rebels saw themselves as opposing: "We were rebelling against the experience of apathy, not against a single specific oppression. . . . Apathy, we came to suspect, was what the administrators and power technicians actually desired. Apathy was not our fault, not an accident, but rather the result of social engineering by those who ran the institutions. . . . The experience of middle-class alienation drew us to Mills's *White Collar*, Albert Camus's *The Stranger*, or Paul Goodman's *Growing Up Absurd*" (4, 8). In short, the student left saw their opponent in terms laid out by fifties social critics such as Mills, Riesman, the Vonnegut of *Player Piano*, and William "Organization Man" Whyte—not advanced capitalism or imperial ambition, but regimentation, bureaucratic management, and postindustrial depersonalization, akin to Ken Kesey's "Combine."

What the student left initially saw itself as fighting *for* is even more telling. Hayden explains, "We chose to put 'values' forward as the first priority in challenging the conditions of apathy and forging a new politics. Embracing values meant making choices as morally autonomous human beings. . . . Henry David Thoreau called on Americans to vote 'not with a strip of paper, but *with your whole life*.' . . . We believed, based on our own experience, that participation in direct action was a method of psychic empowerment, a fulfillment of human potential, a means of curing alienation . . ." (5, 6, 7). What Hayden here describes, and what other mid-sixties icons advocated, is close to what Marianne DeKoven styles "Politics of the Self" and overlaps the form of resistance that scholar James J. Farrell praises using the theological term, "Personalism." It assumed moral autonomy and normalized middle-class experience in order to argue for a kind of self-realization, a mode of activism that is good for the individual psyche. DeKoven explains, "The emphasis . . . for Hayden is clearly on the self—on changing history through personal, risk-taking involvement and direct action, rather than on communally instituting new social and political structures that would create a more democratic society. The personal meaningfulness derived from political activism seems at least as important to Hayden as the social and political change that are activism's goals" (124). Historians have faulted the New Left program for having ignored organizational strategies that the Old Left might have taught (Isserman 1987 219, 244); but there is a deeper ideological fault here. Listening to "Chimes of Freedom" and "Masters of War" in lieu of reading *The German Ideology* and "Left Communism: An Infantile Disorder," or the thirties classics of Lewis Corey and Kenneth Burke,[4] the student left came to believe in a Romantic ethos of the lone man against "the System,"[5] of millenarian acts of conscience (culminating in the Days of Rage and the Weather Underground), in short, in *voluntarism*—what the great Marxist scholar/activist H. Bruce Franklin has styled "the bourgeois myth of free will" (48 *passim*).

The voluntarist ethos saw no contradiction in making heroes of the conservative Democrat Kesey or the Republican bigots Kerouac and Heinlein, inasmuch as all three celebrated "the morally autonomous self" in the form of the unfettered male ego as a source of authenticity in the face of the crushing and apathetic System. Vonnegut's and Dick's personalism, based upon a more pessimistic view of human agency and social change, constitute bright spots in the early sixties. Although they may not have been aware of Dodd's *Sowing the Wind*, they probably had encountered antifascist thrillers by the likes of Stan Ellin and Dorothy Belle Hughes; and their 1962 novels address the possibility of ethical resistance in the face of Nazism, deforming the antifascist novel of earlier years into a tale of individual conscience and bureaucratic oppression that the sixties could understand. *The Man in the High Castle* has no Kerouacian free spirits among its heroes: its climax occurs when a timid, hidebound Japanese bureaucrat finds the wherewithal to use strong language, holding a Nazi official responsible for the crimes of his party:

> The consul said, "You're holding me responsible for general conditions beyond my jurisdiction."
>
> "Chicken shit," Mr. Tagomi said. "I say that to that." (239)

But the synecdochic work for the New Left, as Sean McCann and Mike Szalay have observed, is Pynchon's least favorite of his books, 1967's *The Crying of Lot 49*. Here a thoroughly middle-class consumerist Young Republican goes on an unresolved odyssey with apocalyptic foreshadowings, wherein she is moved by student activism of the Left and Right, discontent among America's mental laborers, and the discovery of urban poverty. Hayden, Mills, and Harrington become the new trinity for the salvation of the sixties soul.

Fortuitously, 1967 and the subsequent two years saw four dramatic changes in Left culture and ideals that boded well for literary and critical thought: black liberationists sought various new directions, women and gays struck out with their own movements, the poststructuralist revolution erupted in the elite academy, and a new generation of artists, often mentored by Old Left figures, came of age. What the poststructuralists rediscovered, and what the new identity movements that were to incorporate their insights in later decades already began to enact, was the rejection of liberal universalism. Kazin and Trilling in the previous decade had smugly asserted that they stood "outside ideology," something Burke and Dewey would have assured them was impossible: now admirers of Foucault, Deleuze, and Derrida were reasserting that impossibility, while women and minorities were pointing out how universalism had consistently been used as a tool of exclusion. The war and the environmental movement had illuminated what DeKoven styles a postmodern critique of modernist aspirations: "Reason and science become in their turn a force of domination, when allied with modernity's dominant bourgeois capitalist class [in opposition to] this Other [who] encompasses body, psyche, nature, and materiality, which are in turn allied with modernity's others of race, gender, class, sexuality, and geographic location" (13). On the individual level, oppressed groups found that it was possible to enact other agendas than strategic outreach to benevolent patrons from the dominant class. Showing more and more resistance to demands that they live up to the standards of an imagined able-bodied, empowered, straight white audience who could aid in the liberation struggle, members of liberatory movements reclaimed the position that Richard Wright had described in his reminiscence of the thirties: "Out of the magazines I read came a passionate call for the experiences of the disinherited, and there were none of the same lispings of the missionary in it. It did not say, 'Be like us and we will like you, maybe.' It said: 'If you possess enough courage to speak out what you are, you will find that you are not alone'" (Denning 1997 61).

The diversification of radical voices that appeared in narrative arts of the late sixties and early seventies often engaged directly with those who, like Wright, had responded to the "passionate call" of an earlier radicalism. When women in Left organizations decided no longer to work alongside the Randle Patrick McMurphy worshippers who adhered to the old American dogma that Women Are Society, the Valentine Michael Smith aspirants who sought a Heinleinesque bevy of handmaidens at their service, or the Majors Bennett Marco who saw the female population as providing a combination of both Evil Authoritarians and Gentle Subordinates, they found an earlier generation of female artists eager to take their part.[6] Tillie Olsen most famously became an iconic theorist and artist for feminists, while two of Muriel Rukeyser's pupils, Alice Walker and Marge Piercy, gained prominence as novelists of female activism and community (Walker had first been celebrated by another Old Left giant, Langston Hughes, for her short fiction). Other novelists refunctioned contemporary narrative modes to articulate alternative or oppositional views. Attitudes that closely paralleled Philip Dick's paranoid (and increasingly misogynist) terror of postindustrial depersonalization were articulated by Diane Johnson as paranoid terror of patriarchal norms. Ursula Le Guin and Kate Wilhelm, although neither would define herself as a feminist until the late seventies,[7] wrote science-fictional denunciations of the military-industrial complex that indicted the standards of Cold War masculinity. Toni Morrison tried to create a new set of myths that located moral and social agency in African American women; Ishmael Reed, seeking to build upon the legacy of Chester Himes, wrote ruthless carnivalesque satires starring black schlemiels and confidence-men. Of course, minority authors seeking to speak on their own behalf accepted the assistance of straight white patrons, of which there was no shortage. N. Scott Momaday saw his early work published in the New Left journal *Ramparts*; a few years later, Samuel Delany's magnum opus, *Dhalgren*, was brought out by ex-Communist Frederik Pohl in the middle of the 1970s.[8]

By the seventies, enough barriers had fallen that artists with Old Left connections and those building upon Cultural Front genres possessed a new prominence in many media. In rock music, John Hammond signed the Woody Guthrie-worshipping Bruce Springsteen to Columbia Records; and Delmore Schwartz protégé Lou Reed became a star as he embarked upon a solo career. Novels by Nathanael West, Chester Himes, Horace McCoy, and Jim Thompson made it into the movies, and Red Scare survivors such as Waldo Salt, Martin Ritt, and Albert Maltz did some of their best cinematic work. The renewed respectability of Cultural Front stories also facilitated the new visibility of heirs to thirties literary modes: the Dos Passos-influenced William Gaddis and the "ghetto pastoral" author Paule Marshall, whose works in those genres had been overlooked when they appeared in the fifties, finally gained some recognition as they continued to produce innovative art in the seventies. Mary Gordon, William Kennedy, Toni Cade Bambara, and John Sayles were part of new generations of authors dealing in working-class themes.[9]

By the end of the seventies and the beginning of the eighties, as the age of American prosperity gave way to economic decline, sixties authors, like their predecessors thirty years earlier, were generating deformations of older progressive traditions for a new era. Kurt Vonnegut's fiction started to invoke 1920s progressive heroes such as Sacco and Debs, and Russell Banks tried his hand at proletarian novels; both invoked Nelson Algren as a precursor to their brand of protest literature. But far earlier, it seems, even the personalist heroes of the mid-sixties could serve as bridges for readers to the progressive works of earlier and later eras: there are readers who "graduated" from Kerouac to Guthrie, from Lawrence Block to Jim Thompson, from Richard Matheson to Shirley Jackson. In each case, the less politically engaged author can be seen as an "effect" by which a more radical author changed the "conditions of reception" for his or her work, or for work sharing some of his or her values, as in Pierre Bourdieu's account: "[W]riters' efforts to control the reception of their own works are always partially doomed to failure . . . if only because the very effect of their work must transform the conditions of reception and because they would not have had to write many things they did write and write them as they did . . . if they had been granted from the outset what they are granted retrospectively" (31).

The fact that *Invisible Suburbs* and other revisionist works on the fifties are appearing many years after these social changes is an indication of how slowly the conditions of reception change in some fields. The values I have associated with the student left and the mid-sixties were something of an anomaly in the history of protest movements, but demographics of the academic and journalistic public spheres seem to have contributed to a mistaken conviction that those values were the norm, as a result of which perceptions of earlier decades suffered from a certain inertia and temporal chauvinism. As Richard Wright's statement indicates, and as this volume has shown, the social innovations of the late sixties, in which voices that Haywire Mac had much earlier ridiculed as "these pressure groups" spoke up for themselves and for their group identities, were manifestations of a very longstanding phenomenon. Michael Denning, drawing connections between the thirties and the nineties, explains that "The concepts that produce a people . . . and the national and imperial discourse that underlie these fantasies of racial and ethnic identity inform much of contemporary cultural studies. This concern for what they called 'the racial-cultural situation' was also at the center of Popular Front social and cultural theory. . . . In part . . . it was overshadowed by the explosion of studies of the national culture and 'character' of the United States" (*Cultural Front* 445). During and after World War II, Denning explains, Henry Luce and the Cultural Cold Warriors refunctioned this "discourse of national character" into a repressive force; only when the war in Vietnam had put paid to celebrations of Americanism did progressives recover the multicultural approach. But some on the New Left were mystified by the movements of the late sixties, unable to think beyond fifties liberal politics of integration, and in effect saying "We offered those people a chance to be just like us, and they weren't satisfied—they must be chauvinists/essentialists/factionalists/fifth columnists."

And still those who try to carry on the legacy of Himes, Dodd, Bannon, and even Algren (whose universalism rarely went beyond the axiom that "Nobody deserves to live this way," and whose insights into the specific stigmas faced by women Ian Peddie has touched upon) are often challenged on the Left as special-interest groups. Liberal universalists style such authors' focus "merely cultural," asserting that "the racism/sexism/homophobia crowd . . . appear to be losers. Class-based leftists have the New Deal . . . where is the analogous model of successful coalition-building and progressive legislation for would-be identity politicians?"[10] As in the Second World War, the disenfranchised in America are supposed to stop whining and join together to fight the greater crisis.

Why the Left should jettison those values with which it has been most successful at raising consciousness is rarely explained: at a time when polls suggest that the majority of Americans are more tolerant than ever of interracial relationships, working mothers, and homosexuality, disavowing the racism/sexism/homophobia crowd in favor of an ascetic politics of economic equality seems counterintuitive, as well as practically unsound: if by some miraculous social reorganization America's economic inequalities could be mitigated by Wednesday, racism and sexism, as they always have, would be used to reinstitute them by Friday. Many astute scholars and activists have built important critiques of specific antiracist, feminist, homophile, or antiableist strategies, often resting upon the failure of those strategies to incorporate useful Marxist insights.

But the conviction on the part of some New Left relics and avatars that "identity politics," broadly construed, are a novel distraction from the great tradition of class struggle is, as Ellen Willis has shown, a travesty of history. *Invisible Suburbs* seeks to recover some specifics of that history from the memory hole into which Cold War ideologies consigned them. It is a great accomplishment of Harry Thomas, Kathlene McDonald, Ian Peddie, and Ladislava Khailova to have demonstrated that even in the repressive fifties, authors knew that oppression on the basis of class, race, gender, and disability were inextricably connected in practice; similarly, Jennifer Worley and Stephanie Brown have offered indispensable reminders that the assertion of group identity, the claim of the subordinated to contest obliteration by the dominant discourse, was alive even in the second decade of Luce's "American Century." The ability of authors and readers in the fifties to maintain and invent such insights and assertions in an oppressive age, eventually to find that the conditions for their reception improved in later decades, may stand as a sign of hope and encouragement amid the conflicts of the present day.

Notes

1. Those novels which succeed at creating a subculture or interpellating a group—*Waiting to Exhale, The Turner Diaries, Left Behind, Harry Potter*—are often of limited artistic worth by the standards of scholars trained in evaluative criticism. Fortunately, the new generation of historicist critics, while interested in first-rate writing and able to discriminate aesthetically, shows great patience with flat prose: Andrew Hoberek on Ayn Rand and Walter Benn Michaels on Orson Scott Card are exemplary.

2. A telling indication of what kind of thirties culture was acceptable in the mid-sixties is the swift canonization of James Agee, who had despised Paul Robeson and ridiculed the idea that *Birth of a Nation* was a racist movie.

3. This perception is ironic in light of both the range of American traditions that the SDS remained ignorant of and the actual influence of foreign ideas, such as those of Herbert Marcuse. The organization was given its name by French immigrant André Schiffrin, who as a publisher introduced Americans to R. D. Laing, Jan Myrdal, and Michel Foucault. See Schiffrin's account of his attempts to offer readers a cosmopolitan Left catalog and to revive blacklisted thinkers in his *A Political Education*.

4. Actually, Old Left origins did not immunize authors against the personalist approach, as witness the sixties antics of Allen Ginsberg and Norman Mailer.

5. The term was originated in 1966 and is distinctive for its vagueness: see McCann/Szalay.

6. The characters mentioned are protagonists of *One Flew Over the Cuckoo's Nest, Stranger in a Strange Land*, and *The Manchurian Candidate*, respectively. The last-mentioned novel was a product of the fifties but became a very influential movie in 1962.

7. Suzy McKee Charnas and Joanna Russ grasped feminism much earlier, and began writing powerful science fiction in that mode close to 1970.

8. Delany's early life was a perfect storm of residual and emergent Left influences: he attended socialist summer camps in the forties and fifties (Kinderland and Woodland), had contact as a child with Pete Seeger and Alger Hiss, attended elementary school with future radical playwrights Wallace Shawn and Ariel Dorfman, and knew future activists

Stokely Carmichael and Todd Gitlin at the Bronx High School of Science. His uncles included radical sociologist E. Franklin Frazier and blacklisted judge Hubert Delany; his maternal grandfather was an associate of labor leader Asa Philip Randolph: see my "About Samuel Delany." Few if any other people with such backgrounds seem to have become novelists.

9. Thanks to the voluntarist tradition, the thirties movement that took longest to resurge was the disability-rights movement; hence recognition of fiction that advances its ideals has only just begun. Seventies authors interested in the struggles of people with disabilities and dysmorphisms include Stanley Elkin (himself disabled), Rosellen Brown, John Irving, and Toni Morrison.

10. Quotes from Butler 33, Willis xiii. Willis was quoting Eric Alterman; Butler sought to leave her opponents anonymous. Perhaps the most dramatic articulation of the universalist stance, in the sense in which I am using the term, came from media critic Mark Crispin Miller in the middle of a credible critique of obscure academic language and its revolutionary pretentions: "More fundamentally, the whole 'progressive' vision that has long preoccupied the universities is itself profoundly non- or even anti-leftist. . . . For any group that fixates on the grievances of three or four selected blocs of 'powerless' types, 'the people' finally don't exist at all; and without them—a mass of disparate groups, united in (I blush to say it) a genuine and altruistic solidarity—no progressive change is possible. . . . Gender and ethnicity per se don't fill the bill. Far from permitting an authentic leftist politics, those purely physical categories, with their defining pigmentational and/or hormonal traces, smack more of Hitler's worldview than of Marx's" (Miller, *Class Dismissed*). That "authentic" and "altruistic" smack more of the sixties than of Marx.

Works Cited

Aaron, Daniel. *Writers on the Left: Episodes in American Literary Communism.* New York: Columbia University Press, 1992.

Aldridge, Jack. "As to Academic Freedom." Rev. of *The Searching Light,* by Martha Dodd. *St. Louis Post-Dispatch* 31 Mar. 1955. Press Clippings File 12.6. Dodd Papers.

Aldridge, John. *After the Lost Generation: A Critical Study of the Writers of Two Wars.* New York: McGraw-Hill, 1951.

Algren, Nelson. *Chicago: City on the Make.* 1952. Chicago: University of Chicago Press, 1983.

——. "Eggheads Are Rolling: The Rush to Conform." *The Nation* 177 October 17 (1953): 306–7).

——. "If You Must Use Profanity." *American Mercury* 31 (April 1934), 430–36.

——. *The Man with the Golden Arm.* 1949. New York: Four Walls Eight Windows, 1990.

——. The Neon Wilderness. New York: Hill and Wang, 1960.

——. *Nonconformity: Writing on Writing.* New York: Seven Stories Press, 1998.

——. "The Role of the Writer in America." *Michigan Voices* 2 (Spring 1962): 3–26.

——. "Spoon-fed Universe." Rev. of *The Golden Spike,* by Hal Ellson. *Saturday Review* 33 (1952): 35.

——. *A Walk on the Wild Side.* 1956. New York: Noonday Press, 1989.

Anderson, Benedict. *Imagined Communities: Reflections on the Origin and Spread of Nationalism.* London: Verso, 1984.

Anderson, Hilton. "Elizabeth Spencer's Two Italian Novellas." *Notes on Mississippi Writers* 13.1 (1981): 18–35.

Andrews, William, and Henry Louis Gates Jr. *The Civitas Anthology of African American Slave Narratives.* Washington, D.C.: Civitas/Counterpoint, 1999.

Aristotle. *Generation of Animals.* Cambridge: Harvard University Press, 1944.

Bak, John S. "'sneakin' and spyin" from Broadway to the Beltway: Cold War Masculinity, Brick, and Homosexual Existentialism." *Theatre Journal* 56 (2004): 225–49.

Baldwin, James. "Everybody's Protest Novel." 1949. *Baldwin: Collected Essays.* New York: Library of America, 1998.

Banks, Russell. "Foreword." *A Walk on the Wild Side,* by Nelson Algren. New York: Noonday Press, 1989. vii-xi.

Bannon, Ann. *Beebo Brinker.* New York: Gold Medal, 1962. In *The Beebo Brinker Chronicles.* New York: Quality Paperback Book Club, 1995.

——. "Foreword." *Strange Sisters.* New York: Viking Studio, 1999. Pp. 9–19.

——. *I Am a Woman.* In *The Beebo Brinker Chronicles.* Rpt. of *I Am a Woman in Love With a Woman. Must Society Reject Me?* New York: Gold Medal-Fawcett, 1959.

——. *Journey to a Woman.* New York: Gold Medal-Fawcett, 1960. Tallahassee: Naiad Press, 1986.

——. *Odd Girl Out.* New York: Gold Medal-Fawcett, 1957. Tallahassee: Naiad Press, 1986.

——. *Women in the Shadows*. New York: Gold Medal-Fawcett, 1959. In *The Beebo Brinker Chronicles*.
Baxandall, Rosalyn. "The Question Seldom Asked: Women and the CPUSA." *New Studies in the Politics and Culture of U.S. Communism*. Ed. Michael Brown, et al. New York: Monthly Review Press, 1993. 141–61.
——. *Words on Fire: The Life and Writing of Elizabeth Gurley Flynn*. New Brunswick: Rutgers University Press, 1987.
Beirne-Smith, Mary, Richard F. Ittenbach, and James R. Patton. *Mental Retardation*. 5th ed. Upper Saddle River, NJ: Merrill, 1998.
Bellow, Saul. "Man Underground." *Commentary* (January 1952): 608–10.
Benjamin, Jessica. *The Bonds of Love: Psychoanalysis, Feminism, and the Problem of Domination*. New York: Pantheon, 1988.
Bennett, James R. "Questioning the Supreme Obsession: Novels about Anti-communism in the United States Since World War II." *Works and Days* 20 (Fall 1992): 89–118.
Bentley, Elizabeth. *Out of Bondage*. New York: Devin-Adair, 1951.
Bergman, David. *The Violet Hour: The Violet Quill and the Making of Gay Culture*. New York: Columbia University Press, 2004.
Bergson, Henri. "Laughter." 1900. Reprinted in *Comedy*, ed. Wylie Sypher. Baltimore: The Johns Hopkins University Press, 1956.
Berlant, Lauren and Elizabeth Freeman. "Queer Nationality." *Fear of a Queer Planet: Queer Politics and Social Theory*. Ed. Michael Warner. Minneapolis: University of Minnesota Press, 1993. 193–229.
Bersani, Leo. *Homos*. Cambridge, MA: Harvard University Press, 1995.
Bibler, Michael P. "'A Tenderness which was Uncommon': Homosexuality, Narrative, and the Southern Plantation in Tennessee Williams's *Cat on a Hot Tin Roof*." *The Mississippi Quarterly* 55 (2002): 381–400.
Bourdieu, Pierre. "The Field of Cultural Production, or: The Economic World Reversed." 1983. *The Field of Cultural Production*. New York: Columbia UP, 1993: 29–73.
Breines, Wini. *Young, White, and Miserable: Growing Up Female in the Fifties*. Boston: Beacon Press, 1992.
Broadwell, Elizabeth P. and Ronald W. Hoag. "A Conversation with Elizabeth Spencer." *Southern Review* 18.1 (Winter 1982): 111–30.
Bronski, Michael. *Pulp Friction*. New York: St. Martin's Press, 2003.
Broughton, Irv. "Elizabeth Spencer." *The Writer's Mind: Interviews with American Authors, Volume II*. Ed. Irv Broughton. Fayetteville: University of Arkansas Press, 1990. 97–125.
Brysac, Shareen Blair. *Resisting Hitler: Mildred Harnack and the Red Orchestra*. New York: Oxford University Press, 2000.
Budenz, Louis. *This Is My Story*. New York: McGraw Hill, 1947.
Buhle, Mari Jo. *Women and the American Left: A Guide to Sources*. Boston: G.K. Hall, 1983.
Buhle, Mari Jo, Paul Buhle, and Dan Georakas, eds. *Encyclopedia of the American Left*. Urbana: University of Illinois Press, 1992.
Bunting, Charles T. "'In That Time and at That Place': The Literary World of Elizabeth Spencer." *Mississippi Quarterly* 28.4 (1975): 435–60.
Butler, Judith. "Imitation and Gender Insubordination." *The Second Wave*. Linda Nicholson, ed. New York and London: Routledge, 1997.

——. "Merely Cultural." *New Left Review* I/227 (1998). 33–44.

Campbell, Joseph. *The Hero with a Thousand Faces*. New York, Pantheon Books, 1949.

Carlson, Licia. "Cognitive Ableism and Disability Studies: Feminist Reflections on the History of Mental Retardation." *Hypatia* 16.4 (2001): 124–46.

Carter, Paul A. *Another Part of the Fifties*. New York: Columbia University Press, 1983.

Case, Sue-Ellen. "Toward a Butch-Femme Aesthetic." *The Lesbian and Gay Studies Reader*. Ed. Henry Abelove, Michèle Aina Barale, David Halperin. London: Routledge, 1993.

Caserio, Robert L. "Queer Passions, Queer Citizenship: Some Novels about the State of the American Nation 1946–1954." *Modern Fiction Studies*. 43.1: 170–205.

Cash, W. J. *The Mind of the South*. 1941. New York: Vintage, 1991.

Chasin, Alexandra. *Selling Out*. New York: St. Martins Press, 2000

Chauncey, George. *Gay New York: Gender, Urban Culture, and the Making of the Gay Male World, 1890–1940*. New York: Basic Books, 1994.

Cheung, Floyd, and Keith Lawrence, eds. *Recovered Legacies: Authority and Identity in Early Asian American Literature*. Philadelphia: Temple University Press, 2005.

Christian, Paula. *Amanda*. New York: Belmont, 1965.

Citron, Alice. "Searching Light on a University." Rev. of *The Searching Light*, by Martha Dodd. *National Guardian* 2 May 1955. Press Clippings File 12.6. Dodd Papers.

Cochran, David. *America Noir: Underground Writers and Filmmakers of the Postwar Era*. Washington, DC: Smithsonian Institution Press, 2000.

Coiner, Constance. *Better Red: The Writing and Resistance of Tillie Olsen and Meridel Le Sueur*. 1995. Urbana: University of Illinois Press, 1998.

Coleman Means, Robin R. *African-American Viewers and the Black Situation Comedy*. New York: Garland, 1998.

Coontz, Stephanie. *The Way We Never Were: American Families and the Nostalgia Trap*. New York: BasicBooks, 1992.

Corber, Robert J. *Homosexuality in Cold War America: Resistance and the Crisis of Masculinity*. Durham: Duke University Press, 1997.

——. *In the Name of National Security: Hitchcock, Homophobia, and the Political Construction of Gender in Postwar America*. Durham: Duke University Press, 1993.

Crane, Sylvia. Comments at Memorial Service for Alfred Stern. 19 Nov. 1986. Ts. 4.3. Dodd Papers.

Creet, Julia. "*Voyage from Lesbos:* Aggression, Ambivalence, and Psychoanalysis in the Fifties." *Fifties Fictions* (ed. Josh Lukin and Samuel R. Delany). *Paradoxa*, No. 18 (2003): 251–78.

Crossman, Richard, et al. *The God That Failed*. New York: Harper Bros, 1949.

Cuordileone, K.A. *Manhood and American Political Culture in the Cold War*. London: Routledge, 2005.

Davis, Chandler. "Critique and Proposals-1949." Reprinted on Ray Davis, ed. *Pseudopodium: Repress*, http://www.pseudopodium.org/repress/chandler-davis/critique-1949.html.

——. ". . . From an Exile." 1960. Reprinted on Ray Davis, ed. *Pseudopodium. Repress*, http://www.pseudopodium.org/repress/chandler-davis/FromAnExile.html

——. "It Walks in Beauty." 1958. Scifiction.com, Posted Sept., 2003.

Davis, Chandler, with Josh Lukin. "Trying to Say Something True: *Paradoxa* Interview with Chandler Davis." Lukin/Delany, "*Fifties Fictions*": 49–80.

Davis, Lennard J. *Enforcing Normalcy: Disability, Deafness, and the Body*. London: Verso, 1995.

Dean, Robert D. *Imperial Brotherhood: Gender and the Making of Cold War Foreign Policy.* Amherst, MA: University of Massachusetts Press, 2001.
Dearborn, Mary V. *Mailer: A Biography.* Boston: Houghton Mifflin, 1999.
DeKoven, Marianne. *Utopia Limited: The Sixties and the Emergence of the Postmodern.* Durham, NC: Duke University Press, 2004.
Delany, Samuel. "More and Less Than Human: Allegories of Human Impediment in the Tales of Theodore Sturgeon." 2006 MLA Convention. Grand Ballroom Salon I, Philadelphia Marriott, Philadelphia. 27 Dec. 2006.
——. "Velocities of Change." In Lukin/Delany, *Fifties Fictions*: 279–312.
Deleuze, Gilles. *Cinema-2: The Time-Image.* 1985. Trans. Hugh Tomlinson and Robert Galeta. Minneapolis: University of Minnesota Press, 1989.
D'Emillio, John. "Capitalism and Gay Identity." *The Lesbian and Gay Studies Reader.* Ed. Henry Abelove, Michéle Aina Barale and David M. Halperin. London: Routledge, 1993.
——. *Sexual Politics, Sexual Communities: The Making of A Homosexual Minority in the United States, 1940–1970.* Chicago: University of Chicago Press, 1983.
D'Emilio, John, and Estelle B. Freedman. *Intimate Matters: A History of Sexuality in America.* 1988. 2nd Ed. Chicago: U of Chicago P, 1997.
DeMott, Benjamin. *The Imperial Middle: Why Americans Can't Think Straight About Class.* New York: William Morrow and Company, 1990.
Denning, Michael. *The Cultural Front: The Laboring of American Culture in the Twentieth Century.* London: Verso, 1997.
——. *Mechanic Accents: Dime Novels and Working Class Culture in America.* London: Verso, 1987.
Derrida, Jacques. "Structure, Sign, and Play in the Discourse of the Human Sciences." 1966. Richard Macksey and Eugenio Donato, Eds. *The Structuralist Controversy: The Languages of Criticism and the Sciences of Man.* 1970. Baltimore: The Johns Hopkins University Press, 1972.
Dick, Philip K. *The Man in the High Castle.* 1962. New York: Vintage, 1990.
Dickstein, Morris. *Gates of Eden: American Culture in the Sixties.* 1977. Cambridge, MA: Harvard University Press, 1997.
——. *Leopards in the Temple: The Transformation of American Fiction 1945–1970.* Cambridge, MA: Harvard University Press, 2002.
Dodd, Bella. *School of Darkness.* New York: P.J. Kenedy & Sons, 1954.
Dodd, Martha. Biographical Note for *The Searching Light.* Ms. 12.7. Dodd Papers.
——. "Biography of William Dodd, Sr." Ms. 2.13. Dodd Papers.
——. "Daughter of Earth." Ms. 10.24. Dodd Papers.
——. "Hoyerswerda: Socialist New Town." *World News* 27 Feb. 1960: 107–12.
——. "Imprison a Flame?" Ms. 11.3. Dodd Papers.
——. Letter to Charles Humboldt. 30 April 1959. Correspondence File 12.18. Dodd Papers.
——. Letter to David Klopfer. 27 Apr. 1981. Correspondence File 6.2. Dodd Papers.
——. Letter to D. N. Pritt. 20 June 1959. Correspondence File 8.10. Dodd Papers.
——. Letter to Italian Publisher of *The Searching Light.* 12 July 1955. Correspondence File 12.2. Dodd Papers.
——. "Maria." *Masses and Mainstream* 3.10 (1950): 19–25.
——. Martha Eccles Dodd Papers. Library of Congress, Washington, DC.
——. "Paul Robeson." *Mainstream* 16.5 (1963): 53–56.
——. "Poet's Wife." Ms. 14.18. Dodd Papers.

———. Postscript to Czech Edition of *The Searching Light*. Ms. 12.7. Dodd Papers.
———. Postscript to German Edition of *Sowing the Wind*. Ms. 12.11. Dodd Papers.
———. Press clippings File. 2.15. Dodd Papers.
———. "Prisoner #4678860." Ms. 11.3. Dodd Papers.
———. "Reflections on a Novel." Ms. 12.11. Dodd Papers.
———. *The Searching Light*. New York: Citadel, 1955.
———. *Sowing The Wind*. New York: Harcourt, 1945.
———. *Through Embassy Eyes*. New York: Harcourt, 1939.
———. "To Those Who Sit in Darkness." Ms. 11.31. Dodd Papers.
———. "The Twain Have Met." Ms. 11.32. Dodd Papers.
———. "Waiting at Poprad, CSSR." Ms. 11.37. Dodd Papers.
———. "World Without Weapons." Ms. 11.41. Dodd Papers.
Dodd, Martha and Alfred K. Stern. Press Release. Prague, Czechoslovakia. 6 Sept. 1957. Ms. 13.4. Dodd Papers.
Donohue, H.E.F. *Conversations with Nelson Algren*. New York: Hill and Wang, 1963.
Douglas, Ann. "Periodizing the American Century: Modernism, Postmodernism, and Postcolonialism in the Cold War Context." *Modernism/Modernity* 5.3 (1998): 71–98.
Drew, Bettina. *Nelson Algren: A Life on the Wild Side*. New York: G. P. Putnam's Sons, 1989.
Du Bois, W. E. B. Letter to Martha Dodd. 18 Apr. 1955. Correspondence File. Dodd Papers.
Duchamp, L. Timmel. "Old Pictures: The Discursive Instability of Feminist SF." *Extrapolation* 45 (2004): 15–33.
Duggan, Lisa. *The Twilight of Equality?: Neoliberalism, Cultural Politics, and the Attack on Democracy*. Boston: Beacon Press, 2004.
DuPlessis, Rachel Blau. *Writing Beyond the Ending: Narrative Strategies of Twentieth-Century Women Writers*. Bloomington: Indiana University Press, 1985.
Ehrenreich, Barbara. *The Hearts of Men: American Dreams and the Flight from Commitment*. New York: Doubleday/Anchor, 1983.
Einstein, Albert. Letter to Martha Dodd. 6 July 1953. Correspondence File 12.5. Dodd Papers.
Elliott, Jane. "Time Changes: The Temporality of Politics and the Narration of 1960s Radicalism in America." PhD Dissertation. Rutgers U, 2004.
Ellis, Havelock. *Studies in the Psychology of Sex, Vol. II*. Philadelphia: F. A. Davis, 1901.
Epstein, Irene. "Women in the USSR." *Masses and Mainstream* 4.5 (1951): 92–94.
Fabre, Michel, and Robert Skinner, eds. *Conversations with Chester Himes*. Jackson, MS: University Press of Mississippi, 1995.
Faderman, Lilian. *Odd Girls and Twilight Lovers: A History of Lesbian Life in Twentieth-Century America*. New York: Penguin, 1992.
———. *Surpassing the Love of Men*. New York: William Morrow, 1981.
Farrell, James J. *The Spirit of the Sixties: The Making of Postwar Radicalism*. New York: Routledge, 1997.
Faulkner, William. *The Sound and the Fury*. 1929. New York: Vintage, 1990.
Favor, J. Martin. *Authentic Blackness: The Folk in the New Negro Renaissance*. Durham: Duke University Press, 1999.
Feuchtwanger, Lion. "Mirror of America." Rev. of *The Searching Light*, by Martha Dodd. *Nation* 9 July 1955. Press Clippings File 12.6. Dodd Papers.
Fiedler, Leslie. "The Noble Savages of Skid Row." *Reporter* 15 (July 1956): 43–44.

——. *No! In Thunder: Essays on Myth and Literature.* New York: Stein and Day, 1960.
Flynn, Elizabeth Gurley. "Hitler's 3 K's for Woman—An American Rehash." *Political Affairs* 26.4 (1947). Rpt. in Baxandall, *Words* 202–8.
——. "Life of the Party." *Daily Worker* 7 June 1948: 10.
——. *Woman's Place—in the Fight for a Better World.* New York: New Century, 1947.
Foley, Barbara. *Radical Representations: Politics and Form in U.S. Proletarian Fiction.* Durham: Duke University Press, 1993.
Forbidden Love: The Unashamed Stories of Lesbian Lives. Dir. Aerlyn Weissman and Lynne Ferme. National Film Board of Canada. 1992.
Ford, Nick Aaron. *The Contemporary Negro Novel: A Study in Race Relations.* 1936. Reprinted College Park MD: McGrath Publishing, 1968.
Foreman, Joel, ed. *The Other Fifties: Interrogating Midcentury American Icons.* Urbana: University of Illinois Press, 1997.
Foster, William Z. "On Improving Our Party's Work Among Women." *Political Affairs* 27.11 (1948): 984–90.
Foucault, Michel. *Madness and Civilization: A History of Insanity in the Age of Reason.* 1965. New York: Vintage, 1973.
——. *The History of Sexuality, Volume I.* 1978. Trans. Robert Hurley. New York: Vintage, 1990. Trans. of *La Volenté de savoir*, 1976.
Franklin, H. Bruce. *Robert A. Heinlein: America as Science Fiction.* New York: Oxford University Press, 1980.
Freedman, William. "From Bernard Malamud, with Discipline and Love." Warren French, ed. *The Fifties: Fiction, Poetry, Drama.* Deland, FL: Everett/Edwards Inc., 1970.
Friedan, Betty. *The Feminine Mystique.* 1963. New York: Bantam, 1983.
Fuller, Edmund. *Man in Modern Fiction.* New York: Random House, 1958.
Garland-Thomson, Rosemarie. *Extraordinary Bodies: Figuring Physical Disability in American Culture and Literature.* New York: Columbia University Press, 1997.
Geismar, Maxwell. "Against the Tide of Euphoria." *Nation* 182 (1956): 473.
Gilbert, James. *Men in the Middle: Searching for Masculinity in the 1950s.* Chicago: University of Chicago Press, 2005.
Giles, James. *Confronting the Horror: The Novels of Nelson Algren.* Kent OH: Kent State University Press, 1989.
Girard, Anne-Marie. "Elizabeth Spencer b. 1921." *Journal of the Short Story in English* 41 (2003): 325–44.
Giroux, Henry A. "Memory and Pedagogy in 'The Wonderful World of Disney': Beyond the Politics of Innocence." Bell et alia, *From Mouse to Mermaid.* 43–61.
Gitlin, Todd. *The Sixties: Years of Hope, Days of Rage.* New York: Bantam, 1987.
——. *The Twilight of Common Dreams: Why America Is Wracked by Culture Wars.* New York: Henry Holt, 1995.
Gloster, Hugh M. *Negro Voices in American Fiction.* Chapel Hill: University of North Carolina Press, 1948.
Gold, Michael. "A Word as to Uncle Tom." *Negro: An Anthology.* Ed. Nancy Cunard. London: Negro Universities Press, 1934. 136.
Goodin, George. *The Poetics of Protest: Literary Form and Political Implication in the Victim-of-Society Novel.* Carbondale, IL: Southern Illinois University Press, 1985.
Goodman, Paul. *Parents'Day.* 1951. Santa Barbara: Black Sparrow Press, 1985.
Grotjahn, Martin. *Beyond Laughter: Humor and the Subconscious.* New York: Blakiston Division, 1957.

Halberstam, Judith. *In a Queer Time and Place*. New York and London: New York University Press, 2005.
Haley, Josephine. "An Interview with Elizabeth Spencer." *Notes on Mississippi Writers* 1 (1968): 42–55.
Hall, Radclyffe. *The Well of Loneliness*. 1928. New York: Doubleday, 1990.
Halsey, Margaret. *Color Blind: The White Woman Looks at the Negro*. New York: Simon and Schuster, 1946.
Hardwick, Elizabeth. *A View of My Own: Essays in Literature and Society*. New York: Farrar, Strauss and Cudahy, 1962.
Hamer, Diane. "'I Am a Woman': Ann Bannon and the Writing of Lesbian Identity in the 1950s." *Lesbian and Gay Writing*. Ed. Mark Lilly. Philadelphia: Temple University Press, 1990.
Harrington, Michael. *The Other America: Poverty in the United States*. New York: Macmillan, 1963.
Harvey, Brett. *The Fifties: A Women's Oral History*. New York: HarperCollins, 1993.
Hastings, March. *Three Women*. New York: Universal, 1958. New York: Quality Paperbacks by arrangement with Naiad Press, 2000.
Hayden, Tom. "The Way We Were and the Future of the *Port Huron Statement*." *The Port Huron Statement: The Visionary Call of the 1960s Revolution*. New York: Thunder's Mouth Press, 2005. 1–42.
Haynes, John Earl and Harvey Klehr. *Venona: Decoding Soviet Espionage in America*. New Haven: Yale University Press, 1999.
Hellman, Lillian. *Scoundrel Time*. Boston: Little, Brown, 1976.
Hesford, Victoria. "A Love Flung Out of Space: Lesbians in the City in Patricia Highsmith's *The Price of Salt*." *Paradoxa* 18: Fifties Fictions. Josh Lukin and Samuel L. Delany, ed. 118–35.
Hicks, Granville. *Where We Came Out*. New York: Viking, 1954.
Highsmith, Patricia. *The Price of Salt*. 1952. New York: Norton, 2004.
Hill, Rebecca. "Fosterites and Feminists, Or 1950s Ultra-Leftists and the Invention of AmeriKKKa," *New Left Review* 228 (1998): 67–90.
Himes, Chester. *The End of a Primitive*. 1956. New York: Allison and Busby, 1990.
——. *If He Hollers Let Him Go*. New York: Doubleday, 1945.
——. *The Quality of Hurt*. New York: Doubleday, 1972.
Hoberek, Andrew. "Cold War Culture to Fifties Culture." *the minnesota review* 55–57 (2002): 143–52.
——. *The Twilight of the Middle Class: Post-World War II American Fiction and White Collar Work*. Princeton: Princeton University Press, 2005.
Hoffman, Daniel. *Form and Fable in American Fiction*. 1961. New York: Oxford University Press, 1965.
Holzman, Michael. "Café CIA Roma: Mary McCarthy's Cold War." *Prospects: An Annual of American Cultural Studies* 25 (2000): 683–706.
hooks, bell. "Postmodern Blackness," *PMC* 1.1 (1990).
Horowitz, Daniel. *Betty Friedan and the Making of* The Feminine Mystique: *The American Left, The Cold War, and Modern Feminism*. Amherst: University of Massachusetts Press, 1998.
Howard, Gerald. "Pynchon from A to V." *Bookforum*, Summer 2005. http://www.bookforum.net/archive/sum_05/pynchon.html
Howard, John. Introduction. *The Bitterweed Path*. 1950. Chapel Hill, NC: University of North Carolina Press, 1996. v-xxi.

——. *Men Like That: A Southern Queer History*. Chicago: University of Chicago Press, 1999.

——. "The Talk of the County: Revisiting Accusation, Murder, and Mississippi, 1895." *Queer Studies: An Interdisciplinary Reader* Ed. Robert J. Corber and Stephen Valocchi. Malden, MA: Blackwell, 2003. 142–58.

Howe, Irving. *A Margin of Hope*. New York: Harcourt Brace Jovanovich, 1982.

Hughes, Carl Milton. *The Negro Novelist 1940–1950*. New York: Citadel Press, 1953.

Irigaray, Luce. *The Irigaray Reader*. Ed. Margaret Whitford. Cambridge, MA: Basil Blackwell, 1991.

Isserman, Maurice. *If I Had a Hammer . . . : The Death of the Old Left and the Birth of the New Left*. New York: Basic Books, 1987.

——. *Which Side Were You On?: The American Communist Party During the Second World War*. Middletown, CT: Wesleyan University Press, 1982.

Jablon, Madelyn. *Black Metafiction: Self-Consciousness in African-American Literature*. Iowa City: University of Iowa Press, 1997.

Jackson, Charles. *The Fall of Valor*. 1946. New York: Arbor House, 1986.

Janoff, Bruce J. "Black Humor, Existentialism and Absurdity: A Generic Confusion." *Black Humor: Critical Essays*. Ed. Alan R. Pratt. New York: Garland Publishing, 1993.

Jay, Gregory. *America the Scrivener: Deconstruction and the Subject of Literary History*. Ithaca, NY: Cornell University Press, 1990.

Jezer, Marty. *The Dark Ages: Life in the United States 1945-1960*. Boston: South End Press, 1982.

Johnson, David K. *The Lavender Scare: The Cold War Persecution of Gays and Lesbians in the Federal Government*. Chicago: The University of Chicago Press, 2004.

Jones, Anne Goodwyn. *Tomorrow Is Another Day: The Woman Writer in the South, 1859–1936*. Baton Rouge: Louisiana State University Press, 1981.

Jones, Anne Goodwyn, and Susan V. Donaldson, eds. *Haunted Bodies: Gender and Southern Texts*. Charlottesville, VA: University Press of Virginia, 1997.

Jordan, Glenn. "Can the Postmodern Subject be Black?" At "Postmodernism and the Fin de Siècle International Symposium," Jan 8–11, 1998, Rauischholzhausen, Germany

Jurca, Catherine. *White Diaspora: The Suburb and the Twentieth-Century American Novel*. Princeton: Princeton University Press, 2001.

Kaiser, Ernest. "A Critical Look at Ellison's Fiction and at Social and Literary Criticism by and about the Author." *Black World* (December 1970): 82.

Kanner, Leo. *A History of the Care and Study of the Mentally Retarded*. Springfield, IL: Thomas, 1964

Karem, Jeff. *The Romance of Authenticity: The Cultural Politics of Regional and Ethnic Literatures*. Charlottesville: University of Virginia Press, 2004.

Kaye, Richard Allen. "Mary McCarthy and the Politics of Impersonality: An Urban Anthropologist in New York's Racial and Sexual Underground." 2005 MLA Convention. Park Tower Suite 8212, Marriott, Washington, D.C. 29 Dec. 2005.

Kazin, Alfred. *Contemporaries*. Boston: Atlantic Monthly Press, 1962.

Keller, Yvonne. *"Was It Right to Love Her Brother's Wife So Passionately?: Lesbian Pulp Novels and U.S. Lesbian Identity, 1950–1965"* *American Quarterly* 57.2, June 2005. 385–410.

Kelly, George M. "An Interview with Thomas Hal Phillips." *Notes on Mississippi Writers* 6 (1972): 3–13.

Kennedy, Elizabeth Lapovsky and Madeline D. Davis. *Boots of Leather, Slippers of Gold.* 1993. New York: Penguin, 1994.

Khailova, Ladislava. *"Where the Average White Male Scored in the Imbecile Range": Changing Paradigms of Mental Retardation in Twentieth-Century Southern Fiction.* PhD Dissertation. University of South Carolina, 2004.

Kimmel, Michael. *Manhood in America: A Cultural History.* New York: Free Press, 1996.

King, Martin Luther Jr. "Showdown for Non-Violence." *Look* 16 Apr. 1968. 24.

——. *Stride Toward Freedom: The Montgomery Story.* New York: Harper & Row, 1958.

Klein, Christina. *Cold War Orientalism: Asia in the Middlebrow Imagination, 1945–1961.* Berkeley, CA: University of California Press, 2003.

——. "The Sentimental Culture of Global Integration." *the minnesota review* 55–57 (2002): 153–166.

Klein, Marcus. *After Alienation: American Novels in Mid-Century.* Cleveland: Meridian Books, 1962.

Krentz, Christopher. "A 'Vacant Receptacle'? Blind Tom, Cognitive Difference, and Pedagogy." PMLA: Publications of the Modern Language Association of America, 120.2 (2005): 552–57.

Kristeva, Julia. *Powers of Horror: An Essay on Abjection.* Tr. Leon S. Roudiez. New York: Columbia University Press, 1982.

Kristol, Irving. "Ten Years in a Tunnel: Reflections on the Thirties." *The Thirties: A Reconsideration in the Light of the American Political Tradition.* Eds Morton J. Frisch and Martin Diamond. DeKalb, IL: Northern Illinois University Press, 1968. 6–27

Kuznick, Peter J., and James Gilbert, eds. *Rethinking Cold War Culture.* Washington, DC: Smithsonian, 2001.

Ladder, The. San Francisco: Daughters of Bilitis, 1956–1972

Larbalestier, Justine. *The Battle of the Sexes in Science Fiction.* Middletown, CT: Wesleyan University Press, 2002.

Larbalestier, Justine and Helen Merrick. "The Revolting Housewife: Women and Science Fiction in the 1950s." Lukin/Delany, *Fifties Fictions*: 136–56.

Lasch, Christopher. *The Agony of the American Left.* New York: Vintage, 1969.

Lears, T. J. Jackson. "A Matter of Taste: Corporate Cultural Hegemony in a Mass-Consumption Society." May, Lary. *Recasting America.*

Lerner, Max. *America as a Civilization.* New York: Simon and Schuster, 1957.

Levine, Lawrence W. *Black Culture and Black Consciousness: Afro-American Folk Thought from Slavery to Freedom.* Oxford: Oxford University Press, 1997.

——. *The Opening of the American Mind: Canons, Culture, and History.* Boston: Beacon Press, 1996.

Lhamon, W. T. *Deliberate Speed: The Origins of a Cultural Style in the American 1950s.* Washington, D.C.: Smithsonian Institution Press, 1990, Cambridge: Harvard University Press, 2002.

Lipton, Lawrence. "A Voyeur's View of the Wild Side: Nelson Algren and his Reviewers." *Chicago Review Anthology.* Ed. David Ray. Chicago: University of Chicago Press, 1959. 31–41.

"Love Goes On Strike." *True Story Magazine* vol. 57, no. 6 (January 1948): 23–25+.

Lukin, Josh. "About Samuel Delany." *the minnesota review*, issue 65–66 (2006). 75–82.

——. "Cold War Masculinity in the Early Work of Kate Wilhelm." *Daughters of Earth: Twentieth Century Feminist Science Fiction*, ed. Justine Larbalestier. Middletown, CT: Wesleyan University Press, 2006.

Lukin, Josh, and Samuel R. Delany, eds. *Fifties Fictions: Paradoxa: Studies in World Literary Genres*, No. 18 (2003).

Macklin, Ruth, and Williard Gaylin, eds. *Mental Retardation and Sterilization: A Problem of Competency and Paternalism.* New York: Plenum, 1981.

Mailer, Norman. *Advertisements for Myself.* 1959. Cambridge: Harvard University Press, 1992.

———. *The Naked and the Dead.* New York: Rinehart, 1948.

Maltz, Albert. Letter to Martha Dodd. Correspondence File 7.7. Dodd Papers.

Mann, William. *Behind the Screen: How Gays and Lesbians Shaped Hollywood 1910–1969.* New York: Viking, 2001.

Margolies, Edward, and Michael Fabre. *The Several Lives of Chester Himes.* Jackson, MS: University Press of Mississippi, 1997.

Massing, Hede. *This Deception.* New York: Duell, Sloan & Pierce, 1951.

May, Elaine Tyler. *Homeward Bound: American Families in the Cold War Era.* New York: HarperCollins, 1988.

May, Lary. *The Big Tomorrow: Hollywood and the Politics of the American Way.* Chicago: The University of Chicago Press, 2000.

———, ed. *Recasting America: Culture and Politics in the Age of Cold War.* Chicago: The University of Chicago Press, 1989.

McCann, Sean. *Gumshoe America: Hard-Boiled Crime Fiction and the Rise and Fall of New Deal Liberalism.* Durham: Duke University Press, 2000.

McCann, Sean, and Michael Szalay. "Do You Believe in Magic? Literary Thinking after the New Left." *Yale Journal of Criticism* 18 (2005): 435–68.

McCarthy, Mary. *The Humanist in the Bathtub.* New York: NAL, 1964.

McClintock, Harry K. "Darky Uncle Ned." On *Haywire Mac.* Stamford, CT: Cook Records, 1950.

McGilligan, Patrick and Paul Buhle. *Tender Comrades: A Backstory of the Hollywood Blacklist.* New York: St. Martin's, 1997.

McLendon, Jacquelyn Y. "'A Round, Unvarnished Tale': Misreading *Othello*, or, African-American Strategies of Dissent." *Othello: New Essays by Black Writers.* Ed. Mythili Kaul. Washington, D.C.: Howard University Press, 1997.

McRuer, Robert. "Crip Eye for the Normate Guy: Queer Theory and the Disciplining of Disability Studies." PMLA: Publications of the Modern Language Association of America, 120.2 (2005): 586–92.

Meaker, Marijane [Vin Packer]. *Spring Fire.* Gold Medal-Fawcett, 1952. San Francisco: Cleis, 2004.

Medovoi, Leerom. "Cold War American Culture as the Age of Three Worlds." *the minnesota review* 55–57 (2002): 167–86.

———. *Rebels: Youth and The Cold War Origins of Identity.* Durham: Duke University Press, 2005.

Meeker, Martin. "A Queer and Contested Medium: The Emergence of Representational Politics in the 'Golden Age' of Lesbian Paperbacks, 1955–1963." *Journal of Women's History* 17.1 (2005) 165–88.

Meyer, Gerald. "American Labor Party." Buhle, *Encyclopedia* 24–25.

Meyerowitz, Joanne. *Not June Cleaver: Women and Gender in Postwar America, 1956–1960.* Philadelphia: Temple University Press, 1994.

Michaels, Walter Benn. "Race into Culture: A Critical Genealogy of Cultural Identity," *Critical Inquiry* 18: 655–85.

——. *The Trouble with Diversity: How We Learned to Love Identity and Ignore Inequality.* New York: Metropolitan Books, 2006.

Mickenberg, Julia L. *Learning from the Left: Children's Literature, the Cold War, and Radical Politics in the United States.* New York: Oxford University Press, 2006.

Miller, Douglas T., and Marion Nowak. *The Fifties: The Way We Really Were.* New York: Doubleday, 1977.

Miller, Mark Crispin. "Class Dismissed." *CONTEXT* No. 4 (2000). http://dalkeyarchive.com/context/1859/class-dismissed-by-mark-crispin-miller.

Mitgang, Herbert. "Books of the Times." Rev. of *The Searching Light*, by Martha Dodd. *New York Times* 26 Mar. 1955. Press Clippings File 12.6. Dodd Papers.

"Morros Testified Mrs. Stern Spied for Soviet Hire." *New York Times* 18 Aug. 1957: 1:6+.

Mullen, Bill V. "Breaking the Signifying Chain: A New Blueprint for African-American Literary Studies." *Modern Fiction Studies* 47:1 (2001): 145–63.

Mullen, Bill V. and James Smethurst (eds.), *Left of the Color Line: Race, Radicalism and Twentieth-Century Literature of the United States.* Chapel Hill, NC: University of North Carolina Press, 2003.

Murphy, Timothy S. *Wising Up the Marks: The Amodern William Burroughs.* Berkeley: University of California Press, 1997.

Nadel, Alan. *Containment Culture: American Narratives, Postmodernism, and the Atomic Age.* Durham: Duke University Press, 1995.

National Security Council. "NSC-68: United States Objectives and Programs for National Security." 14 April 1950. *Documents Relating to American Foreign Policy—The Cold War.* Ed. Vincent Ferraro. 13 Jan. 2001. International Relations Program, Mt. Holyoke College. 2 Sept. 2001 http://www.mtholyoke.edu/acad/intrel/nsc-68/nsc68-2.htm.

Navasky, Victor. "Cold War Ghosts." *The Nation* 16 July 2001: 36–43.

Nealon, Christopher S. "*Invert-History: The Ambivalence of Lesbian Pulp Fiction.*" *New Literary History* (31. 4) Autumn 2000. 745–64.

Nettels, Elsa. "Elizabeth Spencer." *Southern Women Writers: The New Generation.* Ed. Tonette Bond Inge. Tuscaloosa: University of Alabama P, 1990. 70–96.

Newman, Charles *The Postmodern Aura: The Art of Fiction in the Age of Inflation.* Evanston, IL: North Western University Press, 1985.

Noll, Steven. *Feeble-Minded in Our Midst: Institutions for the Mentally Retarded in the South, 1900–1945.* Chapel Hill: University of North Carolina Press, 1995.

Nussbaum, Martha C. *Hiding from Humanity: Disgust, Shame, and the Law.* Princeton: Princeton University Press, 2004.

Oakley, J. Ronald. *God's Country: America in the Fifties.* New York: Dembner Books, 1986.

O'Casey, Sean. Letter to Martha Dodd. 14 June 1955. Correspondence File 12.5. Dodd Papers.

Ohmann, Richard. "The Shaping of a Canon: U.S. Fiction, 1960–1975." 1978. In his *Politics of Letters.* Hanover, NH: Wesleyan University Press, 1987: 68–91.

O'Meally, Robert G. "On Burke and the Vernacular: Ralph Ellison's Boomerang of History." *History and Memory in African-American Culture.* Ed. Genevieve Fabre and Robert G. O'Meally. Oxford: Oxford University Press, 1994.

Orvell, Miles. *The Real Thing: Imitation and Authenticity in American Culture, 1880–1940.* Chapel Hill, NC: University of North Carolina Press, 1989.

Owens, Craig. "The Discourse of Others: Feminism and Postmodernism." Hal Foster, ed., *The Anti-Aesthetic: Postmodernism and Culture*. Port Townsend, WA: Bay Press, 1983.

Packer, Vin [Marijane Meaker]. *Spring Fire*. Gold Medal-Fawcett, 1952. San Francisco: Cleis, 2004.

Parent, Wayne, and Peter A. Petrakis. "Populism Left and Right: Politics of the Rural South." *The Rural South Since World War II*. Ed. R. Douglas Hurt. Baton Rouge, LA: Louisiana State University Press, 1998.

"Parents Urge Inter-Group Textbooks." *The New York Post* 25 February 1950: 18.

Pease, Donald E. "Citizen Vidal and Mailer's America." *Raritan* 11.4 (1992): 72–98.

Perlongo, Bob. "Interview with Nelson Algren." *Arizona Quarterly* 45:1 (Spring 1989): 101–6.

Peters, Fritz. *Finistère*. New York: Farrar, Straus, 1951.

——. *The World Next Door*. New York: Farrar Straus, 1949.

Peters, H.F. "American Culture and the State Department." *The American Scholar* 21.3 (Summer 1952): 265–74.

Phillips, Robert. "Elizabeth Spencer." *The Madness of Art: Interviews with Poets and Writers*. Syracuse, NY: Syracuse University Press, 2003. 121–48.

Phillips, Thomas Hal. *The Bitterweed Path*. 1950. Chapel Hill, NC: University of North Carolina Press, 1996.

Phillips, William and Philip Rahv. "Literature in a Political Decade." *New Letters in America*. Ed. Eleanor Clark and Horace Gregory. New York: Norton, 1937. 174–75.

Podhoretz, Norman. "The Man with the Golden Beef." *New Yorker* 2 June 1956: 134, 135.

Polito, Robert. *Savage Art: A Biography of Jim Thompson*. New York: Knopf, 1995.

Prenshaw, Peggy Whitman. *Elizabeth Spencer*. Boston: Twayne Publishers, 1985.

——. "Elizabeth Spencer." *The History of Southern Women's Literature*. Ed. Carolyn Perry and Mary L. Weaks. Baton Rouge, LA: Louisiana State University Press, 2002. 508–11.

——. "Mermaids, Angels and Free Women: The Heroines of Elizabeth Spencer's Fiction." *Southern Quarterly* 22.1 (1983): 13–31.

Rabinowitz, Peter. *Before Reading: Narrative Conventions and the Politics of Interpretation*. 1987. Columbus: Ohio State University Press, 1998.

Rahv, Philip. "Proletarian Literature: A Political Autopsy." 1939. *Essays on Literature and Politics 1932–1972*. Ed. Arabel J. Porter and Andrew J. Dvosin. Boston: Houghton Mifflin, 1978. 293–309.

Ray, David. "A Talk on the Wild Side: A Bowl of Coffee with Nelson Algren." *The Reporter* 11 June, 1959: 32–34.

Reed, John Shelton. *Southern Folk, Plain and Fancy: Native White Social Types*. Athens, GA: University of Georgia Press, 1986.

Reed, Lou. "Rock'N'Roll." 1969. *Between Thought and Expression: Selected Lyrics of Lou Reed*. New York: Hyperion, 1991.

Reiner, Margrit. "The Fictional American Woman: A Look at Some Recent Novels." *Masses and Mainstream* 5.6 (1952): 1–10.

Reissman, Leonard. "Review." *American Journal of Sociology* (September 1960).

Richardson, Mark. "Peasant Dreams: Reading On the Road." *Texas Studies in Literature and Language* 43:2 (2001): 218–42.

Riesman, David. *Individualism Reconsidered and Other Essays*. Glencoe, IL: Free Press, 1954.

Riesman, David, with Nathan Glazer and Reuel Denny. *The Lonely Crowd: A Study of the Changing American Character.* 1951. New Haven: Yale University Press, 1989.

Rimmon-Kenan, Shlomith. *Narrative Fiction.* New York and London: Routledge, 1983.

Ro, Sigmund. "Coming of Age: The Modernity of Postwar Black American Writing." *The Black Columbiad: Defining Moments in African American Literature and Culture.* Eds. Werner Sollors and Maria Diedrich. Harvard English Studies 19. Cambridge, MA: Harvard University Press, 1994. 226–33.

Roberts, Terry. "Italy: Dream and Nightmare." *Self and Community in the Fiction of Elizabeth Spencer.* Baton Rouge, LA: Louisiana State University Press, 1994. 50–62.

——. "This Crooked Narrative Way." *Mississippi Quarterly* 46.1 (1992–93): 61–75.

Rogin, Michael. Ronald Reagan, *The Movie, and Other Episodes in Political Demonology.* Berkeley: University of California Press, 1987.

Roosevelt, Eleanor. "Two Books." Rev. of *The Searching Light*, by Martha Dodd. *New York World-Telegram* 23 Aug. 1945.

Rosenfelt, Deborah. Commentary. *Salt of the Earth.* By Michael Wilson. New York: Feminist Press, 1978. 93–168.

Rothberg, Michael. "Against Zero-Sum Logic: A Response to Walter Benn Michaels." *American Literary History* 18:2 (2006): 303–11.

Ross, Andrew. *Nor Respect: Intellectuals and Popular Culture.* New York: Routledge, 1989.

Rubinstein, Annette. "Scholar as Hero." Rev. of *The Searching Light*, by Martha Dodd. *Masses and Mainstream* 8.6 (1955): 63.

Rupp, Leila J. and Verta Taylor. *Survival in the Doldrums: The American Women's Rights Movement, 1945 to the 1960s.* New York: Oxford University Press, 1987.

Saunders, Frances Stonor. *The Cultural Cold War: The CIA in the World of Arts and Letters.* 1999. New York: The New Press, 2000.

Savran, David. *Communists, Cowboys, and Queers: The Politics of Masculinity in the Work of Arthur Miller and Tennessee Williams.* Minneapolis, MN: University of Minnesota Press, 1992.

Sayre, Nora. *Previous Convictions: A Journey Through the 1950s.* New Brunswick, NJ: Rutgers University Press, 1995.

Schaub, Thomas Hill. *American Fiction in the Cold War.* Madison: University of Wisconsin Press, 1991.

Scheiner, C.J. *The Encyclopedia of Erotic Literature, vol. I.* New York: Barricade Books, 1996.

Schiffrin, André. *A Political Education: Coming of Age in Paris and New York.* Hoboken: Melville House, 2007.

Schraufnagel, Noel. *From Apology to Protest: The Black American Novel.* Deland, FL: Everett Edwards, 1973.

Schrecker, Ellen. *Many Are the Crimes: McCarthyism in America.* Boston: Little, Brown, 1998.

——. *No Ivory Tower: McCarthyism and the Universities.* New York: Oxford University Press, 1986.

Sedgwick, Eve Kosofsky. *Between Men: English Literature and Male Homosocial Desire.* New York: Columbia University Press, 1985.

——. *Epistemology of the Closet.* Berkeley, CA: University of California Press, 1990.

Seidel, Kathryn Lee. "Madonna of the Marketplace: Art and Economics in Elizabeth Spencer's *The Light in the Piazza.*" *Southern Quarterly* 35.2 (1997): 16–22.

Shklar, Judith N. *American Citizenship: The Quest for Inclusion*. Cambridge: Harvard University Press, 1991.
Siegel, Carol. *Male Masochism: Modern Revisions of the Story of Love*. Bloomington: Indiana University Press, 1995.
Sillen, Samuel. "Behind the Ivy Curtain." *Masses and Mainstream* 2.3 (1949): 7–17.
Smith, William Gardner. "The Negro Writer: Pitfalls and Compensations." *Phylon* 11.4 (1950): 297–303.
Spencer, Elizabeth. *The Light in the Piazza*. New York: McGraw-Hill, 1960.
Steinberg, Julian. *Verdict of Three Decades: From the Literature of Revolt Against Soviet Communism, 1917–1950*. New York: Duell, Sloan &Pierce, 1951.
Stephens, Gregory. *On Racial Frontiers: The New Culture of Frederick Douglass, Ralph Ellison, and Bob Marley*. Cambridge: Cambridge University Press, 1999.
Stewart, George R., and Joseph M. Backus. "'Each in Its Ordered Place': Structure and Narrative in 'Benjy's Section' of *The Sound and the Fury*." *American Literature* 29.4 (1958): 440–56.
Stimpson, Catherine. "Zero Degree Deviancy: The Lesbian Novel in English." *Writing and Sexual Difference*. Ed. Elizabeth Abel. Chicago: University of Chicago Press, 1982. 243–59.
Stryker, Susan. *Queer Pulp*. San Francisco: Chronicle Books, 2001.
Susman, Warren. *Culture as History: The Transformation of American Society in the Twentieth Century*. New York: Pantheon, 1984.
——. "Did Success Spoil the United States?: Dual Representations in Postwar America." May, Lary. *Recasting America*.
Swerdlow, Amy. "The Congress of American Women: Left-Feminist Peace Politics in the Cold War." *U.S. History as Women's History: New Feminist Essays*. Eds. Linda K. Kerber, Alice Kessler-Harris, and Kathryn Kish Sklar. Chapel Hill: University of North Carolina Press, 1995. 196–312, 429–34.
Tarry, Ellen. *The Third Door: The Autobiography of an American Negro Woman*. Introduction by Nellie Y. McKay. Tuscaloosa: University of Alabama Press, 1992.
Taylor, Valerie. *The Girls in 3-B*. New York: Gold Medal-Fawcett, 1959. New York: The Feminist Press, 2002.
——. *Whisper Their Love*. New York: Gold Medal-Fawcett. 1957.
Teres, Harvey M. *Renewing the Left: Politics, Imagination, and the New York Intellectuals*. New York: Oxford University Press, 1996.
Thompson, E.P. "Homage to Thomas McGrath." *The Revolutionary Poet in the United States: The Poetry of Thomas McGrath*. Ed. Frederick C. Stern. Columbia: University of Missouri P, 1988. 104–50.
"Three Women of Leningrad." *Daily Worker* 8 Mar. 1950: 5.
Torgovnick, Marianna. *Gone Primitive: Savage Intellects, Modern Lives*. Chicago: University of Chicago Press, 1990.
Torres, Tereska. *Women's Barracks*. New York: Fawcett, 1950. New York: Quality Paperbacks by arrangement with Naiad Press, 2000.
Tracy, Henry. "Answered in Fiction." *Common Ground*, Summer 1946. 109–10.
Trask, Michael. *Cruising Modernism: Class and Sexuality in American Literature and Social Thought*. Ithaca, NY: Cornell University Press, 2003.
Trend, David. *Cultural Pedagogy: Art/Education/Politics*. New York: Bergin & Garvey, 1992.
Trilling, Lionel. *A Gathering of Fugitives*. Boston: Beacon Press, 1956.
——. *The Liberal Imagination: Essays on Literature and Society*. 1950. New York: Anchor Books, 1953.

Tumanov, Vladimir. "A Tale Told by Two Idiots: Krik idiota v 'Skhole dlia durakov' S. Sokolova i v 'Shume i iarkosti' U. Folknera." *Russian Language Journal* 48.159–61 (1994): 137–54.

Tyor, Peter. "Denied the Power to Choose the Good: Sexuality and Mental Defect in American Medical Practice, 1850–1920." *Journal of Social History* 10 (1977): 472–89.

United States Bureau of Labor Statistics. *How American Buying Habits Change*. Washington: United States Department of Labor, [1959].

Vanden Heuvel, Katrina. "Obituary." *Nation* 24 Sept. 1990: 297.

Vidal, Gore. *The City and the Pillar*. New York: E.P. Dutton, 1948.

Von Eschen, Penny M. *Race Against Empire: Black Americans and Anticolonialism 1937–1957*. Ithaca: Cornell University Press, 1997.

Vonnegut, Kurt. "Introduction." *Never Come Morning*, by Nelson Algren. (1941). New York: Seven Stories Press, 1986.

Wald, Alan. *Exiles from a Future Time: The Forging of the Mid-Twentieth-Century Left*. Chapel Hill, NC: University of North Carolina Press, 2002.

——. "The 1930s Left in U.S. Literature Reconsidered." Mullen, Bill and Sherry Linkon, Eds. *Radical Revisions: Rereading 1930s Culture*. Urbana: University of Illinois Press, 1996.

——. *Writing From the Left: New Essays on Radical Culture and Politics*. London: Verso, 1994.

Walters, Susanna. "'Her Hand Crept Slowly Up Her Thigh': Ann Bannon and the Politics of Pulp." *Social Text*, Fall/Winter 1989.

Warner, Michael. *The Trouble with Normal: Sex, Politics, and the Ethics of Queer Life*. Cambridge, MA: Harvard University Press, 2000.

Warshow, Robert. *The Immediate Experience: Movies, Comics, Theatre and Other Aspects of Popular Culture*. 1962. New York: Atheneum, 1974.

Watkins, Mel. *On the Real Side: Laughing, Lying, and Signifying*. New York: Simon and Schuster, 1994.

Watson, Steven. *The Birth of the Beat Generation*. New York: Pantheon, 1995.

Weaver, Richard M. *The Southern Tradition at Bay: A History of Postbellum Thought*. 1968. Ed. George Core and M. E. Bradford. Washington, DC: Regnery Gateway, 1989.

Weber, Donald. "Memory and Repression in Early Ethnic Television." Foreman, ed. *The Other Fifties*.

Weigand, Kate. *Red Feminism: American Communism and the Making of Women's Liberation*. Baltimore: Johns Hopkins University Press, 2001.

Weinstein, Allen and Alexander Vassiliev. *The Haunted Wood: Soviet Espionage in America—the Stalin Era*. New York: Random House, 1999.

Weisenburger, Steven. *Fables of Subversion: Satire and the American Novel 1930–1980*. Athens, GA: University of Georgia Press, 1995.

Whitfield, Stephen J. *The Culture of the Cold War*. Second Edition. Baltimore: The Johns Hopkins University Press, 1996.

Whyte, William H. *The Organization Man*. New York: Doubleday, 1956.

Williams, John A. "My Man Himes: An Interview with Chester Himes." *Amistad I: Writings on Black History and Culture*. Ed. John A. Williams and Charles F. Harris. New York: Vintage Books, 1970. 25–94.

Williams, Raymond. *Problems in Materialism and Culture*. London: Verso, 1980.

Williams, Tennessee. *Cat on a Hot Tin Roof. The Theater of Tennessee Williams. Vol. 3*. New York: New Directions, 1971. 1–215.

Williamson, Joel. *New People*. New York: Free Press, 1980.
Willingham, Calder. *End as a Man*. New York: Vanguard, 1947.
Willis, Ellen. *Don't Think—Smile! Notes on a Decade of Denial*. Boston: Beacon, 1999.
———. "Escape from Freedom: What's The Matter With Tom Frank (And The Lefties Who Love Him)?" *Situations: Project of the Radical Imagination* 1.2 (2006). http://ojs.gc.cuny.edu/index.php/situations/article/view/30/26.
Wilson, Michael. *Salt of the Earth*. (film Prod. 1953). New York: Feminist Press, 1978.
Wilson, Sloan. *The Man in the Gray Flannel Suit*. New York: Simon & Shuster, 1955.
Winchell, Mark R. "A Golden Ball of Thread: The Achievement of Elizabeth Spencer." *Sewanee Review* 97.4 (Fall 1989): 580–86.
Wittner, Lawrence. *Cold War America: From Hiroshima to Watergate*. New York: Praeger, 1974.
"Woman's Day in the War." *Worker* 4 Mar. 1945: 8.
"Women Active in Congress of Writers." *New York Evening Post* 31 May 1939: 4.
Wright, Richard. "Blueprint for Negro Writing." 1937. Reprinted in *Within the Circle: An Anthology of African-American Criticism from the Harlem Renaissance to the Present*. Ed. Angelyn Mitchell. Durham, NC: Duke University Press, 1994.
Yaszek, Lisa. "Domestic Satire as Social Commentary and Mid-Century Women's Media Landscape SF" *Foundation: The International Review of Science Fiction*. Vol 34, No. 95 (Autumn 2005): 29–39.
———. "Unhappy Housewife Heroines, Galactic Suburbia, and Nuclear War." *Extrapolation* 44, 1 (Spring, 2003): 97–111.
Yee, Jennifer. "The Colonial Outsider: 'Malgérie' in Hélène Cixous' Novel *Les rêveries de la femme sauvage*." *Tulsa Studies in Women's Literature* 20: 2 (2001): 189–216.
Zimet, Jaye. *Strange Sisters*. New York: Viking Studio, 1999.

Contributors

Stephanie Brown is currently an assistant professor of English at the Ohio State University-Newark, where she teaches African American literature and film. She has lectured and written on subjects ranging from twentieth-century African American fiction to popular culture, film, and French literature; she also recently co-edited a collection on pedagogical approaches to contemporary black writers (*New Voices: Teaching Emerging African-American Fiction*, forthcoming from Cambridge Scholars Press). Her current project is a critical study of marginalized African American writers of the immediate post–WW II period. When not teaching or writing, Stephanie spends most of her time answering questions for her three-year-old daughter Clara, and isn't sure which activity is most challenging. She would like to thank Tara McGann, Samuel Delany, and Doug Goldstein for reading early versions of this article; Ann Douglas for having introduced her to Himes's *End of a Primitive*; her husband Stephen for his general patience, forbearance, and support; and Josh Lukin for encouraging her to amend the original essay so that it would have more depth and substance.

Ladislava Khailova is an assistant professor at Northern Illinois University, serving as a Humanities and Social Sciences Subject Specialist (Founders Memorial Library). She earned a Ph.D. in English and an M.L.I.S. from the University of South Carolina and an M.A. in Russian and American studies from Charles University in Prague, Czech Republic. Her research interests gravitate towards the historical and cultural factors that shape constructions of disabilities. This chapter evolved from her dissertation, titled "'Where the average white male scored in the imbecile range': Changing Paradigms of Mental Retardation in Twentieth-Century Southern Fiction" (2004). Khailova has published articles on various genres of twentieth-century American literature (in particular, texts by Roethke, Baraka, and Welty); she has also written on the implementation of the Americans with Disabilities Act in libraries and translated a UNESCO publication titled *Teacher Education Resource Pack: Special Needs in the Classroom* into Czech.

Josh Lukin is a lecturer in English at Temple University. He has published articles on the work of Walt Whitman, Oscar Wilde, Grant Morrison, Neil Gaiman, Jim Thompson, Patricia Highsmith, Kate Wilhelm, and Philip K. Dick as well as four interviews with radical science fiction writers. Lukin is the co-editor of *Paradoxa: Studies in World Literary Genres* Volume 18, "Fifties Fictions," and has given presentations on disability studies. He would like to acknowledge that this volume would not have been possible without the support, advice, and insights of David R. Willingham, Samuel R. Delany, Christopher Schelling, Christopher Barzak, Tom Welsh, Alan Wald, Ann Keefer, Leerom Medovoi, Christopher Breu, Chandler Davis, Robert Caserio, Derrick Johnson, Andrew Hoberek, Jeffrey J. Williams, Walter Biggins, Tom Duchamp, Seetha Srinivasan, Robert McRuer, Rich Puchalsky, and the University Press of Mississippi's anonymous outside reader.

Kathlene McDonald is an assistant professor of English at the City College Center for Worker Education/CUNY. She has published essays on labor and working-class culture and is completing a book on Left feminist culture in the postwar era. She is indebted to Alan Wald for first calling her attention to Martha Dodd's work years ago. The staff at the Library of Congress was enormously helpful in providing her access to the Martha Eccles Dodd Papers. Members of the Columbia University Women and Society Seminar provided invaluable feedback and insights, as did Norah Chase. And Michael Garland provided the support and careful editing advice that nurtured this piece toward completion.

Ian Peddie teaches English at the University of Sydney. His work ranges widely across post-1900 British and American literature and popular culture. He has published work on topics such as radical American poetry, Langston Hughes, Thomas McGrath, Irvine Welsh, and Nelson Algren as well as on popular music. He edited the 2006 collection *The Resisting Muse: Popular Music and Social Protest* (Ashgate) and is currently completing a book on Irvine Welsh. He thanks Josh Lukin for the comments and emendations that helped him to sharpen and organize his essay.

Harry Thomas is a graduate student in English at the University of North Carolina at Chapel Hill. Thus far his scholarly work has focused on representations of masculinity and sexuality in American literature, especially literature from the U.S. South. He has critical articles forthcoming in the *North Carolina Literary Review* and the *Mississippi Quarterly*, and his fiction has appeared online in *Lodestar Quarterly* and *Six Little Things*. He is grateful for the assistance of William Ferris, Tyler Curtain, Fred Hobson, and John Howard, all of whom provided valuable feedback on early versions of the essay found here. Thanks are also due to Meredith Raimondo, who for years and years pushed him to read "that queer southern book that John Howard got back into print." Having finally done so, he is extremely glad that he did.

Jennifer Worley teaches English, film and gender studies at the University of San Francisco and City College of San Francisco. She is currently at work on her first book, *Word and Flesh*, a cultural study of twentieth-century lesbian narrative and the production of queer communities. She would like to thank Josh Lukin, Monica Nolan, Renee Rivera, Bill Basquin, Ed Cohen, and Judith Halberstam for reading and offering valuable feedback on earlier drafts of this article.

Index